OECD Reviews of Digital Transformation: Going Digital in Sweden

OECD
BETTER POLICIES FOR BETTER LIVES

Please cite this publication as:
OECD (2018), *OECD Reviews of Digital Transformation: Going Digital in Sweden*, OECD Publishing, Paris.
http://dx.doi.org/10.1787/9789264302259-en

ISBN 978-92-64-30224-2 (print)
ISBN 978-92-64-30225-9 (PDF)

Photo credits: Cover © Adobe Stock; image design: Taï Marc Le Thanh.

Corrigenda to OECD publications may be found on line at: *www.oecd.org/about/publishing/corrigenda.htm*.

Foreword

OECD Reviews of Digital Transformation: Going Digital in Sweden is part of a new series of OECD country reviews. The *OECD Reviews of Digital Transformation* analyse recent developments of the digital economy in countries, review policies related to digitalisation and make recommendations to increase policy coherence in this area.

Going Digital in Sweden examines recent developments in infrastructures for the digital economy, telecom markets and related regulations and policies in Sweden. It reviews trends in the use of digital technologies by individuals, businesses and the government, and examines policies to foster diffusion. Digital security policies are discussed with a view to assess its strengths and limitations. The Review also examines opportunities and challenges raised by digitalisation in key areas and analyses policy responses to these changes. The areas covered range from global value chains and innovation to jobs, skills and work in the digital economy.

The Review reconsiders these policies in relation to their coherence among different domains and in order to foster synergies across government ministries, levels and institutions, based on the policy framework of the OECD-wide "Going Digital: Making the Transformation Work for Growth and Well-being" project.

Going Digital in Sweden was undertaken following an invitation by the Minister for Housing and Digital Development, Mr Peter Eriksson, and supported by a financial contribution from the government of Sweden. The review was carried out by the OECD Directorate for Science, Technology and Innovation under the auspices of the OECD Committee on Digital Economy Policy.

The review was prepared by a team led by Vincenzo Spiezia and including Laurent Bernat, David Gierten and Alexia Gonzalez-Fanfalone, under the supervision of Anne Carblanc, Head of the Digital Economy Division.

The authors owe much to the support and co-operation of Alf Karlsson, State Secretary for Housing and Digital Development; Anders Hektor, Deputy Director at the Department for Digital Development; and Katarina Isaksson, Counsellor, Swedish Permanent Delegation to the OECD.

The Review draws on the results of a series of interviews with a wide range of stakeholders during two fact-finding missions to Sweden in June 2017 and January 2018: Danny Aerts (Internet Foundation), Jörgen Ahlström (Office of the Digitalisation Council), Anette Ahmens (Ministry of Justice), Leif Andersson (Ministry of Education), Per-Arne Andersson (SKL), Sara Andersson (PTS), Emilie Anér (Ministry of Enterprise and Innovation), Andreas Aurelius (Vinnova), Helena Bäckström (Ministry of Enterprise and Innovation), Ingolf Berg (Ministry of Enterprise and Innovation), Susanne Bergman (Ministry of Enterprise and Innovation), Sofia Berlin Kolm (Higher Education Authority), Nina Björesten(Ministry of Enterprise and Innovation), Erik Borälv (Vinnova), Patrik Bystedt (PTS), Anna Carlsson (SKL), Lena Carlsson (Regional Growth Agency), Maria

Caryll (SKL), Maria Cederholm (Ministry of Enterprise and Innovation), Irene Ek (Growth Analysis), Mikael Ek (SSNF), AnnMari Eklund Löwinder (Internet Foundation), Bente Ellend National Library of Sweden), Per Engström (National Innovation Council), Magnus Enzell (Ministry of Finance), Johanna Essemyr Pauldin (Regional Growth Agency), Patrik Fältström (Netnod), Anna Felländer (Stockholm School of Economics), Margareta Groth (Vinnova), Peter Haglund (Ministry of Enterprise and Innovation), Mikael Halén (Ericsson), Maria Häll (SUNET), Johan Harvard (Ministry of Enterprise and Innovation), Tord Hermansson (Volvo Cars), Nils Hertzberg (Office of the Digitalisation Council), Sofia Holmgren (Ministry of Enterprise and Innovation), Lars Ilshammar (National Library of Sweden), Staffan Ingvarsson (Stokab), Darja Isaksson (national Innovation Council), Marita Jansson (TeliaCompany), Susanna Jansson (Ministry of Enterprise and Innovation), Erik Joachimsson (Ministry of Enterprise and Innovation), Stig Johansson (Financial Supervisory Authority), Anders Jörnesten (Ministry of Education), Vahid Kalhori (Sandvik), Peter Karlberg (Skolverket), Christoffer Karsberg (MSB), Erik Kruse (Ericsson), Robert Liljeström (TeliaCompany), Anders Lindh (Sandvik), Staffan Lindmark (PTS), Lars Lingman (Skolverket), Nicklas Liss-Larsson (Broadband Council), Mikael Ljungblom (Ministry of Enterprise and Innovation), Lars Lundberg (Federation of ICT enterprises), Anders Lundkvist (Seniornet), Mats Lundquist (Telenor Connection), Matilda Malmquist Glas (Ministry of Finance), Mari Mild (Ministry of Enterprise and Innovation), Freenasp Mobedjina (TeliaCompany), Gustaf Molander (Ministry of Education), Åsa Möller (PTS), Bengt Mölleryd (PTS), Lars Nicander (Swedish Defense University), Linda Norman (Ministry of Education), Pär Nygårds (Federation of ICT enterprises), Anders Nyström (Ministry of Finance), Tobias Öhman (Vinnova), Annika Pontén (Higher Education Authority), Maria Ramstedt (Ministry of Foreign Affairs), Mattias Revelius (Riksdagen), Henrik Ringmar (IP-only), Jörgen Samuelsson (Ministry of Enterprise and Innovation), Fredrik Sandberg (Ministry of Enterprise and Innovation), Patrik Sandgren (Broadband Council), Eva Sartorius (Swedish E-identification Board), Jan Shierbeck (Ministry of Education), Cecilia Sjöberg (Vinnova), Emilie Smiding (Ministry of Justice), Fredrik Söderqvist (Unionen), Adrian Solitander (Vinnova), Jonas Stier (Dalarna University), Lena Svendsen (Ministry of Enterprise and Innovation), Karin Svensson Smith (Riksdagen), Mats Tinnsten (Mid Sweden Univeristy), Susanna Torbrand Rosmarus (Ministry of Finance), Åsa Vagland (Ministry of Enterprise and Innovation), Jonas Valdringer (Statistics Sweden), Fredrik von Essen (Federation of ICT enterprises), Peter von Wovern (PTS), Marie Wall (Ministry of Enterprise and Innovation), Peter Wallström (PTS), Erik Wennerström (National Council for Crime Prevention), Anna Wibom (Broadband Council), Luciana Widengren (Telenor Connection), Maria Wieslander (Ministry of Enterprise and Innovation), Andreas Wigren (PTS), Jens Zander (Royal Institute of Technology) and Åsa Zetterberg (Ministry of Enterprise and Innovation).

On 3 May 2018, the OECD Council invited Lithuania to become a Member. At the time of publication the deposit of Lithuania's instrument of accession to the OECD Convention was pending and therefore Lithuania does not appear in the list of OECD Members and is not included in the OECD zone aggregates.

On 25 May 2018, the OECD Council invited Colombia to become a Member. At the time of publication the deposit of Colombia's instrument of accession to the OECD Convention was pending and therefore Colombia does not appear in the list of OECD Members and is not included in the OECD zone aggregates.

Table of contents

Tables

Figures

Boxes

Acronyms and abbreviations

5GEM	5G-Enabled Manufacturing
ADE	Automated data exchange
ADSL	Asymmetric digital subscriber line
AI	Artificial intelligence
AIC	Availability, integrity and confidentiality
AIDA	Analytic Imaging Diagnostics Arena
ANSSI	Agence nationale de la sécurité des systèmes d'information
API	Application programming interface
APNIC	Asia Pacific Network Information Centre
BDA	Big data analysis
CDO	Chief Digital Officer
CERT	Computer emergency response team
CRM	Customer relationship management
CSIRT	Computer Security Incident Response Team
DDI	Digital and data-driven innovation
DNS	Domain Name System
DNSSEC	Domain Name System Security Extensions
DSL	Digital subscriber line
EDI	Electronic data interchange
e-ID	Digital identity
EPL	Employment protection legislation
ERP	Enterprise resource planning
FFI	Strategic vehicle research and innovation programme
FI	Finansinspektionen
FTTB	Fibre to the building
FTTC	Fibre to the cabinet
FTTH	Fibre to the home
FTTP	Fibre to the premises
GB	Gigabyte
Gbps	Gigabits per second

GDP	Gross domestic product
GHz	Gigahertz
HPWP	High-performance Work Practices
ICT	Information and communication technology
IIS	Internet Infrastructure Foundation
IoT	Internet of Things
IP	Internet Protocol
IPv4	Internet Protocol version 4
IPv6	Internet Protocol version 6
IPP	Innovation partnership programme
ISP	Internet service provider
IXP	Internet exchange point
JSC	Job security council
kbps	Kilobits per second
LAN	Local area network
LTE	Long-term evolution
M2M	Machine-to-machine
MB	Megabyte
Mbps	Megabits per second
MHz	Megahertz
MNO	Mobile network operators
MoJ	Ministry of Justice
MSB	Swedish Civil Contingencies Agency
NDS	National digital strategy
NGA	Next-generation access
NIS	Network and Information Security
NTCG	National Telecommunications Coordination Group
OFR	Public Employees' Negotiation Council
PB	Petabyte
PES	Public Employment Services
PIAAC	OECD Survey of Adult Skills
PiiA	Process Industrial IT and Automation
PIMM DMA	Pilot for Industrial Mobile communication in Mining, Digitalised Mining Arena
PISA	Program for International Student Assessment
PPP	Purchasing power parity
PSTN	Public switched telephone network

PTK	Federation of Salaried Employees in Industry and Services
PTS	Post and Telecom Authority
R&D	Research and development
RAN	Radio access network
RFID	Radio-frequency identification
Saco	Swedish Confederation of Professional Associations
SAMFI	Cooperation Group for Information Security
SCM	Supply-chain management
SIP	Strategic innovation programme
SKL	Swedish Association of Local Authorities and Regions
SMEs	Small and medium-sized enterprises
SMP	Significant market power
STEM	Science, technology, engineering, and mathematics
TCO	Swedish Confederation of Professional Employees
TLD	Top-level domain
WTL	Writing to Learning

Executive summary

Sweden is among the leading countries in the diffusion and use of digital technologies. Internet use by individuals and businesses is widespread and the digital divides along lines of age, education, income and firm size are narrower than in most OECD countries. Broadband availability, quality and affordability score among the best in the OECD.

Sweden's capability to embrace the digital transformation has been a main driver of its strong economic performance in recent years. The economy has the highest share of value added produced by the information and communication technologies (ICTs) sector among OECD countries and is among the top ten exporters of ICT services worldwide. Through digitalisation, Swedish firms have moved up along global value chains in manufacturing, focusing their activities on high value-added services.

As the digital economy evolves at a rapid pace, Sweden faces new opportunities and new challenges:

- increasing tradability of digital services is opening up new markets at the time when international competition in manufacturing is getting stronger
- labour productivity growth has slowed down but investment in knowledge remains high and can be better used for innovation
- "big data" and artificial intelligence are enabling new business models and new services, but require that digital risks and privacy be effectively managed
- policy coherence has become essential to seize the benefits of the digital transformation while preserving the societal values of the Swedish people.

Building on the OECD project "Going Digital: Making the Transformation Work for Growth and Well-being", the *Policy Review of Sweden* provides recommendations in key areas of the digital economy as well as on the implementation of the government's Digital Strategy, as outlined below.

Expanding connectivity

Sweden has set an ambitious target for its broadband network: 98% of households and firms should have access to 1 gigabit per second by 2025. Achieving this goal requires a few targeted measures:

- enhance co-ordination among national, regional and local broadband strategies, by strengthening the role of the Broadband Forum
- promote deployment of high-speed broadband networks in sparsely populated areas, through concerted actions by the Swedish Post and Telecom Authority (PTS), the Broadband Forum and the newly established Digitalisation Council
- foster competition in infrastructure provision by private players and municipalities, based on a closer assessment of current network models by the PTS and the Swedish Competition Authority.

Increasing adoption and use of digital technology

Use of digital technologies by individuals, firms and the government is higher in Sweden than in most OECD countries. Yet, there is significant room for improvement in a number of specific areas:

- foster usage among individuals with a lower education and low income and promote the uptake of online activities in remote areas
- promote the diffusion of advanced digital technologies in firms, particularly small and medium-sized enterprises, by strengthening the "Digital Lift" programme and its focus on big data and digital business processes
- enhance digital public services in remote areas, by increasing capacity at the local level and building on existing initiatives under the "Digital First" policy
- open up public sector information and open government data to citizens, an area where Sweden seems to be lagging behind.

Upgrading skills for the digital transformation

A key goal of Sweden's Digital Strategy is that "everyone will be able to develop and use his/her digital skills". In recent years, Sweden has launched several reforms of the education system, including the National Digitalisation Strategy for the School System in 2017. Building on these policy initiatives, the government should:

- support the effective use of digital technologies in schools as a learning tool
- strengthen foundation skills, particularly writing, numeracy and ICT skills, in primary and secondary education
- increase tertiary education courses on ICT and data analysis and attract more students to these disciplines
- strengthen the incentives for professional training in ICT and data analysis, in co-ordination with social partners
- reduce the gender divide in programming skills and ICT-related occupations
- consider developing a comprehensive Digital Skills Strategy.

Fostering digital innovation

Sweden is an international hub of scientific excellence and technological leadership. The share of gross domestic product (GDP) spent on research and development is among the highest worldwide, although it has been declining since 2000. There are a large number of initiatives, publicly funded and in co-operation with businesses, to foster research in ICTs and promote the development of advanced digital tools for businesses. The government, through its innovation and research agencies, could further improve the performance of the Swedish innovation system:

- continue current efforts to set priorities for innovation policies related to digitalisation
- scale up programmes for digital innovation in order to exploit economies of scale in research and testing

- undertake a more systematic evaluation of research projects and innovation programmes supported by public funds
- strengthen policy labs and regulation sandboxes as an innovative approach to the design and implementation of policies and regulations in the digital economy.

Strengthening labour market institutions

Effective labour market policies and institutions are essential to accompany workers along the digital transformation. The Swedish model, based on a strong dialogue between the social partners and the active role of job security councils (JSCs) seems well-equipped to facilitate a smooth transition for workers affected by the digital transformation. There is room, however, to improve the coverage and the quality of JSC services and Public Employment Services (PES) services. Social partners may want to:

- extend the provision of JSC services to all displaced workers, including blue-collar, youth and other vulnerable groups
- promote successful job-transition services, e.g. the Early Risk Service, in all JSCs
- improve co-ordination between the JSCs and PESs at an early stage of the dismissal procedure, in co-operation with the government
- establish a negotiation council for platform-mediated jobs, where platforms and trade unions may negotiate collective agreements
- promote regulatory sandboxes to facilitate the compliance of new forms of work with existing regulations and the development of new regulations for digital labour markets.

Enhancing digital security

The 2017 National Cybersecurity Strategy aims to better integrate digital security policy within the broader digital transformation agenda. The strategy marks a turning point towards a more holistic approach to digital security in Sweden and should be further developed in several directions:

- promote a clear vision of digital security risk management as an economic and social responsibility of leaders and decision makers in public and private organisations
- provide policy leadership on the economic aspects of digital security, by strengthening ministerial co-ordination
- promote the role of the Digitalisation Council as a hub for co-operation on digital security issues
- develop adequate mechanisms for policy co-ordination around digital security, taking stock of the different approaches adopted by other OECD countries.

Turning the Digital Strategy into policy actions

In 2017 the Swedish government launched a new Digital Strategy, whose overall goal is for Sweden to be the best in the world in the use of digitalisation opportunities. The strategy set a number of targets to achieve this goal: digital literacy, digital security, digital innovation, digital leadership and digital infrastructure. To translate these targets into effective policy actions, the government should:

- link the Digital Strategy's targets to specific policy instruments, with well-defined and quantifiable objectives
- assign institutional responsibilities for the Digital Strategy's targets, in order to facilitate policy co-ordination and increase accountability
- provide for clear appropriations in the Budgetary Bill, in order to signal the government's commitment and strengthen the political credibility of the strategy
- set up stronger co-ordination mechanisms among ministries, agencies and across levels of government, possibly supported by an appropriate matching grants scheme.

Chapter 1.

Sweden in the digital transformation: Opportunities and challenges

This chapter sets the scene for the review. Building on OECD work, it examines recent economic performance in Sweden with a focus on policies and initiatives related to the digital economy, in particular Sweden's new Digital Strategy.

The statistical data for Israel are supplied by and under the responsibility of the relevant Israeli authorities. The use of such data by the OECD is without prejudice to the status of the Golan Heights, East Jerusalem and Israeli settlements in the West Bank under the terms of international law.

Sweden has been among the best performing economies in recent years. Real gross domestic product (GDP) per capita has grown faster than in most OECD countries, despite a large population increase mainly driven by immigration. The unemployment rate has receded from its 2010 peak (8.9%) and is now just below 7%.

Sweden is also among the leading countries for the diffusion and use of digital technologies. The economy has the highest share of valued added produced by the information and communication technologies (ICTs) sector among OECD countries and is among the top ten exporters of ICT services worldwide. Internet use is widespread, both among individuals and businesses, and the digital divides along lines of age, education, income and firm size among the narrowest in the OECD.

Strong economic performance and the digital transformation are tightly entwined in Sweden. The ICT sector and ICT investments together accounted for over 40% of labour productivity growth over 2006-13 (Growth Analysis, 2014). Use of digital technologies has enabled the successful integration of Swedish firms into global value chains in manufacturing, where different stages of production are located across different countries. Through digitalisation, Swedish firms have moved up the value chain, focusing their activities on high value-added services, e.g. product design and marketing, rather than on production activities (OECD, 2015b).

As the digital economy continues to evolve at a rapid pace, Sweden is facing new opportunities as well as new challenges. Increasing tradability of digital services is opening up new markets at a time when international competition in manufacturing has become stronger. Labour productivity growth has slowed down but investment in knowledge remains high and can be better used for innovation. "Big data" and artificial intelligence (AI) are enabling new business models and new services for consumers and citizens, but require that these opportunities be nurtured by appropriate management of digital risks and effective protection of privacy. More fundamentally, policy coherence is essential to help the whole economy seize the benefits of the digital transformation while preserving the societal values of the Swedish people.

Fostering advanced services via digitalisation

By creating opportunities for new services and new production processes, digitalisation has triggered a structural transformation in economic activities away from manufacturing and towards services. In California for example, the (subnational) economy with the strongest specialisation in digital and digitally related activities, services account for over 70% of the business sector value added.

Compared to other areas in the OECD, Sweden is characterised by a relative specialisation in manufacturing and a lower weight of business services (Figure 1.1). In 2015, manufacturing accounted for 25% of the business sector value added – excluding mining and real estate – less than in Germany (34%) and Finland (27%) but more than in all other partner economies, notably the United Kingdom (15%), Norway (16%), the Netherlands (17%) and California (19%). The share of business services was 59% in Sweden against 71% in California and the Netherlands, and 70% in the United Kingdom.

Sweden's relative specialisation in manufacturing should be considered in light of the high content of services embedded in manufactured goods. Digital technologies are reshaping the characteristics of the manufacturing of goods and services, and production processes and customer relations are being digitalised. An increasing share of value added in Swedish manufacturing is generated in upstream (e.g. research and development

[R&D]) and product design and downstream services (e.g. marketing and customer services). Rather than simply selling a product, manufacturing firms in Sweden are providing a complete solution (Government Offices of Sweden, 2016b).

Figure 1.1. **Value added in manufacturing and services in selected economies, 2015**

As a proportion of business sector value added

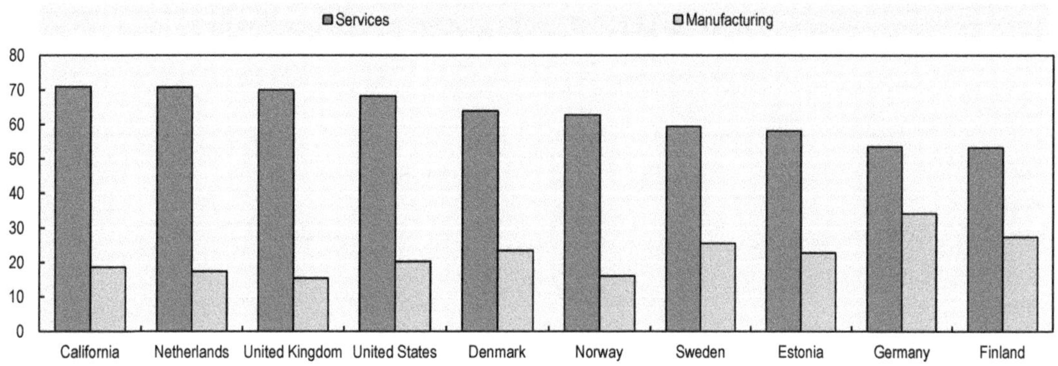

Note: Total business sector value added, excluding mining and real estate.

Source: Author's calculations based on OECD (2017f), *STAN Structural Analysis Database*, http://oe.cd/stan and BEA (2017), *Regional Economic Accounts*, https://www.bea.gov/regional.

Within the services sector (Figure 1.2), information technology (IT) and information services in Sweden accounted for 4.8% of the business sector value added, in line with Estonia (4.8%) and Finland (5.4%) but well behind California (8%). Similarly, the share of professional, scientific and technical activities in Sweden (11%) is close to the share in the Netherlands and the United Kingdom (12%) but significantly lower than in California (15%).

Figure 1.2. **Value added in professional and IT services in selected economies, 2015**

As a proportion of business sector value added

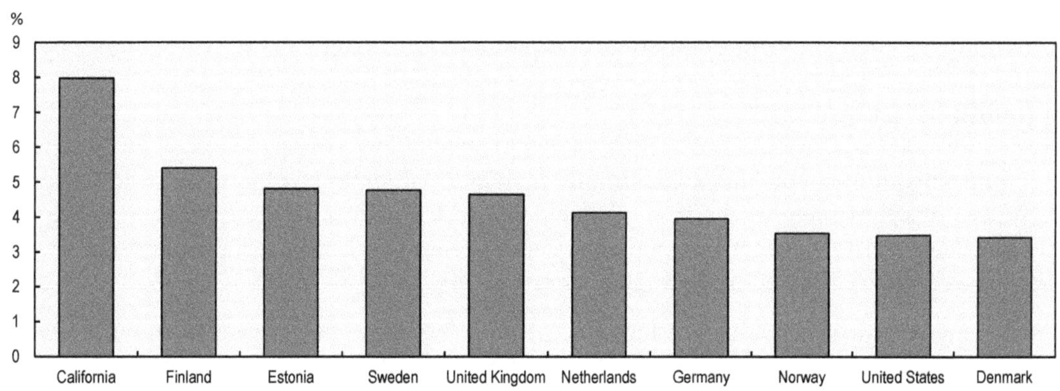

Source: Author's calculations based on OECD (2017f), *STAN Structural Analysis Database*, http://oe.cd/stan.

Strengthening comparative advantages in the world economy

A strong manufacturing industry has been a key engine of exports in Sweden over the last two decades. However, there are signs that this engine is slowing down (Figure 1.3).

While the trade balance in commodities remains positive, its surplus has been shrinking since 2008. Global competition in this sector has intensified in recent years, and advanced manufacturing is becoming a strategic priority for many governments. Smart Industry (Government Offices of Sweden, 2016b) is the government's strategy to increase the competitiveness of the industrial sector, primarily in the high-quality segments of global value chains.

Figure 1.3. **Net exports of goods and services from Sweden**

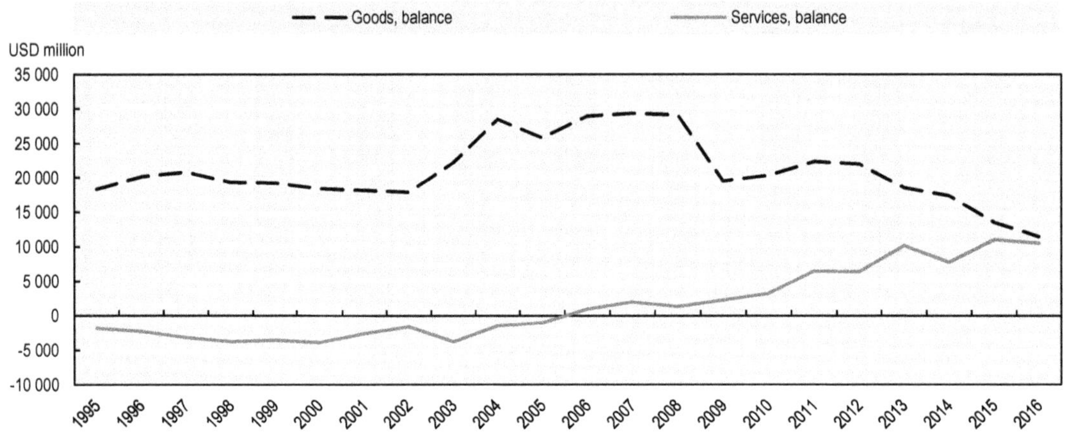

Source: OECD (2017a), "Balance of payments BPM6", https://stats.oecd.org/Index.aspx?DataSetCode=MEI_BOP6.

Unlike manufacturing, the trade balance in services, which was negative until 2005, has been steadily improving since. By 2016, the trade surplus in services was almost as large as the commodities surplus. This increase is mainly accounted for by telecommunications, computer and information services, intellectual property and financial services (OECD, 2018).

These services have a high degree of digitalisation, heavily rely on data and data analytics, and are likely to be deeply transformed by fast developments in AI in the forthcoming years. Further development of advanced services is therefore essential to sustain growth in Sweden and to strengthen its comparative advantages in the world economy.

Raising productivity growth

Specialisation in the most profitable segments of global value chains has allowed Sweden to achieve one of the best productivity performances in the OECD over the past two decades (OECD, 2015b). As in many other economies, however, productivity growth has slowed down in Sweden since 2003 (Figure 1.4).

The slowdown in labour productivity growth has been the largest in manufacturing, where the growth rate dropped from 7.8% a year over 2001-07 to 4.6% in 2009-15. The decrease was less pronounced in business services, where labour productivity growth (2.7% a year in 2009-15) tends to be lower than in manufacturing (OECD, 2017d).

The decrease in investment, both ICT and non-ICT, has contributed to the slowdown in labour productivity growth. Yet the main factor seems to have been the sharp decrease in multifactor productivity, which captures the effects of innovation and intangibles assets on productivity (OECD, 2017d).

Figure 1.4. **Trend in labour productivity growth in Sweden**

Total economy, percentage change at annual rate

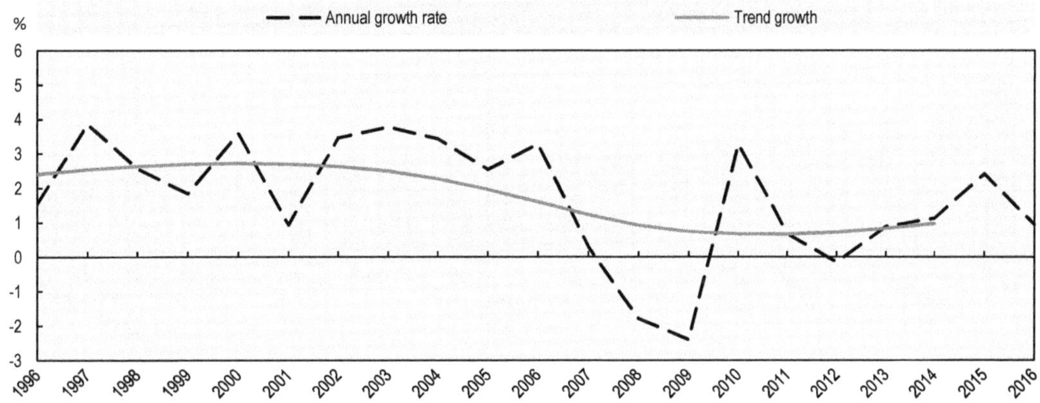

Notes: Labour productivity is defined as GDP per hour worked and its growth rate is calculated as first natural-log difference. Trends are estimated using the Hodrick-Prescott filter.

Source: OECD (2017d), *OECD Compendium of Productivity Indicators 2017*, http://dx.doi.org/10.1787/pdtvy-2017-en.

While the slowdown in productivity is common to most advanced economies, investments in physical (non-residential) and intangible assets in Sweden are among the highest in the OECD. Productivity growth could be increased if these assets were used more efficiently. The digital transformation not only requires the adoption and use of cutting-edge technologies, but is rooted in the capability of firms to leverage technology to do business in new and different ways. Some important tools such as e-purchases, supply chain management and big data analysis are used by fewer firms in Sweden than the OECD average. Small firms, in particular, seem to be lagging behind in terms of digital maturity (see Chapter 3). Although the Swedish government has addressed the need to support ICT use in small firms (Government Offices of Sweden, 2012), the rationale for policy actions in this area remains strong.

Raising productivity growth should be a key objective, both in manufacturing, to face stronger international competition, and in services, to seize the new market opportunities for tradable services.

Improving the Swedish innovation system

Sweden is an international hub of scientific excellence and technological leadership. It is among the global science leaders, both for the number and the quality of its scientific publications. The number of international patents per capita is higher than in most OECD countries.

Sweden also used to have the highest expenditures on R&D relative to GDP in the world. After 2000, however, R&D intensity started to decline, down to 3.3% in 2015 (Figure 1.5). While Sweden still registers a high level, its research performance is losing ground compared to both world innovation leaders (e.g. Denmark, Israel, Korea and Switzerland), and some emerging economies (e.g. the People's Republic of China [hereafter "China"] and Chinese Taipei). The Swedish telecommunication industry has been particularly hit by these changes in the global R&D landscape (OECD, 2016d).

Figure 1.5. **Gross domestic expenditure on R&D in selected economies**

As a percentage of GDP

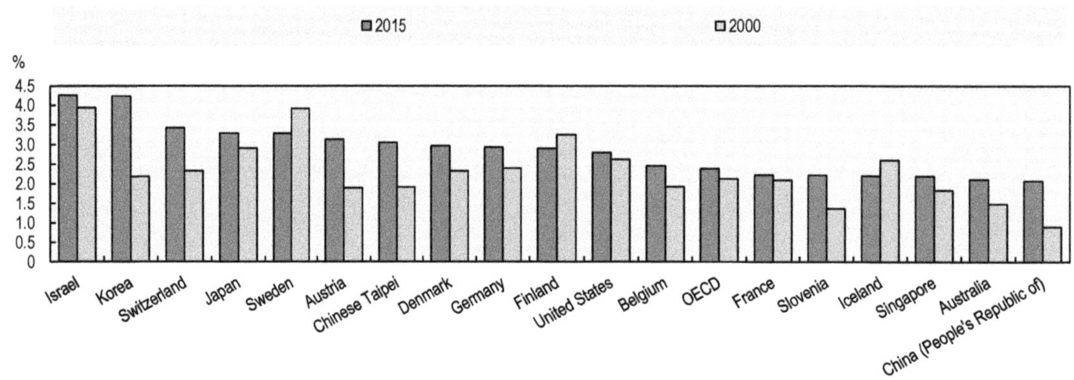

Note: Data refer to: 2001 instead of 2000 for Denmark; 2014 instead of 2015 for Singapore.

Source: OECD (2017c), "Main science and technology indicators", http://dx.doi.org/10.1787/data-00182-en.

The Research and Innovation Bills of 2008, 2012 and 2017 introduced a number of policy initiatives aimed at strengthening the performance of the Swedish innovation system. However, there is room for improving co-ordination and reducing fragmentation in the Swedish funding system for innovation, which comprises many medium-sized agencies, research councils and private foundations, running a host of sometimes overlapping programmes (OECD, 2013a; 2016d).

Fostering innovation requires broadening the scope for businesses and governments to experiment with the opportunities created by digital technologies. More responsive regulation systems, able to provide temporary changes for "testbeds", assess their results and quickly adapt accordingly, are crucial to support innovation in the digital economy. In this respect, the main challenge for the government lies in the effective co-ordination of sector-specific regulations in response to technological opportunities that, by their very nature, cut across established sectors. Given the slow pace of policy making, countries are increasingly allowing experimentation on a limited, controlled basis via policy labs or regulatory sandboxes (OECD, 2017g).

Sweden has taken several initiatives in this direction, through the launch of Testbed Sweden, the establishment of policy labs and the creation of an Innovation Centre for the financial sector (see Chapter 5).

Enhancing digital skills

The pervasiveness of digital technologies in daily life is fundamentally changing the way individuals access and elaborate knowledge. Individuals have to process complex information, think systematically and take decisions weighing different forms of evidence. They also have to continuously update their skills to match rapid technical change in the workplace. More fundamentally, in order to seize the new opportunities that digital technologies are opening in many areas, individuals have to develop the right set of skills to make meaningful use of these technologies (OECD, 2016e).

To ensure that individuals can engage in digital activities and adapt rapidly to new and unexpected occupations and skills needs, a stronger emphasis has to be placed on promoting strong levels of foundation skills, digital literacies, higher order thinking competencies as well as social and emotional skills (OECD, 2016c).

Skill levels are high in Sweden. According the OECD Survey of Adult Skills (PIAAC) the country is among the top performers for literacy and numeracy. Swedish workers have the second highest average score in ICT-related problem solving among OECD countries, though age and gender gaps remain large (Figure 1.6). Readiness to learn and creative thinking are also among the highest in the OECD.

Figure 1.6. **Proficiency in problem solving in technology-rich environments among adults**

Percentage of 16-65 year-olds scoring at each proficiency level

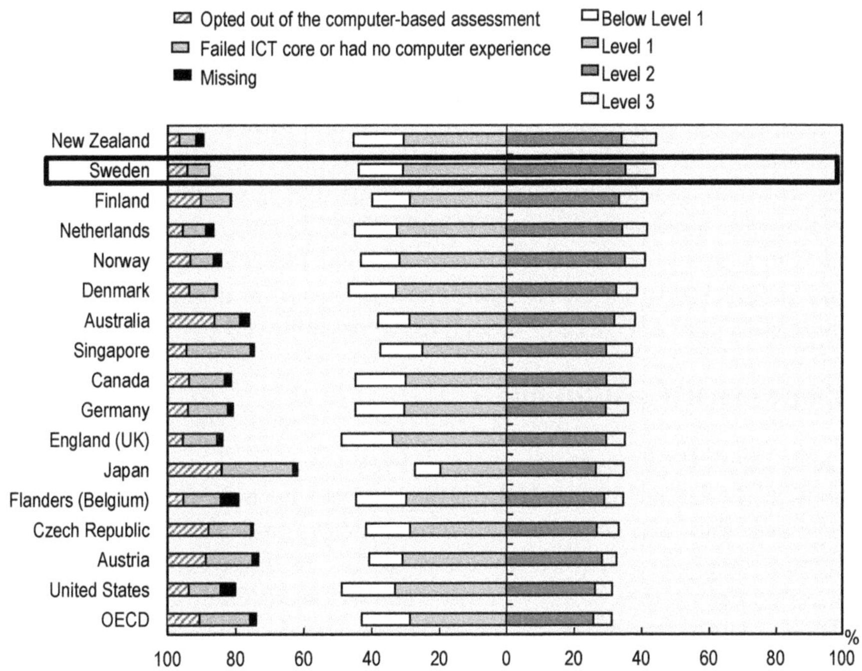

Notes: ICT = information and communication technology. The proficiency scale ranges from Level 1 (low) to Level 3 (high). Economies are ranked in descending order of the combined percentages of adults scoring at Level 2 and at Level 3. Adults included in the missing category were not able to provide enough information because of language difficulties, learning or mental disabilities, or technical problems with the computer used for the survey.

Source: Based on OECD (2016f), *Skills Matter: Further Results from the Survey of Adult Skills*, Table A2.6, http://dx.doi.org/10.1787/9789264258051-en.

Students in Sweden have positive attitudes towards science and believe that science is important for their own future career – more so today than around a decade ago. However, when asked about their own career expectations, only one in five 15-year-old students in Sweden expects to be working in a science-related occupation. This is less than the OECD average of around one in four students. Among those who expect to pursue a science-related career, only 3% expect to have an occupation related to ICTs. This proportion is much lower for females, in line with all OECD countries (OECD, 2016a).

There are signs of growing inequalities in the distribution of learning outcomes in Sweden. The gap between the highest- and lowest-performing students has increased over the last decade and is now wider than the OECD average. The performance gap between socio-economically advantaged and disadvantaged students is also increasing (OECD, 2017e). This challenge is particularly difficult with immigrant students. The share of immigrant students in Sweden (first- and second-generation) is growing and the performance gap between immigrant and non-immigrant students in science is larger than the OECD average.

While raising the demand for new skills, digital technologies are also creating new opportunities for skills development. Massive online open courses and open educational resources modify learning methods and give access to quality resources to a larger population over more flexible hours. The use of digital technologies in formal education and vocational training has the potential to improve learning, although the outcomes depend on the capacity to link these tools to effective pedagogy. Big data analytics can also complement labour market information systems with a more timely and precise monitoring of changing skills demand to adapt skills development and activation policies.

In October 2017, the Ministry of Education and Research launched a National Digitalisation Strategy for the School System (Government Offices of Sweden, 2017c). The strategy's objective is that all children, students and young adults should get the skills they need for their life and work, which in turn provides the basis for talents in future. The strategy aims to identify new solutions enabled by digitalisation, assess their effectiveness, and then develop and use the solutions that have proven successful. It also aims to develop the ability to drive and lead skills development with the support of digitalisation. The strategy has three focus areas: digital literacy for everyone in the school system; equal access and use; and research and follow-up on digitalisation opportunities. Each area includes a goal and several objectives to be achieved by 2022 (see Chapter 3).

Strengthening labour market institutions

Major technological innovations have always been accompanied by extensive transformations in the labour market. Jobs brought about by new technologies are different from the old ones: they are created in different sectors and different occupations; they involve different tasks and require different skills. In today's digital transformation, employment is decreasing in sectors with more scope for automation and slower growth in demand, such as manufacturing, retail and finance. The decrease in employment is more pronounced in routine occupations, both for low- and high-skill jobs, leading to employment polarisation and the decline in middle-income jobs (see Chapter 5).

Internet job platforms bring the potential to dramatically change traditional work arrangements and labour market relationships. Some full-time, long-term jobs are being turned into an uneven flow of "on-demand" tasks for a large global pool of "virtual workers". While these changes create opportunities for workers, jobseekers and firms, they also raise major challenges for job quality, taxation and social security.

In this context, effective labour market policies and institutions are essential to accompany displaced workers along the transition to new jobs and reduce the social costs of this process. Compared to most OECD countries, the Swedish labour market has performed pretty well in recent years, mainly due to the so-called "Nordic model": the strong dialogue between the social partners and the active role of job security councils (JSCs).

Workers with temporary and fixed-term contracts, however, mainly youth and other vulnerable groups, benefit less from JSCs' services, despite the fact that they are more likely to be dismissed. In addition, many of those who qualify for JSC support receive only partial services, especially blue-collar workers. At the same time, the proportion of employees with temporary contracts in Sweden is among the highest in the OECD, particularly for young workers (Figure 1.7). Expanding JSC services to all workers, therefore, should be a priority for labour market institutions in Sweden.

Figure 1.7. **Incidence of temporary workers in dependent employment, 2016**

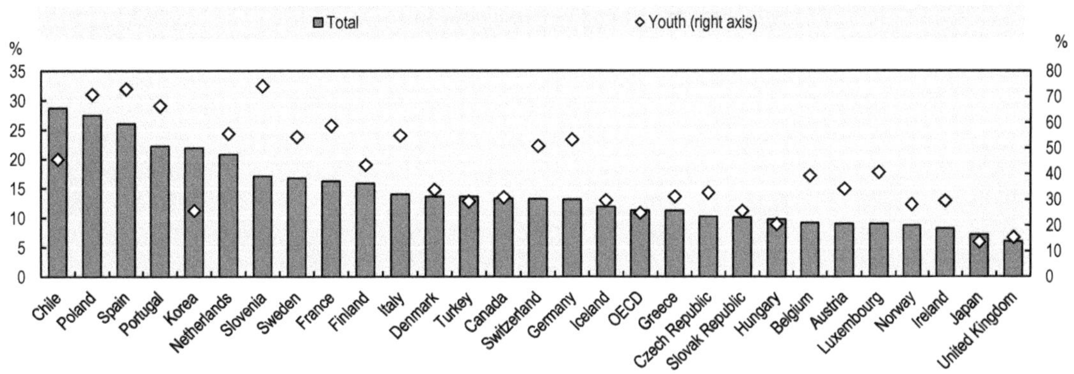

Source: OECD (2016b), "Labour market statistics: Employment by permanency of the job: Incidence", http://dx.doi.org/10.1787/data-00297-en.

Fostering digital security

High-value, digitally advanced services crucially rely on "big data" and, in the context of global value chains, cross-border data. The Internet of Things (IoT), in particular, is already generating a mass of operational and users' data that has major potential for the development of new products and smart services. The value of assets, firms and markets is increasingly underpinned by access to and strategic use of data.

These developments are putting pressure on Sweden's traditional stance for openness and transparency. In a data-driven economy and society, there is a risk that greater information asymmetry may translate into a shift in power away from individuals to organisations, traditional businesses to data-driven businesses, and governments to data-driven businesses (OECD, 2017g).

Policy makers will be challenged by a bundle of new issues as they grapple with data, such as the attribution of responsibility and liability for inappropriate decisions. The potential risk of significant social and economic harm to third parties from automated, data-driven decisions will require careful assessment of when human intervention may no longer be required. Associated with this is the promotion of a systematic culture of digital security and privacy risk management across society (OECD, 2017g).

Overall, Swedish businesses seem to show a relatively high level of digital security risk awareness and willingness to manage this risk but a more limited capability about how to do so (Government Offices of Sweden, 2016a). The same seems to hold for people. Among EU countries, Sweden has the highest percentage of individuals not ordering or buying on line and not sharing personal information to online communities because of security concerns (Figure 1.8).

The basic components of digital security policy are in place in Sweden, with an emphasis on the protection of essential services and critical infrastructure, particularly in the telecommunications sector. The transposition of the EU Directive on Security of Network and Information Systems will help to establish a clearer and more robust framework to strengthen digital security in essential sectors, beyond telecommunications. Other agencies are involved in digital security policy in areas such as innovation and regional growth.

Figure 1.8. **Individuals who did not carry out Internet activities because of security concerns, 2015**

As a proportion of all individuals aged 16-74 years

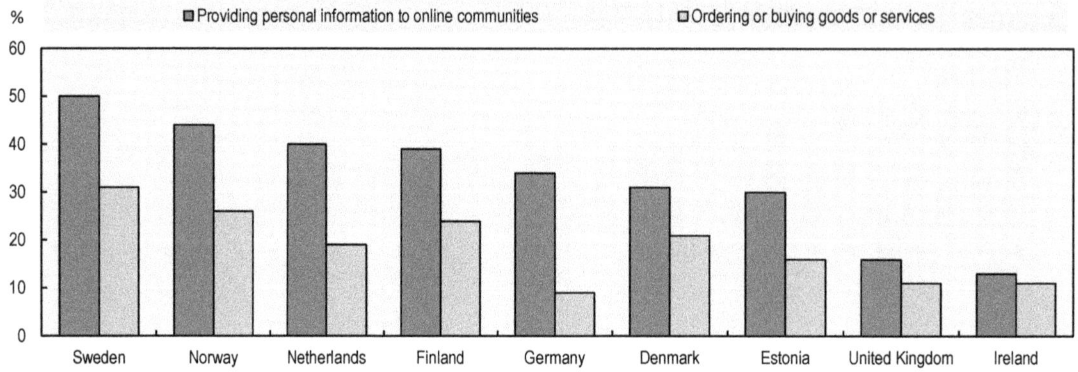

Source: Author's calculations based on Eurostat (2018), *ICT Usage in Households and by Individuals*, http://ec.europa.eu/eurostat/data/database.

A new National Cybersecurity Strategy was adopted in June 2017 (Government Offices of Sweden, 2017a). The strategy, which broadens digital security beyond crisis preparedness, aims to create the long-term conditions for all stakeholders in society to work effectively on digital security and to raise the level of awareness and knowledge throughout society. It includes 19 objectives covering 6 strategic priorities.

Sweden's new national digital security strategy aims to provide an opportunity to better integrate digital security policy within the broader digital transformation agenda, including with respect to the protection of vital societal functions and critical infrastructures. It may also help elevate this issue in order to better manage security and privacy risk raised by the high degree of digital openness that Sweden – and more broadly the OECD – promotes as a source of innovation and growth.

Despite these initiatives, there does not seem to be a clear co-ordination framework to ensure that they serve a common vision and objectives. At the strategic level, the Swedish approach to digital security is characterised by a general focus on the security of information systems and networks rather than on the economic and social activities that rely on them. While strategic documents address many aspects of digital security, they do not yet place a sufficient emphasis on digital security as a business leadership priority and responsibility (see Chapter 4).

Improving the governance of digital policies

Fostering digitalisation requires a coherent policy framework both among ministries and agencies (horizontal co-ordination) as well as across levels of government (vertical co-ordination). Digitalisation also calls for a reconsideration of the roles of public and market services in the delivery of social goods.

The Swedish government system is characterised by two features. The first is administrative dualism: a clear division of roles between ministries in charge of strategic policy development and oversight, on the one hand, and autonomous agencies tasked with policy implementation, on the other. The second feature means a high degree of decentralisation for largely autonomous county councils and municipals governments, which are responsible for key components of the Swedish welfare system.

While these two features are common to other Nordic countries, Sweden has the largest proportion of central government employment in agencies (96%) (OECD, 2013b) and one of the highest shares of general government employment in local governments (81%) (Figure 1.9).

Figure 1.9. **Distribution of general government employment across levels of government, 2014**

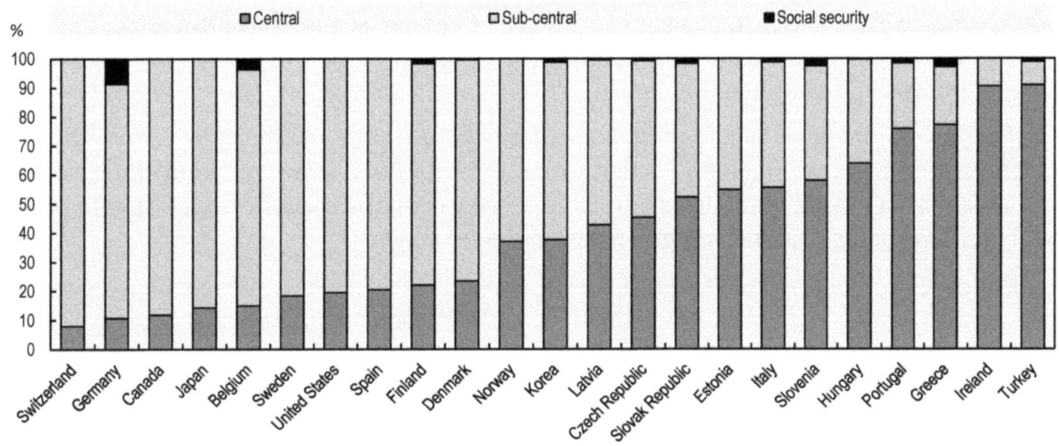

Note: Social security funds are not separately identified (i.e. recorded under central and/or sub-central government) for Canada, Estonia, Ireland, Japan, Norway, Spain, Switzerland and the United States.

Source: OECD (2017b), *Government at a Glance 2017*, http://dx.doi.org/10.1787/gov_glance-2017-en.

In this institutional setting, a political and societal culture towards consensus-building is crucial to ensure a smooth policy-making process. Policy decisions are the collective responsibility of the Cabinet and decisions are taken by consensus. Inter-ministerial committees and working groups play therefore a key role to facilitate discussion between public service officials. Institutionalised contact arrangements among government, employers and the unions enable widespread participation in decision making. Consensus-building helps to reduce potential conflicts by favouring pragmatic solutions and promoting gradual change (Cordova-Novion and Jacobzone, 2011).

Several OECD reports, however, have pointed out areas where administrative dualism and decentralisation may result in duplications of competencies or misalignment of objectives, leading to lower efficiency. The publication *OECD Reviews of Innovation Policy: Sweden 2016* (2016d) calls for better horizontal co-ordination among innovation agencies in setting priorities and designing and implementing programmes. *Value for Money in Government: Sweden* (OECD, 2013b) invited the Swedish government to consider the opportunity to establish common process agencies and wholesale merger of agencies. The 2015 *OECD Economic Survey of Sweden* (2015b) and *Improving Schools in Sweden: An OECD Perspective* (2015a) recommended a clearer definition of responsibility among the state, municipalities, headmasters and teachers and a better alignment of resources and responsibility in education. The 2017 *OECD Economic Survey of Sweden* (2017c) also recommends enhancing co-operation between central and local government in land-use planning and co-ordination in housing policies among municipalities.

Improving policy co-ordination has become even more crucial in the digital economy (see Chapter 6). Ongoing work under the OECD project “Going Digital: Making the Transformation Work for Growth and Well-being” points out that digitalisation cuts across policy domains and level of governments, requiring close policy integration and a more multidisciplinary perspective. The challenge for regulators and policy makers is to improve co-ordination across an array of policy domains: for example, the introduction of automated vehicles will have a direct impact on tax, environmental and labour policies as well as on transportation and urban planning.

Governments also need to be attentive to the interoperability of platforms, portability of data and scope of gatekeeping. Such standards are needed to maintain current levels of safety, ensure trust based on enhanced levels of digital security and privacy, improve energy and resource efficiency, and address emerging social and organisational challenges brought on by the digital transformation.

The development of standards and standards-based interoperability is critical for the development of the IoT, including smart cities and smart mobility. Common standards are also essential to ensure that citizens are able to access public services from different places and by different administrations, e.g. e-health and e-learning.

Policy effectiveness is also at stake when outcomes depend on reaching a critical threshold by improving policy co-ordination, e.g. the public support to R&D expenditures in the ICT field. Digital tools create the potential for greater communications and co-ordination within and across levels of government, but administrative structures change slowly and key differences – political, jurisdictional, cultural and epistemic – persist, often reinforcing each other.

The roles of public and market-based services in the delivery of social goods are also being redefined by digitalisation. Digital platforms are beginning to match or exceed the public role once played by the post office, public broadcasting, libraries or public meeting places, by providing basic public services like maps, libraries, public video, mail, messaging, emergency messages and employment offers. This leads to rethinking how existing public services should be adapted and to consider the opportunity for the delegation of certain policies to private entities, subject to public review, and the use of public-private partnerships where governments can leverage the agility of the private sector (OECD, 2014).

At the same time, some services typically provided by private companies may acquire greater importance due to digitalisation and become part of the core public service. The discussion to create a public digital identity (e-ID) in Sweden, as a complement to the market-based approach chosen in the early 2000s, is an illustration of these changes (see Chapter 4).

For a Sustainable Digital Sweden: A Digital Strategy

In June 2017, the Swedish government launched its Digital Strategy (Government Offices of Sweden, 2017b). The strategy's overall goal is for Sweden to be the best in the world in the use of digitalisation opportunities. The strategy will also be instrumental to reach the government's objective for Sweden to have Europe's lowest unemployment rate in 2020. In order to achieve this overall goal, the strategy sets five targets: digital literacy, digital security, digital innovation, digital leadership and digital infrastructure (Table 1.1).

Table 1.1. **For a Sustainable Digital Sweden: Five targets**

Targets	Description
Digital competence	In Sweden, everyone will be able to develop and use his/her digital skills.
Digital security	In Sweden, there are the best conditions for everyone to safely participate, take responsibility and have the confidence in the digital society.
Digital innovation	In Sweden, there are the best conditions for digitally driven innovations to be developed, disseminated and used.
Digital leadership	In Sweden, improvements in efficiency and quality through digitalisation should be relevant, purposeful and lawful.
Digital infrastructure	The whole of Sweden should have access to infrastructure allowing for fast broadband, stable mobile services and supporting digitalisation.

Source: Government Offices of Sweden (2017b), "For Sustainable Digital Transformation in Sweden: A Digital Strategy".

Digital competence

The target "digital literacy" entails that everyone should be familiar with digital tools and services and have the ability to follow and participate in the digital developments. Digital literacy is partly about the technical skills to use digital tools and services, and on media and information literacy, which covers the knowledge and skills needed to find, analyse, evaluate, and create information in different media and contexts. Digital skills concern, on the one hand, the technical skills to use digital tools and services and, on the other, media and information literacy, which encompasses the knowledge and abilities required to find, analyse, critically evaluate, and create information in different media and contexts. Digital literacy also includes the ability of an individual to keep up with the digital evolution and being able to find and keep a job, start and run a business, or to improve organisation and innovation in firms. The Digitalisation Commission has identified enhanced skills as a strategically important area for digitalisation policy.

Important areas under this target include:

- the ability and possibility of contributing to and participating in the digital society
- the modernisation of the education system
- skills matching
- digital skills in the public sector and state-owned companies.

Digital security

The target digital security entails people, companies and organisations having trust and confidence in the use of digital services and being able to use them easily. Since the digital transformation changes society in more fundamental ways than other technologies in the past, it requires a broader perspective on security. In addition to information security and personal privacy, the views of people and companies on how society handles the risks associated with the digital transformation also need to be taken into account.

Important areas under this target include:

- digital identity
- high security requirements
- privacy in the digital society

- democracy safeguards in digital environments
- a secure and mobile labour market
- functioning digital markets and secure consumers.

Digital innovation

The digital innovation target entails the existence of competitive conditions for the creation and spread of new or improved products and services that are valuable to the society, companies, the environment and people. Innovation can help to solve the challenges facing society and contribute to building a modern and sustainable society by combining knowledge in new ways or by an entirely new way of thinking.

Important areas under this target include:

- increased focus on data-driven and digitally driven innovation and research
- strengthened innovation climate for data-driven and digitally driven innovation
- effective intellectual property law
- digital transformation for strengthened national and international competitiveness
- modern society building.

Digital leadership

The digital leadership goal entails activities being improved, developed and enhanced through governance, measurement and follow-up. It is important that the government's efforts focus on how the opportunities offered by the digital transformation can be harnessed and the risks minimised, not only on how the digital transformation itself can be promoted. Political leadership is needed to create a secure and robust digital space and to co-ordinate public sector development. A cost-effective perspective on available resources is a natural condition for making the best use of the opportunities the digital transformation offers. It is important that companies, organisations and people have easy access to public sector activities.

Resource efficiency and the modernisation of the regulatory framework must not be undertaken at the cost of lower protection for individuals' privacy or weakened national security. The Digitalisation Commission has identified the regulatory framework as a key area for the digital transformation. It has also highlighted the need to develop better statistics to monitor developments.

Important areas under this target include:

- clearer central government leadership in the transformation
- simplification through digital transformation
- continuous analysis of digital maturity and the need for the measures
- governance towards a resource-efficient society helped by the digital transformation
- strengthened local and regional engagement.

Digital infrastructure

The digital infrastructure goal entails an improvement and reinforcement of infrastructure for electronic communications that are crucial for transmitting data. Digital infrastructures cover everything from (hard) physical lines to the (soft) systems for traffic management. Broadband infrastructure provides more opportunities to access social services, run a business and contribute to social cohesion. For a modern society, building infrastructure is a prerequisite, and digitalisation is dependent on efficient infrastructure.

The area can also be linked to the goal of Agenda 2030 for Sustainable Development for building resilient infrastructure, promoting an inclusive and sustainable industrialisation and innovation. The Digitalisation Commission has identified broadband and soft infrastructure as necessary conditions for strengthening competitiveness and for reaching efficiency gains.

Important areas under this target include:

- improved access to "hard" infrastructure
- development of "soft" infrastructure.

OECD Reviews of Digital Transformation: Going Digital in Sweden

This review examines opportunities and challenges raised by digitalisation in Sweden in the areas highlighted above. It also looks at the policies in place and makes recommendations to improve them.

Chapter 2 examines trends and structural features of the telecommunication markets, broadband infrastructure and services in Sweden. It provides policy recommendations to promote the deployment of high-speed broadband networks in sparsely populated areas, enhance fibre networks and spur the uptake of IPv6.

Chapter 3 reviews recent trends in the use of digital technologies by individuals, businesses and the government in Sweden; analyses the skills required to use these technologies effectively; and provides policy recommendations.

Chapter 4 provides an overarching description of digital security policy in Sweden and discusses its strengths and limitations from the perspective of the *OECD Recommendation on Digital Security Risk Management for Economic and Social Prosperity*.

Chapter 5 examines opportunities and challenges raised by digitalisation in two key areas – innovation and skills – and analyses key policies in these areas and provides recommendations.

Chapter 6 reconsiders the policies analysed in the other chapters in relation to their coherence among policy domains and across levels of government. The chapter presents the policy framework being developed by the OECD project "Going Digital: Making the Transformation Work for Growth and Well-being"; makes recommendations for Sweden's Digital Strategy; and addresses the issue of policy coherence.

References

BEA (2017), *Regional Economic Accounts*, Bureau of Economic Analysis, https://www.bea.gov/regional (accessed 27 November 2017).

Cordova-Novion, C. and S. Jacobzone (2011), "Strengthening the institutional setting for regulatory reform: The experience from OECD countries", *OECD Working Papers on Public Governance*, No. 19, OECD Publishing, Paris, http://dx.doi.org/10.1787/5kgglrpvcpth-en.

Eurostat (2018), *ICT Usage in Households and by Individuals* (isoc_cisci_ax), http://ec.europa.eu/eurostat/data/database.

Government Offices of Sweden (2017a), "A national cyber security strategy", Skr. 2016/17:213, Ministry of Justice, www.government.se/legal-documents/2017/11/skr.-201617213.

Government Offices of Sweden (2017b), "For sustainable digital transformation in Sweden: A digital strategy", Ministry of Enterprise and Innovation, N2017.23.

Government Offices of Sweden (2017c), "National digitalisation strategy for the school system" (in Swedish), U2017/04119/S, www.regeringen.se/pressmeddelanden/2017/10/regeringen-beslutar-om-nationell-digitaliseringsstrategi-for-skolvasendet (accessed 7 December 2017).

Government Offices of Sweden (2016a), "Digitalisation effects on individuals and society: Four thematic reports" (in Swedish), SOU 2016: 85, www.regeringen.se/rattsdokument/statens-offentliga-utredningar/2016/12/sou-201685 (accessed 7 December 2017).

Government Offices of Sweden (2016b), "Smart industry: A strategy for new industrialisation for Sweden", N2016.06, Ministry of Enterprise and Innovation, www.government.se/498615/contentassets/3be3b6421c034b038dae4a7ad75f2f54/nist_statsformat_160420_eng_webb.pdf.

Government Offices of Sweden (2012), *Små företag – stora möjligheter med it* [Small Business: Large Opportunities with IT] (in Swedish), SOU 2012: 63, www.regeringen.se/rattsdokument/statens-offentliga-utredningar/2012/10/sou-201263 (accessed 7 December 2017).

Growth Analysis (2014), "How digitalisation drives productivity and competitiveness in Sweden", Report 2013:14, Swedish Agency for Growth Policy Analysis, Östersund, Sweden, www.tillvaxtanalys.se/in-english/publications/reports/reports/2015-01-15-how-digitalisation-drives-productivity-and-competitiveness-in-sweden.htm (accessed 7 December 2017).

OECD (2018), "Balance of payments BPM6", *Main Economic Indicators* (database), http://dx.doi.org/10.1787/data-00706-en (accessed 19 April 2018).

OECD (2017a), "Balance of payments BPM6", https://stats.oecd.org/Index.aspx?DataSetCode=MEI_BOP6 (accessed 27 November 2017).

OECD (2017b), *Government at a Glance 2017*, OECD Publishing, Paris, http://dx.doi.org/10.1787/gov_glance-2017-en.

OECD (2017c), "Main science and technology indicators", *OECD Science, Technology and R&D Statistics* (database), http://dx.doi.org/10.1787/data-00182-en (accessed 27 November 2017).

OECD (2017d), *OECD Compendium of Productivity Indicators 2017*, OECD Publishing, Paris, http://dx.doi.org/10.1787/pdtvy-2017-en.

OECD (2017e), *OECD Economic Surveys: Sweden 2017*, OECD Publishing, Paris, http://dx.doi.org/10.1787/eco_surveys-swe-2017-en.

OECD (2017f), *STAN Structural Analysis Database*, ISIC Rev.4, http://oe.cd/stan (accessed 27 November 2017).

OECD (2017g), "Vectors of digital transformation", internal document, DSTI/CDEP/GD(2017)4/REV1, OECD, Paris.

OECD (2016a), *Education at a Glance 2016: OECD Indicators*, OECD Publishing, Paris, http://dx.doi.org/10.1787/eag-2016-en.

OECD (2016b), "Labour market statistics: Employment by permanency of the job: Incidence", *OECD Employment and Labour Market Statistics* (database), http://dx.doi.org/10.1787/data-00297-en (accessed 19 April 2018).

OECD (2016c), "New skills for the digital economy", *OECD Digital Economy Papers*, No. 258, OECD Publishing, Paris, http://dx.doi.org/10.1787/5jlwnkm2fc9x-en.

OECD (2016d), *OECD Reviews of Innovation Policy: Sweden 2016*, OECD Publishing, Paris, http://dx.doi.org/10.1787/9789264250000-en.

OECD (2016e), "Skills for a digital world: 2016 ministerial meeting on the digital economy background report", *OECD Digital Economy Papers*, No. 250, OECD Publishing, Paris, http://dx.doi.org/10.1787/5jlwz83z3wnw-en.

OECD (2016f), *Skills Matter: Further Results from the Survey of Adult Skills*, OECD Publishing, Paris, http://dx.doi.org/10.1787/9789264258051-en.

OECD (2015a), "Improving schools in Sweden: An OECD perspective", OECD, Paris, www.oecd.org/edu/school/Improving-Schools-in-Sweden.pdf.

OECD (2015b), *OECD Economic Surveys: Sweden 2015*, OECD Publishing, Paris, http://dx.doi.org/10.1787/eco_surveys-swe-2015-en.

OECD (2014), *Recommendation of the Council on Digital Government Strategies*, OECD, Paris, www.oecd.org/gov/digital-government/Recommendation-digital-government-strategies.pdf.

OECD (2013a), *OECD Reviews of Innovation Policy: Sweden 2012*, OECD Publishing, Paris, http://dx.doi.org/10.1787/9789264184893-en.

OECD (2013b), *Value for Money in Government: Sweden 2013*, OECD Publishing, Paris, http://dx.doi.org/10.1787/9789264200685-en.

Chapter 2.

Infrastructure for Sweden's digital economy

This chapter examines trends and structural features of the telecommunication market as well as broadband infrastructure and services. It concludes with recommendations to continue to spur broadband deployment and use in Sweden.

Connectivity provides access to information and communication technologies (ICTs) – the backbone of today's digital economies and societies. The Swedish government has set an ambitious broadband targets to achieve ubiquitous "ultra-fast" broadband connectivity by 2025 and progress is reviewed in this chapter.

The statistical data for Israel are supplied by and under the responsibility of the relevant Israeli authorities. The use of such data by the OECD is without prejudice to the status of the Golan Heights, East Jerusalem and Israeli settlements in the West Bank under the terms of international law.

This chapter examines trends and structural features of the telecommunication market in Sweden. It provides an overview of investment and revenue in the communication sector, including the fixed and mobile broadband markets, and developments in machine-to-machine (M2M) subscriptions, as well as in the deployment of key enablers such as IPv6. Furthermore, it examines developments in Sweden related to access and connectivity, such as infrastructure sharing, next-generation networks, and the regulatory treatment of communication bundles.

Communication networks are critical for the development of the digital economy. Mindful of their importance, the Swedish government has set forward successive broadband strategies to achieve connectivity goals. The most recent Broadband Strategy of 2016 has set an ambitious agenda for 2025. This chapter examines progress to date and concludes with a consideration of further measures to spur broadband deployment and use in Sweden.

Objectives and challenges for Swedish digital infrastructure

By most measures of telecommunication infrastructure and service development Sweden has always been among the leading OECD countries. Keenly aware of the importance of the sector for economic and social development, successive governments have set out plans and goals to meet their objectives. As early as March 2000, for example, Sweden proposed goals to make information and communication technologies (ICTs) available to all people. This included making funding of USD 0.9 billion available for broadband infrastructure deployment in regional areas, which can in some ways be considered as the policy that kick-started broadband developments in Sweden (Mölleryd, 2015).

In 2009, Sweden set out a strategy for where it would like to be, in terms of broadband infrastructure, by 2020. The ambitious goals surpassed those set by most peers and those found in the Digital Agenda for Europe. The main target was to achieve 90% coverage of households and business with 100 megabits per second (Mbps) by 2020. In 2017, the Ministry of Enterprise and Innovation expected this goal to be fulfilled as planned. While most of the investment has come from market participants, including private as well as publicly owned network operators, investment in the sector was complimented by public funding in the order of USD 0.19 billion for the 2007-13 period, and USD 0.57 billion for the period 2014-20.[1] In addition, property owners contribute to financing the roll-out of next-generation networks by making an upfront payment for the instalment of fibre infrastructure leading to their properties.

Sweden completely connected by 2025: The 2016 Broadband Strategy

Given that the targets established in the 2009 plan are expected to be achieved,[2] the government published a new Broadband Strategy in December 2016 with the aim of achieving "access to high-speed broadband in all of Sweden" by 2025 (Government Offices of Sweden, 2016). This goal has three milestones: achieve 95% of connected households and businesses by 2020 with broadband of at least 100 Mbps; by 2023, all of Sweden should have access to reliable high-quality mobile services; and by 2025, 98% of the population should have access to 1 gigabit per second (Gbps) broadband in their residences and workplaces, the remaining 1.9% with 100 Mbps, and 0.1% with 30 Mbps (Government Offices of Sweden, 2016).

To fulfil the goals set out in the 2016 Broadband Strategy, the Swedish government has focused on, among other things, three strategic areas of work: i) roles and rules; ii) cost-efficient network deployment; and iii) enabling infrastructure and services for everyone (Government Offices of Sweden, 2016). In other words, the different roles and rules for operators in the broadband market still need to be clarified, incentives have to be clear for cost-efficient network deployment, and obstacles for co-operation between players and technologies mitigated or eliminated. Thus, the main emphasis of the Broadband Strategy is to foster the market-driven deployment of broadband networks, supplemented with public support.

The authorities responsible for the Broadband Strategy in Sweden are the Ministry of Enterprise and Innovation, the Swedish Post and Telecom Authority (PTS), and the Broadband Forum, which has its administrative offices within the PTS.[3] The Ministry of Enterprise and Innovation is responsible for topics related to, among other things, regional development, transport and ICTs. The PTS monitors and regulates the communications market to ensure that every citizen has access to affordable and efficient communication services, and the Broadband Forum, established in 2010, is tasked with providing an arena for dialogue among different stakeholders (i.e. government, public authorities and firms) of the Swedish broadband market (European Commission, 2017b).

The Broadband Forum, which has a steering committee headed by the Ministry of Enterprise and Innovation, has served as an important form of co-operation contributing positively to fibre expansion in Sweden. Among other things, namely it has: i) contributed to increasing the collaboration between public and private players in mobile and fixed broadband expansion; ii) provided guidance to municipalities regarding robust fibre networks; iii) identified relevant barriers for infrastructure deployment; iv) provided solutions for establishing "fibre villages"; v) established measures to support for broadband deployment in rural areas; and vi) acted as a Secretariat for regional broadband co-ordinators.

Since 2011, Sweden's functional access to broadband has been defined at a minimum speed of 1 Mbps. In February 2017, however, the Swedish government instructed the PTS to evaluate the minimum connection quality for Internet access for all users in the country. The government decided in January 2018 to raise the level of functional access to broadband from 1 Mbps to 10 Mbps. The government also allocated funding for procurement of solutions to the small amount of households and businesses located where there are no offers on the market to access 10 Mbps.

Challenges to meet the objectives

Notwithstanding Sweden's strong performance in terms of broadband connectivity, when compared to other OECD countries, some challenges persist in meeting objectives for the current and future Digital Agenda. Certain areas for improvement in terms of connectivity include:

- enhancing co-ordination among national, regional, and local strategies and plans for broadband (fibre) deployment, and fostering robust fibre networks
- promoting the deployment of high-speed broadband networks in sparsely populated areas, including the use of European Agricultural Funds for Rural Development and the European Regional Development Fund
- spurring the uptake of IPv6.

In addition, in terms of measurement of the digital economy, where Sweden is a leader, one recommendation is:

- to further develop M2M data collection by introducing a category for subscriptions and data generated by autonomous vehicles.

The remainder of the chapter will provide an overview of communication developments and market structures in order to support these recommendations.

Developments in Swedish communication markets

In Sweden, as in a number of OECD countries, there has been an historically strong relationship between an increase in communication subscriptions and a growth in the size of the sector's revenues. In recent years, also mirroring other countries, this relationship has somewhat decoupled. Overall, revenues and investment in the Swedish telecommunication sector have remained relatively stable since 2006, with the exception of the 2009 crisis (Figure 2.1). By 2015, total revenue and investment in the telecommunication sector in Sweden amounted to SEK 52 billion (USD 6.2 billion) and SEK 12.5 billion (USD 1.5 billion), respectively.

Figure 2.1. **Trends in telecommunication revenues and investment in Sweden**

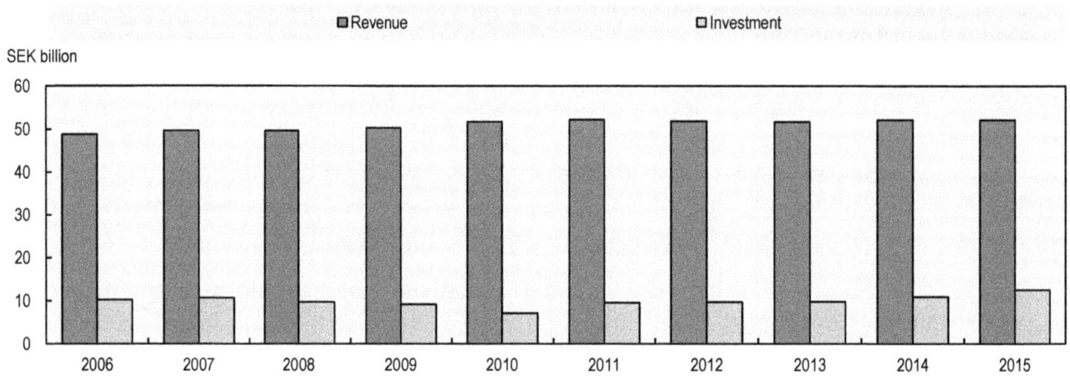

Source: OECD (2018b), "Telecommunications database", http://dx.doi.org/10.1787/tel_int-data-en.

At the same time, the number of telecommunication subscriptions (measured in terms of "access paths"), continues to grow in Sweden, from 21.3 million access paths in 2006 to 36.8 million in 2015 (OECD, 2018a). The growth in communication access paths in Sweden is due to an increase in mobile and fixed broadband subscriptions, as well as the growth of M2M subscriptions in recent years (OECD, 2018a). In contrast, similar to the trend in most OECD countries, the number of fixed telephony lines in Sweden continues to decrease, passing from 5.07 million in 2006 to 1.7 million in 2015 (OECD, 2018a).

Broadband networks

Communication services can be assessed using a number of key measures. These include the availability of services, the quality of those services, and the level of prices faced by business and consumers. Regarding broadband availability, digital agendas aiming to ensure access to broadband can formulate such an objective using a number of metrics. These include indicators such as the number of broadband subscriptions per 100 inhabitants (i.e. broadband penetration rates), the number of households or businesses with access to broadband, or by geographical coverage (e.g. urban, rural and remote areas).

A further indicator for broadband assessment is the quality of communication services. One element of the quality of a broadband service is the download speed of a connection. Some broadband plans or digital agendas, in addition to penetration goals, have the speeds they are expected to enable. For example, the Digital Agenda for Europe has a target of 100% of households having access to broadband at speeds of 30 Mbps by 2020, with a further aim of 50% of households having speeds above 100 Mbps (European Commission, 2010). Sweden, in contrast, went beyond this target, aiming for 90% of households to have 100 Mbps by that date and subsequently raising that to 1 Gbps for 98% of households by 2025.

Finally, the availability of prices at competitive rates is a key indicator for benefiting from the opportunities created by digital economies. The OECD uses a pricing methodology that incorporates usage baskets (e.g. for fixed and mobile broadband) in order to compare prices of communication services. This provides information on how Sweden's prices for fixed and mobile communication services compare to the OECD average for each basket as well to other countries.

The following subsections present indicators of Swedish communication markets over these three aspects (i.e. availability, quality and prices).

Access to broadband

In Sweden, as in most OECD countries, fixed and mobile broadband subscriptions have continued to grow, reflecting the ongoing complementarity of both networks (OECD, 2017b). Fixed broadband subscriptions per 100 inhabitants in Sweden increased from 32% in June 2012 to 37.5% in June 2017 (Figure 2.2).

On the other hand, while Sweden is still among the leaders in broadband penetration, other countries have had higher growth rates in recent years (OECD, 2018a). Over the past five years (i.e. between Q2 2012 and Q2 2017) Sweden had a similar growth of fixed broadband subscriptions per 100 inhabitants (16.7%) as the OECD (16.8%). In terms of fibre subscriptions growth, in 2017 Sweden reported a higher annual growth (i.e. 17.9%) than the OECD average (i.e. 15.3%).

Figure 2.2. **OECD fixed broadband subscriptions per 100 inhabitants**

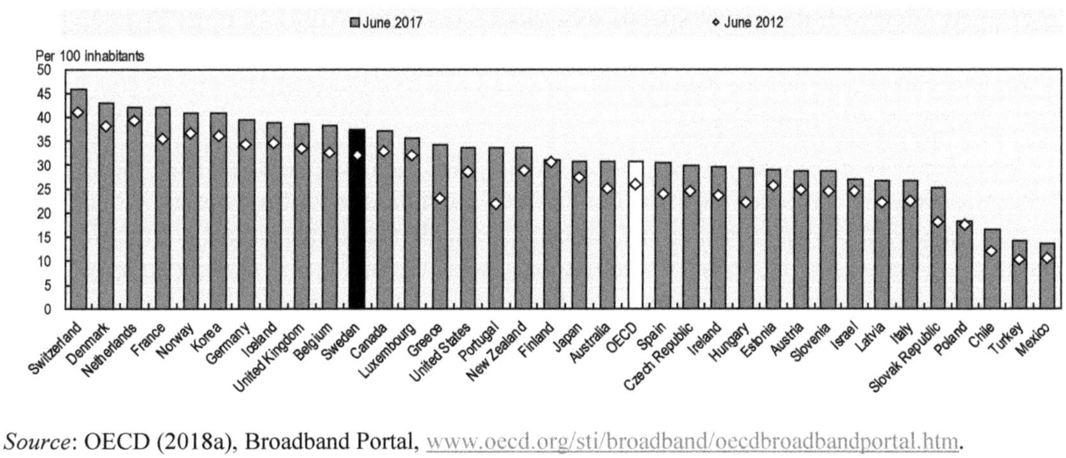

Source: OECD (2018a), Broadband Portal, www.oecd.org/sti/broadband/oecdbroadbandportal.htm.

In June 2017, in terms of mobile broadband subscriptions per 100 inhabitants, Sweden was ranked 7th in the OECD with 122.4% (Figure 2.3). This was up from 105% in 2012. In June 2017, most of these subscriptions (i.e. 102%) were "data and voice subscriptions", whereas 20.4% were "data only" subscriptions (OECD, 2018a).

Figure 2.3. **OECD mobile broadband subscriptions per 100 inhabitants, by technology, June 2017**

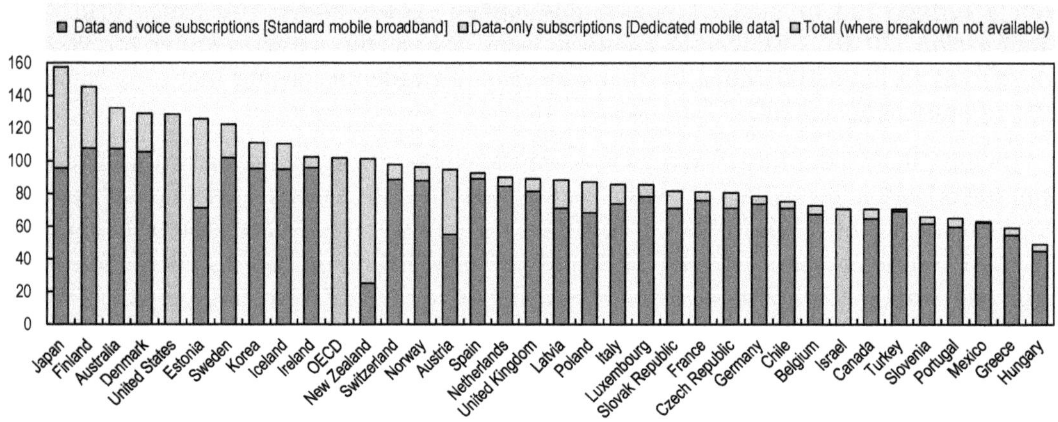

Note: Data for Israel is from GSMA Intelligence; data for Luxembourg, Mexico, Switzerland and the United States are estimates.

Source: OECD (2018a), Broadband Portal, www.oecd.org/sti/broadband/oecdbroadbandportal.htm.

Quality of broadband

A key indicator associated with assessing the quality of fixed and mobile broadband services are the speeds experienced by users. Fixed broadband download speeds in Sweden are high compared to the OECD. Internet speeds are always from the perspective of the networks involved, and as a content distribution network, Akamai provides one of the largest such views (Akamai, 2017). According to Akamai data on fixed network connectivity, Sweden ranks among the leading three countries in the OECD, with an average actual download speed of 22.5 Mbps, compared to an OECD average of 15.3 Mbps in Q1 2017 (Akamai, 2017).

A useful measure to complement any assessment of broadband services is to combine penetration rates with the actual speeds experience by users. Not only does Sweden have a relatively high broadband penetration, it also has among the largest proportion of uses at the highest tier measured by the OECD. In 2016, 16.7% were greater than 100 Mbps, second only to Korea (Figure 2.4).

A further way to consider average download speeds across countries is to look at one of the most Internet Protocol (IP) traffic intensive applications: online games. One source of such data is the platform Steam (Figure 2.5), with the statistics reflecting network performance for one of the most demanding groups of Internet users. Download speed data for the Steam application was retrieved for the week of 10 November 2017 (Steam, 2017). The leading country for average download speed for games played when the sample was taken was Korea with 99 Mbps, followed by Sweden (50.8 Mbps). OECD countries represented 54% of total Steam traffic in terms of total petabytes (PB). The United States alone constituted 16% of worldwide Steam traffic in the week of measurement (with 32.5 PB), whereas Sweden represented 1.3% of total traffic for this gaming application measured in petabytes (with 2.5 PB).

At the time the sample was taken (November 2017), there were 3.15 million active Steam users in Sweden (SteamSpy, 2017). With a population of roughly 9.9 million (2016), a sample of 3.15 million Swedish users comprises almost one-third of the country's population, which is an outstanding sample to measure broadband speeds. The average playtime of Swedish Steam users was 2 hours per day and these players own around 37 Steam games on average (SteamSpy, 2017). This makes Sweden the fifth OECD country, after Luxembourg, Iceland, Japan and Latvia, in terms of average playtime per user for Steam games.

Figure 2.4. **Fixed broadband subscriptions per 100 inhabitants, by speed tiers, December 2016**

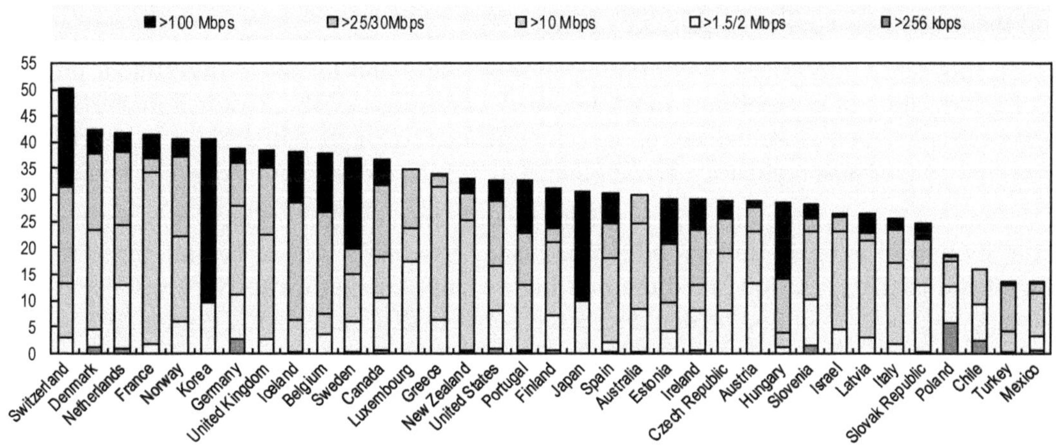

Notes: Mbps = megabits per second; kbps = kilobits per second. In Korea, 96.2% of subscriptions have a speed above 50 Mbps.

Source: OECD (2017a), "Broadband database", www.oecd.org/sti/broadband/oecdbroadband portal.htm.

Figure 2.5. **Average download speed of Steam games, OECD countries, November 2017**

Right hand side of figure shows the average download speed for Sweden disaggregated by Internet service provider

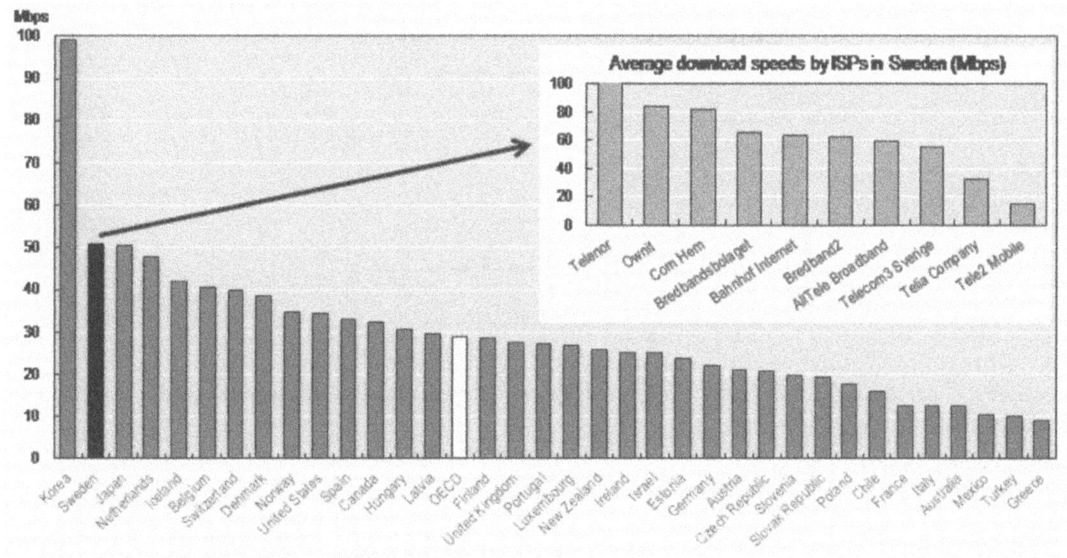

Notes: ISP = Internet service provider; Mbps = megabits per second. Data retrieved 10 November 2017, displaying the average download speed of the past seven days.

Source: Steam (2017), "Steam global traffic map (most recent 7 days)", http://store.steampowered.com/stats/content.

Prices of fixed and mobile broadband services

Prices of communication services depend greatly on the competitive conditions of the market in each country and in some instances regulation for specific services. In a sector with high fixed costs and barriers to entry, as is often the case for some telecommunication segments, the institutional and regulatory framework bears weight on the resulting market structure, and hence, has a direct influence on the affordability of communication services and the disciplines applied to prices by competition.

In this sense, the prices of communication services and levels of investment provide useful indicators of competition and framework conditions of the Swedish market. In the next section, market share indicators of communication markets will also be provided as an overview of the latest regulatory developments in Sweden which complement pricing data.

The OECD telecommunication baskets provide information on how Sweden's prices have evolved for fixed and mobile broadband. Sweden's prices for all three mobile broadband baskets (i.e. low, medium and high usage) are significantly below the OECD average, and prices within Sweden decreased between 2013 and 2017 (Figure 2.6).

Figure 2.6. **Trends in mobile broadband prices in Sweden compared to the OECD average**

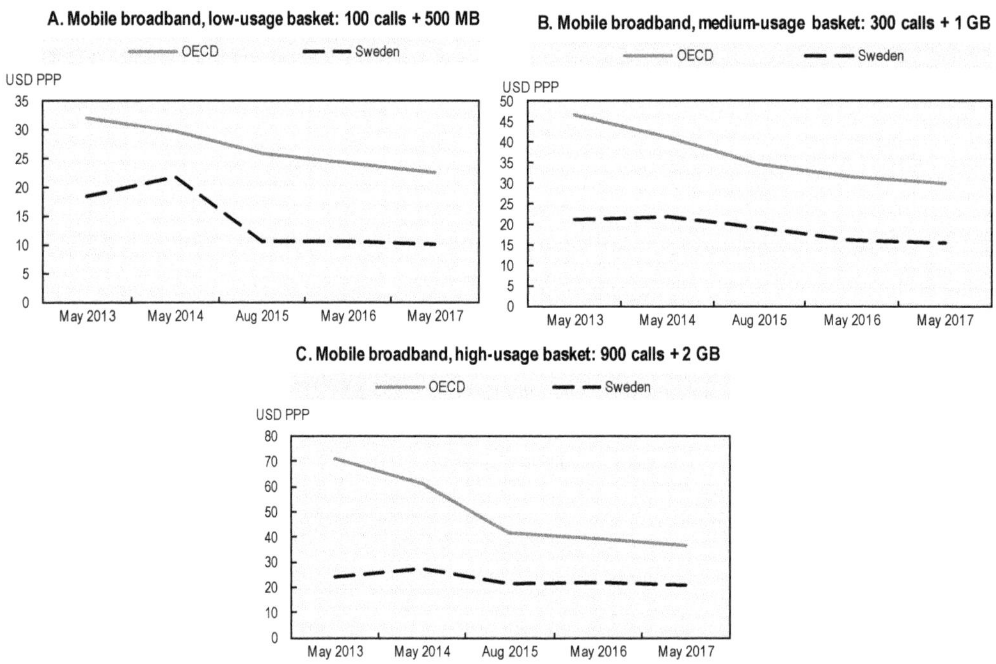

Notes: PPP = purchasing power parity; MB = megabyte; GB = gigabyte. Data for 900 calls + 2 GB are for November 2014 instead of May 2014.

Source: Author's calculations based on Strategy Analytics (2017), "Broadband", https://www.strategyanalytics.com/access-services/service-providers/tariffs---mobile-and-fixed/broadband.

In particular, the price of the low-usage mobile broadband basket (i.e. 100 calls + 500 megabytes [MB]) has experienced a sharp decrease in the last four years, decreasing from 18.48 USD PPP in May 2013 to 9.73 USD PPP in November 2017 (Figure 2.6A). Between 2013 and 2017, the price of the medium-usage basket (i.e. 300 calls + 1 gigabyte [GB]) also decreased, going from 21.09 USD PPP to 14.85 USD PPP, while the price of the high-usage basket (i.e. 900 calls + 2 GB), exhibited a similar drop, with a price of 23.94 USD PPP in 2013 to 14.85 USD PPP in November 2017 (Figures 2.6B and 2.6C).

The difference in prices in Sweden with respect to the OECD average is less striking for the fixed broadband baskets. In fact, during the period of 2013-17, the price of the "low-usage" fixed broadband basket (i.e. 20 GB) in Sweden increased from 26.96 USD PPP in June 2013 to 33.36 USD PPP in December 2017, and this basket exceeds the OECD average over the whole period. For instance, in December 2017, the price for the 20 GB fixed broadband basket in Sweden was 33.36 USD PPP, and compares to the OECD average price of 29.74 USD PPP. That being said, it is likely that there are few offers in the Swedish market that fit this profile. Indeed, in their absence, a tariff with more data included will be used, hence the price being the same for baskets with higher usage levels.

The "high-usage" fixed broadband basket (i.e. 200 GB) prices in Sweden were slightly lower than the OECD average price for such a basket for the period 2013-17 (Figure 2.7). The price of this higher usage basket in Sweden was 33.36 USD PPP in December 2017, slightly lower than the OECD average price for December 2017 of 36.33 USD PPP.

Figure 2.7. **Trends in fixed broadband prices in Sweden compared to the OECD average**

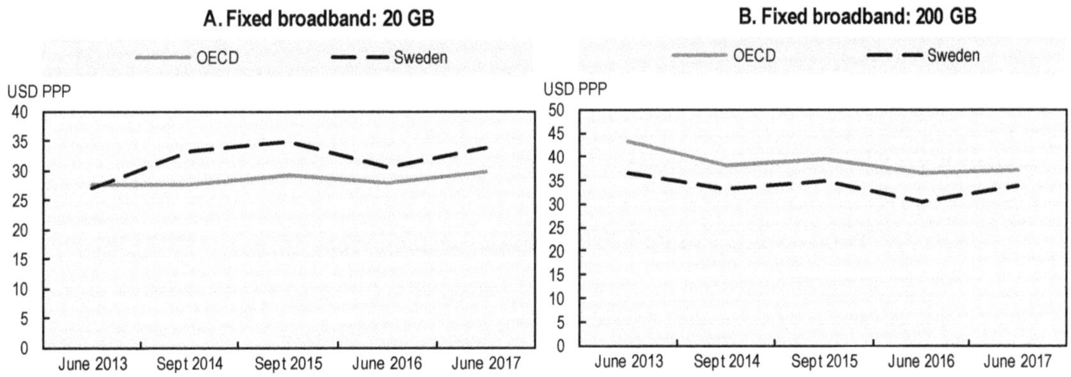

Note: PPP = purchasing power parity; GB = gigabyte.

Source: Author's calculations based on Strategy Analytics (2017), "Broadband", https://www.strategyanalytics.com/access-services/service-providers/tariffs---mobile-and-fixed/broadband.

Data (IP) traffic over broadband networks

Mobile traffic: Complementarities between fixed and mobile networks

One indicator that is closely linked to affordability of broadband packages is the amount of data used by subscribers. Sweden is among the top five OECD countries in mobile data usage per mobile broadband subscription, behind Finland, Latvia and Austria in the past six years (OECD, 2018a). The average mobile broadband subscription in Sweden was 4.38 GB per month, whereas the OECD average was 2.3 GB per month in 2016. Compared to Nordic countries, Sweden comes second after Finland (10.95 GB per month) and has almost the same usage as Denmark of 4.37 GB per month per subscription (Figure 2.8).

The Cisco VNI provides information for 13 OECD countries[4] on the percentage of smartphone data traffic offloaded through fixed networks using Wi-Fi. In 2016 this was 61% of mobile traffic for Sweden. In addition, the *OECD Digital Economy Outlook 2017* surveyed all OECD countries on the amount of mobile traffic generated per mobile broadband subscription through cellular networks. It recorded that the amount of data usage per mobile broadband (cellular) subscription in Sweden was 4.38 GB per month (OECD, 2017b). One way to see the total amount of IP traffic used by smartphones is to combine both sets of data. By doing so, one can estimate the total amount of traffic in terms of gigabytes generated by mobile devices, that is, the sum of the traffic that is offloaded through Wi-Fi, plus the traffic that is transmitted through cellular networks (Figure 2.9). Using this approach, Sweden had the largest amount of total data usage per smartphone device, behind only Korea (Figure 2.9).

Figure 2.8. **Mobile data usage per mobile broadband subscription, 2016**

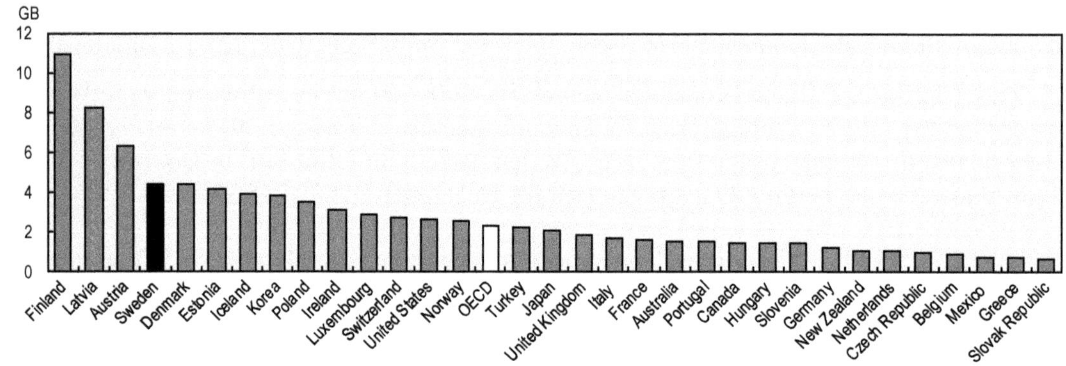

Note: GB = gigabyte.

Source: OECD (2017a), "Broadband database", www.oecd.org/sti/broadband/broadband-statistics.

Figure 2.9. **Total data per mobile broadband user (smartphone) per month, 2016**

Mobile traffic disaggregated by the Wi-Fi offloaded traffic and cellular network traffic

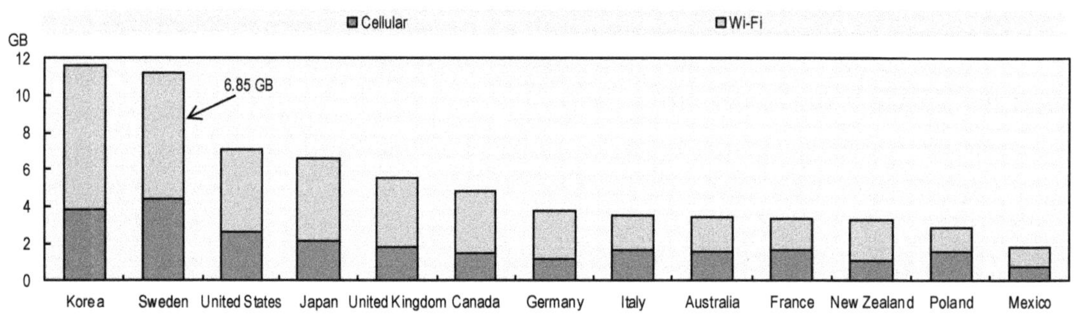

Notes: GB = gigabyte. Offloaded Wi-Fi traffic calculated using Cisco VNI data of percentage of smartphone offloaded traffic (e.g. for Sweden it was 61%).

Source: Author's calculations using data from Cisco VNI (2017), "VNI mobile forecast highlights for Sweden", https://www.cisco.com/assets/sol/sp/vni/forecast_highlights_mobile/#~Country and from OECD (2017b), *OECD Digital Economy Outlook 2017*, http://dx.doi.org/10.1787/9789264276284-en.

Sweden's increasing use of mobile data is expected to continue its upward path in the coming years. According to Cisco VNI, in Sweden, mobile data traffic will double from 2016 to 2021, a compound annual growth rate of 20%. Mobile data are expected to reach 132.8 PB per month by 2021 (i.e. the equivalent data for 33 million DVDs each month), up from 53.2 PB per month in 2016 (Cisco VNI, 2017). In addition, Cisco forecasts that mobile traffic per mobile-connected end user in Sweden will reach 7.6 GB per month by 2021, up from its earlier estimate of 3.59 GB per month for 2016, a compound annual growth rate of 16% (Cisco VNI, 2017). The latter figure by Cisco (i.e. 3.59 GB) turned out to be similar to the actual result reported by the regulatory authority, the PTS (i.e. 4.38 GB).

Internet exchange points and data centres in Sweden

Two elements of Internet infrastructure enabling efficient management of IP traffic are Internet exchange points (IXPs) and data centres. There are 14 IXPs in Sweden (PCH, 2017). Furthermore, Sweden's unique geographical position, extensive connectivity, as well as thriving digital environment makes it very appealing for Internet companies to establish data centres in Sweden (Business Sweden, 2017b). In 2017, for example, Amazon Web Services announced a new data centre region in the Stockholm area, to become operational in 2018 (Business Sweden, 2017a).

Structure of communication markets in Sweden

One characteristic of the Swedish market is that there is coverage in areas with lower population density by multiple providers. A major factor in this outcome has been the lower cost to deploy this infrastructure by the prevalence of infrastructure-sharing agreements. In addition, the use of municipal fibre networks has played an important role in making essential infrastructure available (OECD, 2014c).

Mobile market developments

Competition

Sweden's mobile telecommunication market has exhibited robust levels of competition since the turn of the century, when the first spectrum was awarded for 3G services. Apart from the management of spectrum, the primary regulatory intervention is on mobile termination rates, where by its very nature each operator has a termination monopoly for its own customers. Operators are free to make commercial agreements with mobile virtual network operators and provide wholesale access, but there are no obligations to do so in either respect.

There are five mobile network operators (MNOs) in Sweden. These are Telia, Tele2, Telenor, Hi3G (or 3) and Net 1 (an operator in the 450 megahertz [MHz] band). The 4 mobile operators held 94% of the market in 2016, while 21 mobile virtual network operators held around a 6% share. In December 2016, the market shares of the two largest MNOs (i.e. Telia and Tele2) were 35.8% and 26.5% of the market (Figure 2.10).

Figure 2.10. **Market shares of mobile operators in Sweden, December 2016**

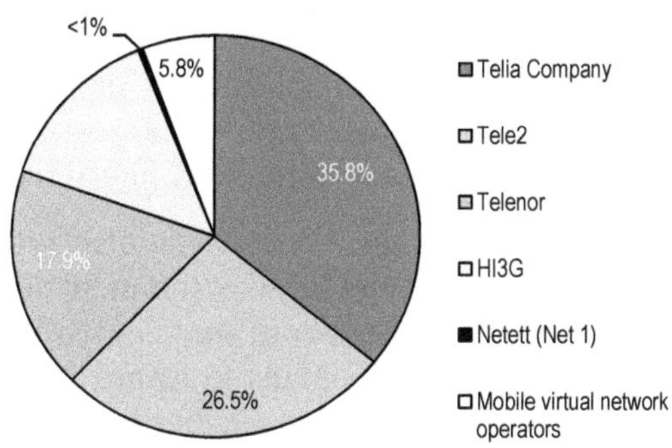

Note: There are 41 mobile virtual network operators and 5 MNOs in Sweden.

Source: PTS (2017i), "Table 1 Key data: The market for electronic communications", http://statistik.pts.se/en/the-swedish-telecommunications-market/tables/electronic-communications/table-1-key-data.

At present, there is nearly 100% 4G and 3G network coverage in Sweden (European Commission, 2017c). Authorities believe a number of factors have contributed to this coverage, including lower costs as a result of allowing infrastructure sharing, sound spectrum management and the extensive geographical availability of fibre networks to provide backhaul.

Infrastructure sharing

Passive and active infrastructure sharing can be viewed as a means to reduce costs, particularly those associated with expanding coverage, while ensuring robust competition under appropriate safeguards. Fixed infrastructure sharing includes all passive equipment such as towers, masts and ducts, as well as wholesale arrangements of dark fibre. Whereas mobile infrastructure sharing includes active parts of the network, such as radio access network (RAN) sharing agreements. A key aspect of successful infrastructure sharing is the agreements put in place between network operators. In Sweden, such agreements, for both mobile and fixed networks, were made before the building of much of today's shared facilities and were subject to careful examination by the Competition Authority and the regulator (OECD, 2014c).

All four MNOs in Sweden have had long-standing arrangements for network sharing. In particular, they all have RAN-sharing agreements, where a site and all equipment are shared.[5] This has contributed to the high network coverage in Sweden.

Fixed and mobile networks continue to be complimentary in many respects, especially given that mobile networks rely on fixed networks for backhaul. Stockholm's Stokab municipal fibre network provides one example of backhaul over shared infrastructure. Net4Mobility, a joint-venture infrastructure company providing backhaul for the long-term evolution (LTE) network of two mobile operators (i.e. Tele2 and Telenor), is one of Stokab's clients. The long-term commitment by Net4Mobility has allowed Stokab to extend its network into new areas of the city. At the same time, Net4Mobility stated that fibre network sharing has allowed the company to deploy its mobile network at a faster pace compared to regions where such shared infrastructure did not exist (OECD, 2014c).

Spectrum management

While a comparative selection process was used for the turn of the century 3G allocations, since that time the PTS has used auctions for all spectrum allocations. In addition, PTS' strategy has been to use spectrum sharing where possible.

According to PTS's "Spectrum Policy", spectrum should be managed as to maximise its social benefit and promote innovation. To achieve this, the PTS highlights three important points: i) licenses should be technologically neutral; ii) auctions should be preferably applied when selection procedures are warranted; and iii) license exemption should be introduced when there is little risk of harmful interference (PTS, 2006).

In February 2017 the PTS published an "Orientation plan for spectrum management" with the aim of presenting updates of spectrum assignment and use in the upcoming years. Several frequency bands are currently being studied, while some are expected to be licensed in the future. For instance, the PTS plans to award the license for the 450 MHz band in the first half of 2018, whereas the 1.5 gigahertz (GHz) and 2.3 GHz band are planned for 2018 or later (PTS, 2017e).

The 700 MHz band auction in Sweden was due to start in December 2016, but the PTS cancelled the planned auction on 31 October 2016 given a decision that the frequencies of this band were still to be used for broadcasting until May 2018. Furthermore, due to an evolving policy situation, there is also a consideration of whether this band should be used to ensure communications of the defence and the emergency services authorities. This overturned a previous decision by the authority in 2014 (PTS, 2017a). In June 2017, the PTS resumed the work for the 700 MHz band by opening a public consultation (PTS, 2017a).

The PTS is at present participating in the preparatory work for the ITU World Radio Conference that will take place in November 2019, where there will be discussion of possible allocation of bands for the new generation of wireless services or "5G" (PTS, 2017e). At the same time, the European Commission, which also decides on harmonisation of frequencies among member countries, has already identified the 700 MHz band, the 3.6 GHz band and the 26 GHz band as pioneer bands for 5G deployment in Europe.

In addition, given many industry developments in 5G in Sweden, the PTS planned to allocate test licences for 5G trials through administrative procedures in the first half of 2017 (PTS, 2017d). During the public consultation that took place in February 2017, market players expressed support of PTS' proposal on the Spectrum Plan for 5G tests, which includes trial licenses in the 3.4-3.6 GHz and 26 GHz bands (PTS, 2017d).

5G developments in Sweden

Industry players in Sweden are undertaking 5G trials in the millimetre wave bands, and collaborations and joint partnerships between different stakeholders are occurring in others to test 5G technology and other related applications. For example, Ericsson, in collaboration with Telia, has performed outdoor testing in Kista, Stockholm (Ericsson, 2016). Also, in August 2017 Telia, Boliden, Ericsson, Volvo, ABB, RISE SICS and LTU Technologies joined forces to test 5G technology for safety communications in the Kankberg underground mine in Boliden, Sweden (RR Media Group, 2017). In January 2016, Telia and Ericsson announced that by 2018 they would launch a 5G network in Stockholm and Tallinn. In November 2016, Telia announced a similar joint venture with Nokia to launch a 5G network in Helsinki (Telia, 2017a).

An application that is closely related to 5G and the Internet of Things (IoT) is autonomous driving. Volvo is planning to offer customers fully autonomous vehicles by 2021, and initiated in January 2017 a massive trial of 100 self-driving vehicles tested by ordinary people in the city of Gothenburg (Carlström, 2017).

Internet of Things: Sweden a leader in machine-to-machine connections

As highlighted at the OECD Cancun Ministerial, following the convergence between fixed and mobile networks and between telecommunication and broadcasting, the IoT represents the next step in convergence between ICTs and economies and societies on an unprecedented scale. It holds the promise of substantially contributing to further innovation, growth and social prosperity, and as with any such development, policy makers and other stakeholders need evidence to inform the decisions they will take in the coming years. The Cancun Ministerial Mandate identified a set of areas for stakeholder engagement to promote IoT deployment. In particular, it highlighted the importance of developing metrics to measure the effects of adoption of the IoT in different policy areas (OECD, 2016).

The IoT is expected to grow exponentially, connecting many billions of devices in a relatively short period of time (OECD, 2015). Sweden has been at the forefront of this market development, especially in terms of M2M communications. M2M connected devices are a small subset of the IoT as, increasingly, IoT connected devices are becoming IP-based and platform-agnostic (i.e. operating on mobile, fixed and other networks).

M2M devices are characterised by autonomous data communication with little or no human interaction (OECD, 2015).

Since 2012, OECD countries have been collecting data on M2M embedded mobile cellular subscriptions.[6] By June 2017 there were 174.5 million M2M communication subscriptions in the OECD, up from 108 million at the end of 2014 (OECD, 2017b). In terms of M2M penetration, Sweden has 101.5 M2M SIM cards per 100 inhabitants – a much higher level than for most other OECD countries, and well above the OECD average of around 16% (Figure 2.11). It is important to note one caveat for M2M data and that is that not all of these devices are located in Sweden.

In regards to enabling robust development of the IoT, the PTS has allocated spectrum that is used by various applications for the IoT and M2M. In addition, as early as 2005, the PTS had identified numbering as one of the regulatory issues surrounding the IoT, and since then has dedicated number series for both fixed and mobile networks allocated exclusively for M2M (i.e. a total of 10 billion numbers).

Figure 2.11. **M2M/embedded mobile cellular subscriptions, June 2017**

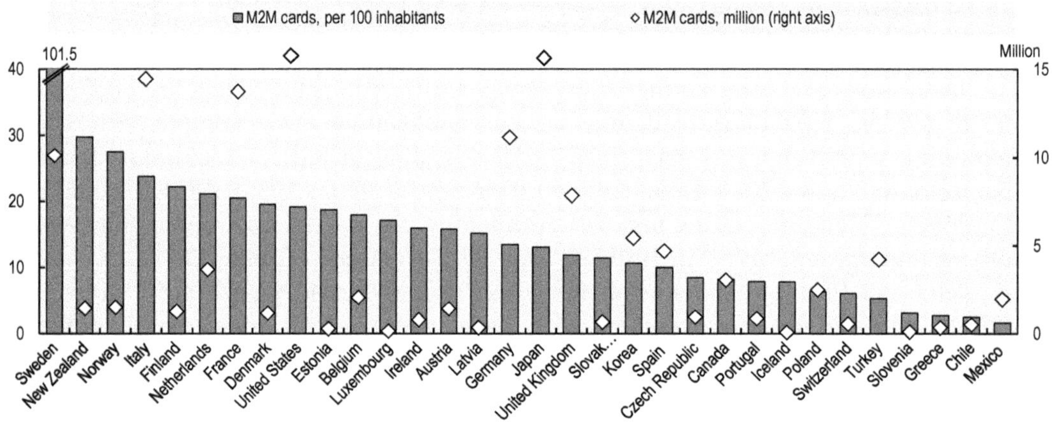

Notes: The OECD defines machine-to-machine (M2M) on mobile networks as "the number of SIM-cards that are assigned for use in machines and devices (cars, smart meters, and consumer electronics) and are not part of a consumer subscription". This means that dongles for mobile data and tablet subscriptions should be counted by countries under the mobile broadband definition; whereas SIM cards in personal navigation devices, smart meters, trains, automobiles, etc., should be counted under the M2M category.

Source: OECD (2018a), Broadband Portal, www.oecd.org/sti/broadband/oecdbroadbandportal.htm.

In June 2017, there were approximately 10.1 million M2M-embedded SIM cards in Sweden (Figure 2.11). Meanwhile, using a different definition of M2M, the number of mobile-connected M2M "modules" or devices in Sweden reached 4 million in 2016, and is expected under this measure to reach 13 million in 2021 (Cisco VNI, 2017).

The policies that the PTS has followed in terms of numbering have undoubtedly contributed to Sweden's leading position in IoT development. Some of this has occurred domestically, but it has also opened opportunities for Swedish firms in foreign markets. This is why Sweden's M2M penetration is recorded as being much higher than that of other OECD countries (Figure 2.11), including in the Nordic and Baltic regions (Figure 2.12). At the forefront Telenor Connexion, which held 81% of the M2M market share in Sweden in 2016 according to PTS figures, uses its numbering (IMSI numbers) not only for Sweden, but also for its clients around the world. For example, if Volvo, a client of Telenor Connexion, sells an automobile with a SIM card and this vehicle is sold outside Sweden anywhere around the world, it shows up in the M2M figures of Sweden provided by the PTS. In this case, the Volvo vehicle shows up in the local network outside Sweden as a foreign roamer. The most recent data for 2016 indicate one or more connectivity providers in Latvia are also likely benefiting from the use of M2M numbering for foreign services.

Figure 2.12. **M2M subscriptions per 100 inhabitants in Nordic and Baltic countries**

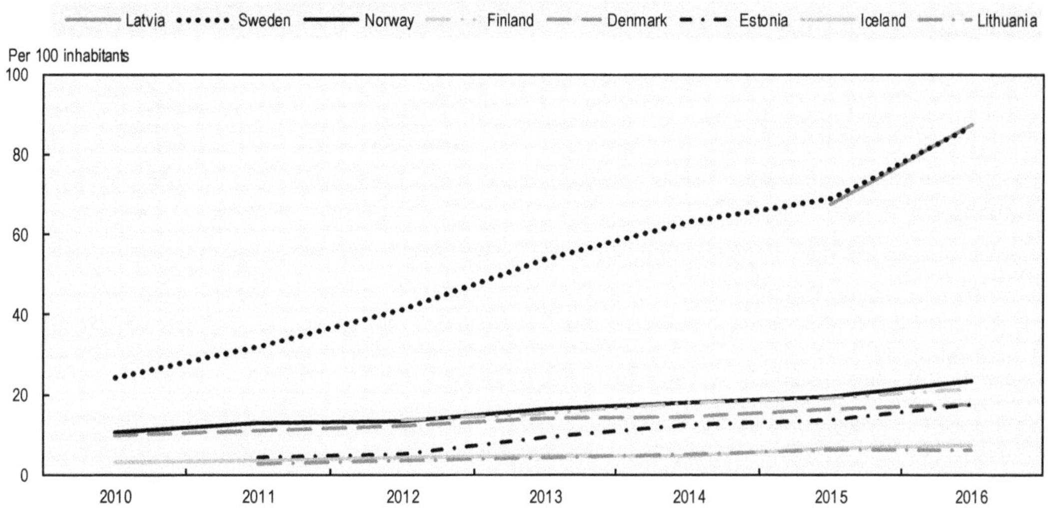

Sources: PTS (2017g), "Telecommunication markets in the Nordic and Baltic countries", http://statistik.pts.se/en/nordic-baltic-telecom-market/tables/mobile-call-and-data-services/table-1-subscriptions; OECD (2018c), Population (indicator), http://dx.doi.org/10.1787/d434f82b-en.

As mentioned previously, since 2012 most OECD countries have been collecting data on M2M subscriptions, and Sweden has gone a step further by complementing these data by gathering information on how much revenue is generated per year by M2M subscriptions. Furthermore, since 2010, the PTS has collected data on the amount of M2M traffic. The collection of data for all these indicators is commendable, as they provide relevant information for all stakeholders, and such information is likely to be increasingly pivotal for informing future developments across the digital economy.

While still relatively small when measured per M2M subscription compared to smartphones, such traffic grew from less than 1 MB per M2M subscription in 2010 to almost 23 MB in 2016 (Figure 2.13B). Notable, however, was the sharp increase in 2016. This is likely due to an evolution in the M2M market, with some application of the technology being used in areas that generate higher amounts of traffic, such as connected automobiles. According to Cisco VNI data, M2M traffic in Sweden will grow tenfold from 2016-21 (compound annual growth rate of 59%), and will account for 9% of total mobile data traffic, compared to 2% at the end of 2016 (Cisco VNI, 2017).

The PTS also collects data on the amount of revenue generated by M2M subscriptions. On a per subscription basis these have declined since 2008, decreasing from a little more than USD 2 per month in 2008-09 to roughly USD 1 in 2016 (Figure 2.13A). Another Nordic communications authority collecting data on M2M revenues is in Norway, where the experience has been similar to that of Sweden, as monthly revenues per M2M subscriptions have declined over the past three years. This may be because of the large increase in M2M devices and new tariff plans.

Figure 2.13. **Monthly M2M revenues and traffic per subscription in Sweden**

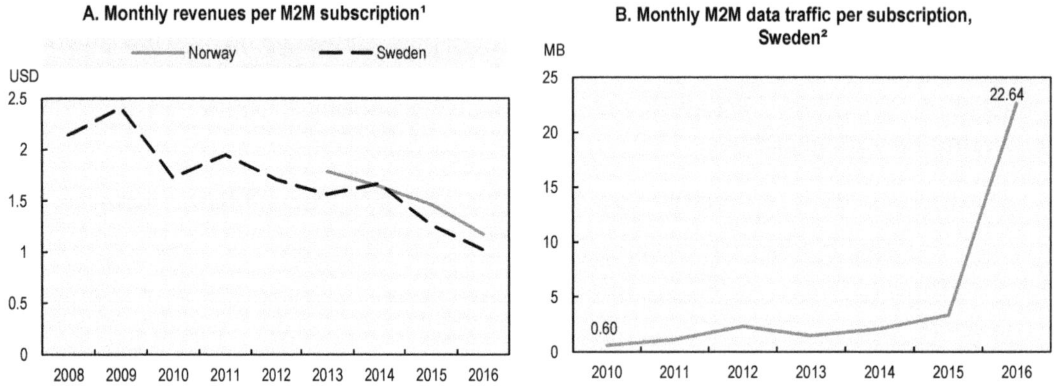

1. Revenues of M2M are compared between Sweden and Norway. The number of M2M subscriptions of both countries was taken from PTS (2017g).

2. The PTS defines M2M as communication between machines used for telematics and telemetry.

Notes: MB = megabyte. The PTS defines subscriptions as contract subscriptions plus pre-paid cards. Pre-paid cards are reported according to the three-month rule. The increase in traffic for data services between 2015 and 2016 depends on Telia's reporting. Telia reported for 2016 around 2 000 Tbytes and for 2015 76 Tbytes. Telia says that the 2015 data are too low, but an actual value is not available.

Source: Author's calculations using data from the PTS and the Norway National Communications Authority (2018), "M2M sales" (in Norwegian), https://ekomstatistikken.nkom.no/#/statistics/details?servicearea=Mobiltjenester &label=Maskin-til-maskin%20-%20omsetning.

In the future, different M2M applications are likely to generate very different usage patterns. Environmental sensors, for example, may only generate very small amounts of data relative to connected bicycles and robots, right up to perhaps the largest amounts in the case of autonomous vehicles. This is why, for the future, the PTS should consider breaking out M2M traffic for categories of devices that may make tremendous demands on networks. As an M2M leader and likely to be one of the first countries to deploy 5G, as well as having leading automobile and telecommunication equipment manufacturers, Sweden is in an ideal position to assess the implications of autonomous transport for the digital economy.

Although OECD countries have witnessed high growth of M2M connected devices, in terms of revenues, M2M is still a nascent market. For instance, according to the PTS, M2M only generated SEK 908 million (USD 106.05 million) in revenues 2016, making up 1.7% of the total Swedish telecommunication market.[7] Nevertheless, M2M as subset of the IoT has the potential to grow in the near future with new business cases emerging. That is, although at present M2M is not large in terms of revenues, with the growth of the IoT and evolving business models, it is expected to become the majority of connections, with implications for infrastructure with the advent of 5G and autonomous vehicles.

Fixed market developments

Competition

In Sweden, 111 fixed network operators owned and controlled their own infrastructure in 2016. Telia is the historical incumbent and owns the only network with public switched telephone network (PSTN)/xDSL technology, with plans to gradually transition its legacy copper network. The total number of subscriptions for the two largest fixed operators (measured in terms of PSTN and broadband) are 3 316 400 and 903 600 for Telia and Com Hem, respectively.

The Swedish government has a 37.3% share in the ownership of Telia. Many networks are fully owned by municipal governments. At the end of 2016, there were 156 providers of fibre subscriptions to end users in Sweden (PTS, 2017h). Out of these fibre providers, 43 were municipality networks (municipalities or municipality-owned enterprises).

In 2017, there were 156 municipal fibre networks in Sweden. However, most of them provided wholesale products such as "dark fibre" and Ethernet capacity. According to the PTS, the municipal networks that do provide broadband subscriptions are typically, though not always, smaller municipalities. In terms of fixed broadband subscriptions to end users, municipal networks accounted for approximately for 4% of the market share, where the largest municipal network registered 9 064 fibre subscriptions at the end of 2016.

The three largest fixed broadband operators, Telia, Telenor and Com Hem, accounted for almost 73% of fixed broadband subscriptions in December 2016 (PTS, 2017h). The fixed broadband market in Sweden is comprised of 3.7 million subscriptions, of which 54% were on either Telia's or Telenor's network in 2016 (Figure 2.14).

Figure 2.14. **Fixed broadband market shares in Sweden, December 2016**

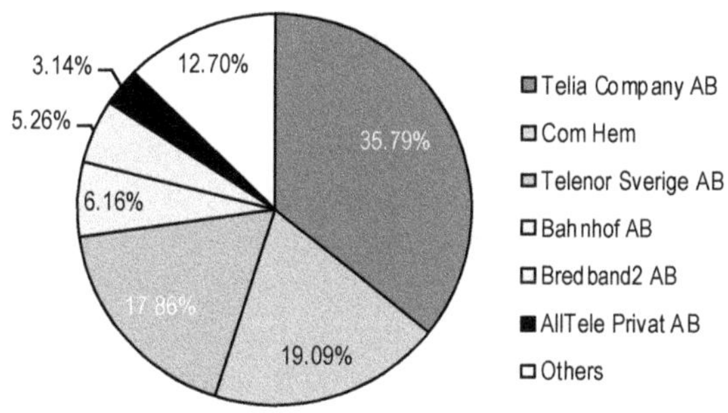

Note: "Others" includes 169 active and smaller ISPs in Sweden.

Source: PTS (2017i), "Table 1 Key data: The market for electronic communications", http://statistik.pts.se/en/the-swedish-telecommunications-market/tables/electronic-communications/table-1-key-data.

Figure 2.15. **Historical investment in fixed networks in Sweden, 2016 prices**

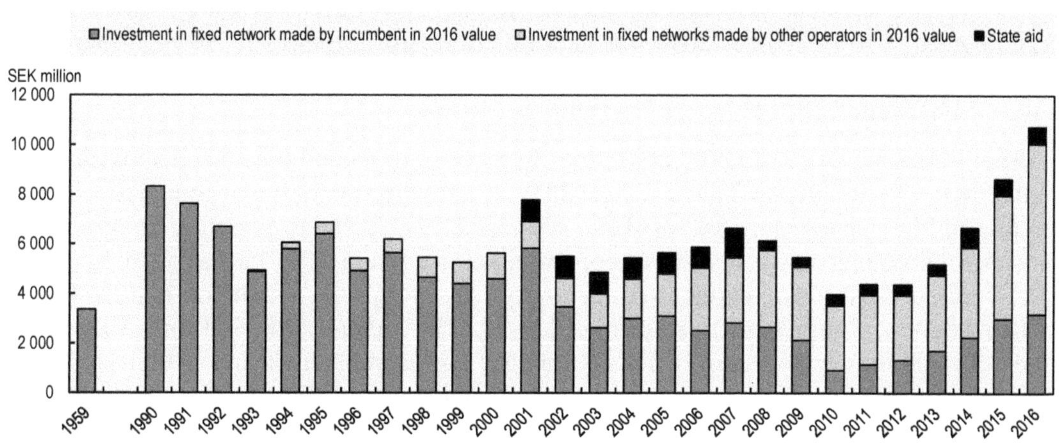

Source: Data provided by the PTS.

Historically, the incumbent, Telia, invested the most in fixed network infrastructure, and a peak can be observed in the mid-1990s, which represented investments in PSTN technology. A decrease in investment levels from the incumbent operator can be observed since 1990. Although Telia still accounted for 50% of investment in fixed infrastructure over the last decade, since 2006, investment by other players (e.g. IP Only and municipal fibre networks), together with state aid, have taken a more prominent role. This has coincided with the PTS reportings that IP Only, an entrant in the fibre infrastructure market, invested SEK 3.3 billion (USD 0.39 billion) during the period 2013-16.[8] Investment in fixed network infrastructure reached a record high in 2016 (Figure 2.15).

Next generation access in Sweden

The OECD has used the term "next-generation" access (NGA) networks to describe the requirement of fibre coming closer to the end user, or providing the direct connection (OECD, 2011). Aside from fibre to the home (FTTH), NGA access can also include wireless technologies, and other access networks with different technologies (e.g. VDSL, fibre to the premises [FTTP] and DOCSIS 3.0). This section considers mostly networks that deliver "ultra-fast broadband" (or speeds higher than 100 Mbps), in line with the connectivity targets that Sweden aims to achieve.

According to the European Commission's definition, the overall NGA coverage in Sweden, measured by the percentage of households with access to broadband via VDSL, FTTP or DOCSIS 3.0 technologies, was 77.7% in 2017, up from 56.6% in 2012 (European Commission, 2018). However, the PTS has mentioned a caveat regarding European comparison of coverage statistics, as it would seem the definition for NGA coverage according to the European Union is FTTP, whereas Sweden reports FTTH figures. In addition, the PTS has pointed out that Sweden's target of remote areas may be more ambitious than that of other EU countries.[9] With this caveat in mind, national coverage of NGA in 2017 in Sweden was similar to the EU28 average of 80.1%; however, there is a sharp difference when compared to the rest of Europe in terms of NGA coverage in rural areas. In Sweden, only 22.7% of rural households had access to NGA networks, whereas the average for the EU28 was 46.9% in 2017 (European Commission, 2018).

In June 2017, the share of fibre in broadband connections in Sweden was one of the highest in the OECD, just behind Japan, Korea and Latvia (Figure 2.16).[10] From December 2012 to December 2016, the share of fibre subscriptions in Sweden increased from 33.7% to 55%, whereas this same share as a percentage of total broadband subscriptions in the OECD went from 14% to 21.2% (OECD, 2018a).

The decreasing share of DSL connections in Sweden in overall broadband subscriptions, from almost 47% in 2012 to 23.4% in June 2017, is an indication of the ongoing reduction in the use of the legacy network of Telia (Figure 2.17). Telia is planning to gradually transition its copper network. These copper lines are planned to be replaced by fibre, fixed wireless services or wireless connectivity. The point of comparison can be Japan, another country with a high fibre penetration rate. In Japan, NTT East and NTT West have both said they will cease to offer asymmetric digital subscriber line (ADSL) services from 2023, citing the declining number of subscriptions and difficulty to get maintenance parts (NTT East, 2017).

Although Telia does not have any universal service obligation, during this ongoing transition from the existing PSTN based on copper to an all IP network, Telia has made a commitment to safeguard communication to all concerned households currently connected to the part of the copper network that will soon be transitioned (PTS, 2015).

Figure 2.16. **Percentage of fibre connections in total broadband among countries reporting fibre subscribers, June 2017**

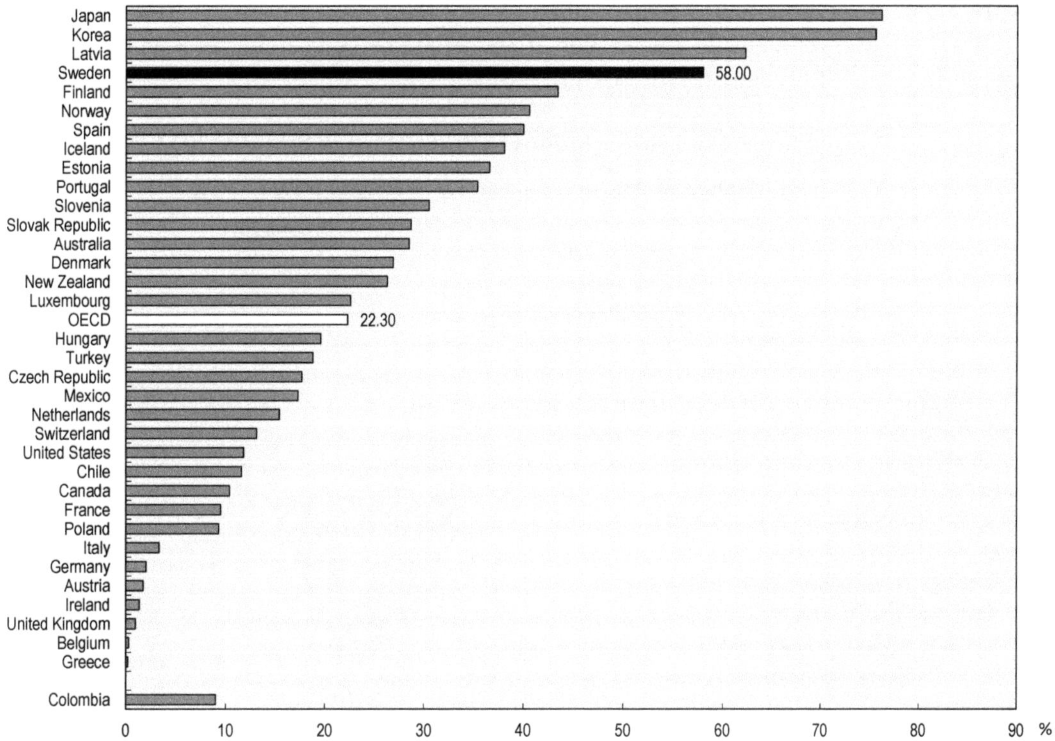

Notes: Fibre subscription data include FTTH, FTTP and fibre to the building (FTTB) and excludes fibre to the cabinet (FTTC). Some countries may have fibre but did not report figures, so they are not included in the graph. Israel, Switzerland and the United States: data for December 2016 are estimates; Germany: fibre includes fibre lines provided by cable operators; United Kingdom: no fibre data are available as digital subscriber line (DSL) includes all fibre technologies (FTTH, FTTP, FTTB and FTTC) because the breakdown between these technologies is not available yet.

Source: OECD (2018a), Broadband Portal, www.oecd.org/sti/broadband/oecdbroadbandportal.htm.

Telia aims to streamline its network and close down small and unprofitable exchanges from its copper legacy network. It is involved in an ongoing project for "the network of the future", which consists of dismantling small exchanges and instead providing consumers with mobile communications (PTS, 2015). This mobile connectivity may be done through 4G and 5G networks. In fact, Telia plans to deploy 5G networks by 2018 (Telia, 2017b). Furthermore, by 2025, the company aspires to build a single "seamless, borderless, roaming free network that delivers 1 Gbps across the entire Nordic and Baltic region" (Telia, 2017b).

The second relevant player in the deployment of NGA networks is a new entrant in the fibre market called IP Only. In 2016, this entrant had a 2.3% share of the fibre access market measured in terms of revenues, whereas Telia held 31% of the same market (PTS, 2017c). Given that IP Only deploys an open network where Internet service providers (ISPs) provide retail services, the subscriber numbers for IP Only do not reveal how large of a share the company has on the infrastructure market. This makes the revenue share more relevant. IP Only is in a race with Telia, the incumbent, as well as with municipal networks, to provide fibre, and the PTS reports that it invested SEK 3.3 billion (USD 0.39 billion) during the period 2013-16.[11] The company says it has invested EUR 1.5 billion since it entered the market, out of which half of its investment in infrastructure is dedicated to rural areas in the country. In fact, in 2017 the European Investment Bank provided IP Only with EUR 125 million in debt financing to extend its fibre network in rural areas (European Commission, 2017a). IP Only is one of the main players selling network capacity or Ethernet to players that are not telecom operators (i.e. leased lines), holding a 17% market share in December 2016, whereas Telia held 30% of this market measured in terms of revenue (PTS, 2017c).

Figure 2.17. **Fixed broadband subscriptions by technology in Sweden, 2012 vs. 2017**

OECD share of fibre over total broadband subscriptions

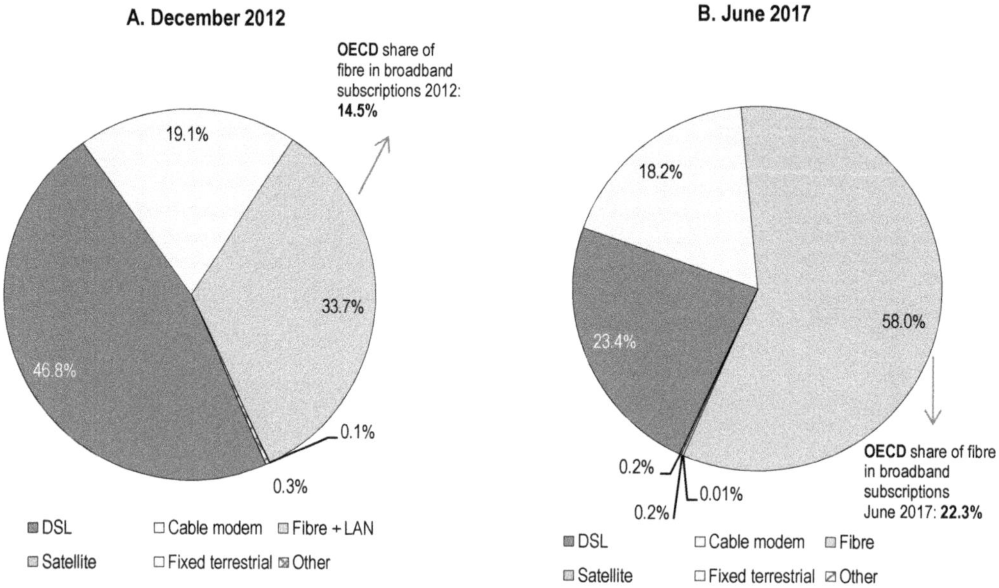

Note: DSL = digital subscriber line; LAN = local area network.

Source: OECD (2017a), "Broadband database", www.oecd.org/sti/broadband/broadband-statistics.

The third group of fixed network players are the 156 municipal fibre networks present in 200 of the 290 municipalities of Sweden. Most of these networks only provide wholesale products such as dark fibre and Ethernet capacity (i.e. bitstream access). There are also 43 municipal networks that provide fibre subscriptions to end users, who hold approximately 4% of the retail fibre market share according to PTS data of December 2016. IP Only accounts for 0.4% of the market, whereas the vast majority of fibre connections to end users are provided by Telia (i.e. 30%) (PTS, 2017c).

The following section provides more details on this group of actors that have played a key role in the deployment of high-speed networks in Sweden since the 1990s.

Ex ante *asymmetric regulatory measures applied to dominant players*

Sweden, as many other European countries, has a set of NGA and local loop unbundling regulations for an operator with significant market power (SMP). These SMP measures are based on EU directives and recommendations. Accordingly, since 2010 Telia, given that it holds SMP status, has the obligation to provide access to the unbundled local loop on copper and wholesale access to fibre. However, the price of fibre access is not regulated by the PTS, whereas the price of local loop unbundling (i.e. copper) is set by the regulator.

Price regulation on wholesale access to fibre was relaxed for Telia in December 2016. Henceforth, with regards to fibre-based local access, Telia is obliged to provide wholesale access on a non-discriminatory basis meeting the requirements of equivalence of inputs (i.e. the same price Telia would charge to its retail unit). That is, rivals should be able to economically replicate services in the retail market based on wholesale access to the fibre. The latter is examined through an economic replicability test, which is not a full-fledged margin squeeze test, but rather a safeguard that Telia is not abusing its dominant position.

Municipal networks in Sweden

A decisive factor in Sweden's high fibre take-up is that municipal networks have been widely deployed in the country since the liberalisation of the communication market (Mölleryd, 2015).

In Swedish municipalities, broadband is viewed as a utility, where local authorities are responsible of providing a significant proportion of public services and infrastructure. Local governments view municipal fibre networks as a basic infrastructure for their communities. Two notable examples of municipal networks are Stokab in Stockholm,[12] leasing dark fibre to ISPs, MNOs and other interested parties, and Fiberstaden in the Hudiksvall municipality.

Most Swedish municipal networks provide retail "operator"-neutral network infrastructure based on fibre to the building or FTTH. That is, their business model relies on open networks where they act as physical infrastructure providers offering wholesale access to retailers on a non-discriminatory basis. This has led to a notion of "open" municipal networks, which contrasts with other business models for backbone and backhaul provision of fibre that rely on completely vertically integrated telecommunication operators present both in wholesale and retail markets (Mölleryd, 2015).

It needs to be noted that the concept of "openness" when it comes to municipal networks depends on the definition of vertical integration. Vertical integration here is understood as a player present in two downstream markets, even if both are on a wholesale level (e.g. infrastructure provider and network operator of active equipment). Some municipal networks act only as dark fibre providers, and are truly "operator neutral" at the active equipment layer (network providers), as well as the service provision level (ISPs), whereas many municipal networks are vertically integrated in both wholesale markets which may limit the players in the bitstream access market. Few municipal networks are present in all three layers (both wholesale markets as well as retail markets).

Municipal networks in Sweden vary in terms of cost structures and commercial strategies, therefore wholesale prices will also exhibit differences. Wholesale prices influence the number of ISPs that will be present in the local broadband market. The competition between ISPs strongly influences retail prices. In 2014, an OECD report found that retail prices of broadband subscriptions in municipal networks in Sweden with several ISPs were 23-38% lower than the prices of Swedish ISPs with national coverage. In addition, broadband prices with several ISPs present in a municipal network were on average 25% lower compared to municipal networks with only one ISP present (Mölleryd, 2015).[13]

For the most part, there are three roles different stakeholders take in fibre networks in Sweden depending on the layer of broadband infrastructure and services:

- infrastructure provider (e.g. dark fibre)
- network operator (e.g. manage and own active network infrastructure, for example bitstream access)
- service provider (e.g. Internet or pay-TV service provider).

Some municipal networks act in one, two or all three of the roles outlined above if they are completely vertically integrated up to the retail level. In the latter case, they could have a dominant position if there were no other ISPs in that area. In Sweden, following the SMP regulatory framework, as a result of the product market definition, the market for "wholesale local access provided at a fixed location" (i.e. EU market "3a") is national in geographic scope. Hence, only one player in Sweden, Telia, has SMP status and is regulated *ex ante* through a decision based on the Electronic Communications Act.[14] This means that municipal networks acting in all three roles, at present, would not be susceptible to competition remedies or regulatory actions.[15] Municipal networks may be regulated if the PTS deems that they have SMP status in specific relevant markets and that these should be regulated.[16]

Depending on how fibre deployment costs in Sweden change when examined at a local level, the model used by municipal networks (i.e. what roles they adopt) will vary. Deployment costs, and hence the models adopted by municipal networks, are likely to depend on several factors, including demand, population density and geography (i.e. urban/rural). In addition, Swedish end users have a high willingness to pay the upfront fee for the roll-out of FTTH. For example, owners of single dwelling units in Sweden in 2014 paid an installation fee of around EUR 2 000 (USD 2 667) (BEREC, 2016).[17]

Some stakeholders have even attributed the lack of upgrading of Swedish networks to support IPv6 to the heterogeneous open access models that exist for fixed networks, suggesting that some models have worked better than others, in the sense of providing incentives to upgrade network equipment. For instance, in the case of municipal networks, different models exist regarding the level of presence of a given player in the passive and active wholesale level which determines the degree of open access of the network.

A common business model for municipal networks is one of open networks where municipal networks act as infrastructure providers, that is they own and maintain the passive infrastructure (e.g. "dark fibre") and offer wholesale access on a non-discriminatory basis to network providers (Mölleryd, 2015).

Municipal networks adopting open network architecture and acting only at the passive level of the infrastructure (i.e. playing only the role of infrastructure provider), may provide more incentives to network operators (and service providers) to upgrade active parts of the networks (or services). One example of a network that plays only the role of infrastructure provider (as it leases dark fibre) is Stokab.

The "Stokab municipal network model" is an open network providing access to dark fibre. Proponents say the key factor behind Stokab's success is that it only provides passive infrastructure (as opposed to bitstream access or active infrastructure), facilitating investment by ISPs and mobile operators as they maintain the incentives to improve services for their customers. One of the outcomes of this "open access" model has been extensive availability of high-speed broadband networks with a dynamic ISP market in Stockholm. This partially reflects the fact that Stokab is present in a location with multiple dwelling units present, but also the success of the wholesale model it follows.

In the 1990s, the liberalisation of the telecommunication market in Sweden not only encouraged alternative operators to expand and the creation of municipal networks, but also local communities to form co-operatives for the roll-out of fibre networks, commonly referred to as village networks. The Broadband Forum estimates that there are around 1 000 village fibre networks, and each of these networks connects on average 150-200 households (Box 2.1).

Box 2.1. **The village fibre approach in Sweden**

Deployment cost savings of village fibre

The "village fibre" approach is based on the premise of community involvement to plan, build and operate local fibre networks in co-operation with municipalities and commercial operators.

Proponents say the village fibre approach facilitates fibre deployment at a considerably lower cost compared to commercial operators through a combination of three factors: i) handling of permissions; ii) excavation work and trenching; and iii) voluntary work in respect to aggregation of demand. Moreover, the deployment of fibre networks through village fibre as well as all other operators is facilitated by consumers' willingness to pay upfront fees of around USD 2 300 to connect single dwelling units, and the possibility to apply for a subsidy from public funds.

Deployment costs of fibre are much higher in sparsely populated areas than in urban ones, and thus, state aid is primarily intended to offset these differences. Given that village networks are deployed in areas where no commercial operators are deploying fibre networks, they meet the key criteria for state aid. Compared to commercial broadband projects, village fibre projects can achieve cost savings of some 50% using an innovative handling of permissions as well as excavation and voluntary work. A further reduction of some 25% is achieved through state aid, making the connection fee equivalent to that of urban areas (Figure 2.18).

Figure 2.18. **Estimated cost savings by village fibre compared to operators**

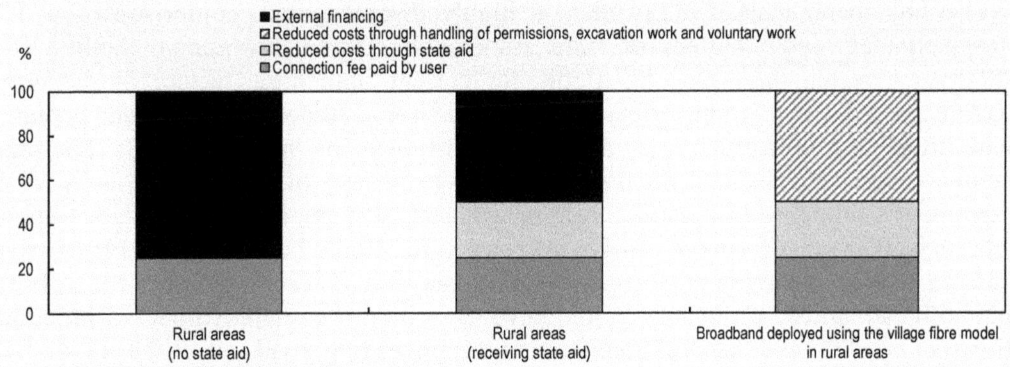

Note: Index based on the commercial cost in rural areas.

Source: PTS.

Coverage objectives: Regional deployment and access

Setting broadband availability targets in terms of speed will have an influence on the network costs that are required to meet the goals within a digital agenda. For instance, broadband speeds above 100 Mbps or, as the case of Sweden at 1 Gbps, may require upgrades of existing infrastructure to NGA networks, which consequently impacts deployment costs depending on the country (given its geography and existent legacy network).

Given the evolution of fibre networks through the municipal open network infrastructure, as well as the deployment in rural areas by IP Only and Telia, Sweden is well ahead of the curve in terms of NGA deployment, and will most likely meet the objectives with a speed of 100 Mbps. This being said, to meet the "last-mile" of the Digital Agenda's objective (i.e. to connect all households, even those in very remote or rural areas), Sweden may face challenges. In addition, the advantages of the municipal network approach that until now have enabled extensive fibre deployments, could represent a challenge going forward when considering a ubiquitous coverage goal at such high speeds with a multiplicity of stakeholders and municipal network models, which may face interoperability issues at a larger scale.

According to the PTS, in 2017, 78.5% of Sweden's households had access to broadband at speeds higher than 100 Mbps, up from 68.7% in 2015. Therefore, it seems likely that Sweden may be able to comply with the broadband target established in 2009, i.e. 90% of households and businesses with broadband access of 100 Mbps by 2020.

For Sweden's new broadband strategy, which aims to provide 98% of households with 1 Gbps broadband by 2025, a wider deployment of NGA networks will perhaps be necessary. In terms of NGA coverage, defined by the European Commission as including VDSL, FTTP and DOCSIS 3.0, 77.7% of households had coverage in 2017, compared to 56.6% in 2012 (European Commission, 2018). There is a difference with household uptake of NGA broadband in rural communities, as this amounted to only 22.7% of rural households in Sweden by 2017, albeit up from 6.3% in 2012 (European Commission, 2018). Thus, there is regional heterogeneity in the access to high-speed broadband in Sweden, as can be seen in the broadband speed maps. For instance, in Stockholm municipality 97% of households have access to 100 Mbps broadband, whereas in the Stromsund municipality only 31% of households and businesses have access to connections at these speeds (PTS, 2018).[18]

The broadband market in Sweden is highly disaggregated, comprised of at least 500 stakeholders and hundreds of fibre associations (Swedish National Audit Office, 2017). As a result, there may be a role for current fibre infrastructure of the central government to be used more effectively, as has been outlined in the recent document "State broadband infrastructure as a resource" (Ministry of Industry, 2016). The report contains several suggestions on how to improve the use of the over-capacity of the government's broadband infrastructure. For instance, how publicly owned dark fibre and ducts, as well as other forms of passive infrastructure, should be made available to private actors to reduce deployment costs by market players. It also highlights the role that regional broadband co-ordinators should have to facilitate "co-deployment" of broadband infrastructure with other network deployment initiatives (e.g. roads, electricity).

With the aim of improving co-ordination among the plethora of actors in the broadband market, in 2017 the Swedish government appointed funds for regional broadband co-ordinators, organised under the Broadband Forum. Albeit the regional broadband co-ordinators cannot fully address the issue, they are specifically tasked with the responsibility to promote and streamline the expansion of both fixed and wireless broadband deployment.

While municipal networks and the village fibre approach can assist in addressing broadband deployment costs, and contribute to achieving Sweden's broadband targets for 2020, it is important to highlight the potential risks of the uneven deployment of "ultra-fast" robust broadband networks. For example, in 2017 the Swedish National Audit Office report highlighted that there is a risk of uneven distribution of "robust" fibre networks in Sweden. Particularly, the report found a lack of robustness in access networks owned by non-profit associations that build broadband infrastructure in rural areas (known as fibre associations or the village fibre approach) as well as some municipal networks that lease active infrastructure, such as bitstream access (Swedish National Audit Office, 2017).

Other than providing state aid through European Union funds (i.e. the Rural Development Programme and the European Regional Development Fund), there are other ways the European Commission is supporting Sweden to extend fibre deployment in rural communities. For example, the European Investment Bank has provided IP Only, the entrant in fibre deployment at the national level in Sweden, with EUR 125 million in debt financing over the next four years to deploy fibre networks in rural areas, covering almost 400 000 households and firms (European Commission, 2017d).

Although initiatives to help fund rural broadband deployment, in addition to the village and municipal network approaches, could help mitigate the current issues of uneven broadband deployment in Sweden between rural and urban households, other potential issues remain to be addressed. Such issues include the incentives to upgrade networks given the degree of vertical integration of municipal networks at a wholesale level (i.e. the presence of one player in both the passive and active infrastructure layers).

Furthermore, given inherent difficulties in terms of business cases for market actors to provide broadband in some rural areas of Sweden, the policy co-ordination among broadband initiatives at the national, regional and municipal level becomes even more critical. Continued broadband support in sparsely populated areas is a key factor for Sweden to meet its ambitious broadband targets. At the same time, Swedish authorities also need to be cautious of the possibility of state aid interfering with deployment incentives by the private sector (Swedish National Audit Office, 2017). For the Swedish government, it is very important for state aid to be targeted to areas where commercial deployment is not available or planned. In its response to the Audit Report, it has outlined the tools in place to ensure this goal. Some of these tools include prior market analysis to identify the areas that are not commercially attractive, and once the areas are detected, public consultations of the planned financed expansions so that private operators can identify if these plans clash with a planned commercial development (Government Offices of Sweden, 2017).

There are many actors involved in the co-ordination and allocation of subsidies for rural deployment of broadband. Such subsidies include the European Agricultural Funds for Rural Development and the European Regional Development Fund. The two funds have different orientations for broadband deployment and are managed by two separate authorities, but the broadband measure in each fund is created to complement each other. The government has instructed the managing authorities to co-operate regarding their respective broadband measure in order to create an efficient deployment.

IPv6 in Sweden

One potential challenge for the future of the Internet is its ability to scale to connect tens of billions of devices and machines, and a key aspect of that scalability is the use of the IP. The IP specifies how communications take place between one device and another through an addressing system (Perset, 2010). There are two versions of the IP in use, one which is largely exhausted in terms of the distribution of unassigned addresses (Internet Protocol version 4 [IPv4]) and another that is plentiful but has had a slower than desirable adoption (Internet Protocol version 6 [IPv6]).

Encouraging the deployment of IPv6 has been a long-standing goal for OECD countries. In the 2008 Seoul Declaration, for example, ministers highlighted the importance of fostering IPv6 adoption, in particular through its deployment by the private sector and by governments through tools such as public purchasing (OECD, 2008).[19] At present, the exhaustion of IPv4 is one reason new entrants with large numbers of users, such as

Reliance Jio in India, have emphasised the use of IPv6 in establishing their network (Ghosh, 2017), and why traditional players such as Verizon have ceased assigning fixed IPv4 addresses to business customers (Sharwood, 2017).[20]

In order to transition to IPv6, previous OECD reports have recognised how multiple players (i.e. ISPs, backbone providers, device manufacturers, content providers and so forth) have to co-ordinate (OECD, 2014a). The IPv6 transition can be thought of as a "technology adoption model" characterised by the presence of direct and indirect network effects that can make it harder for a new platform standard to achieve critical mass because different stakeholders may find it difficult to co-ordinate (OECD, 2014a). This raises the question of whether some of the market structures used in Sweden are ensuring the necessary co-ordination between wholesale and retail providers of infrastructure and services.

There has been a relatively slow take-up in the use of IPv6 in Sweden compared to other OECD countries and this may have a range of potential economic implications. For instance, existing technologies that enable the sharing of limited IP addresses (i.e. Carrier Grade network address translations) may break some applications and disrupt the modularity of the Internet, which in turn may degrade the quality of Internet service for some users. In addition, when resources become scarce, such as IPv4 addresses, innovation may be hampered due to a rise in transaction costs. In this sense, the rise of secondary markets for IPv4 addresses may increase the costs of developing new applications and services (OECD, 2014b).

In respect to the IoT, IPv6 is important not only because of scalability, but also potentially from a security perspective. This is because IPv6 may be more conducive to end-to-end encryption, which may be favourable for the security of industrial IoT applications. In addition, the increase in transaction costs linked to current IP address exhaustion may affect the IoT by making it more difficult and costly to roll out these devices (OECD, 2014b). Hence, promoting the adoption of IPv6 is an effective way to support the development of the IoT (OECD, 2016), and ensure markets are open for new entrants.

Sweden exhibits a strong performance for most communication indicators. It is therefore, somewhat surprising to observe that Sweden fares relatively worse than the OECD average in terms of IPv6 adoption (Figure 2.19).

Measuring an evolving process such as the adoption of IPv6 requires the use of different methodologies to assess different layers of the Internet infrastructure (OECD, 2014b), and thus Figure 2.19 displays three different sources measuring IPv6 adoption (Akamai, Google and APNIC). Using the Asia Pacific Network Information Centre (APNIC), IPv6 adoption in Sweden was 4.7% in 2016 (ranked 21st among OECD countries), compared to a 10% OECD average (Figure 2.19). Sweden is significantly behind OECD leading countries, such as Belgium which had a 55% IPv6 adoption rate as of September 2017 according to APNIC data.

Cisco 6lab using data from Google and APNIC has found that IPv6 adoption in Sweden grew from about 1% at the end of 2014 to a little more than 4% in 2017 (Cisco 6lab, 2017). The bottleneck does not appear to be from terminal devices. Indeed, according to Cisco VNI, in Sweden, 93% of smartphones and tablets were IPv6-capable in 2016 (equivalent to 10.6 million devices) (Cisco VNI, 2017). This points to a potential lack of upgrading in the core network.

The reasons behind the lack of incentives to upgrade network equipment in order to foster IPv6 adoption may be several. That being said, some stakeholders in the Swedish

Internet technical community have pointed to the possibility that the low rate of adoption of IPv6 may be a symptom of a larger issue related to the interoperability of fixed networks stemming from the municipal network model used for fibre deployment.

Figure 2.19. **Country adoption of IPv6**

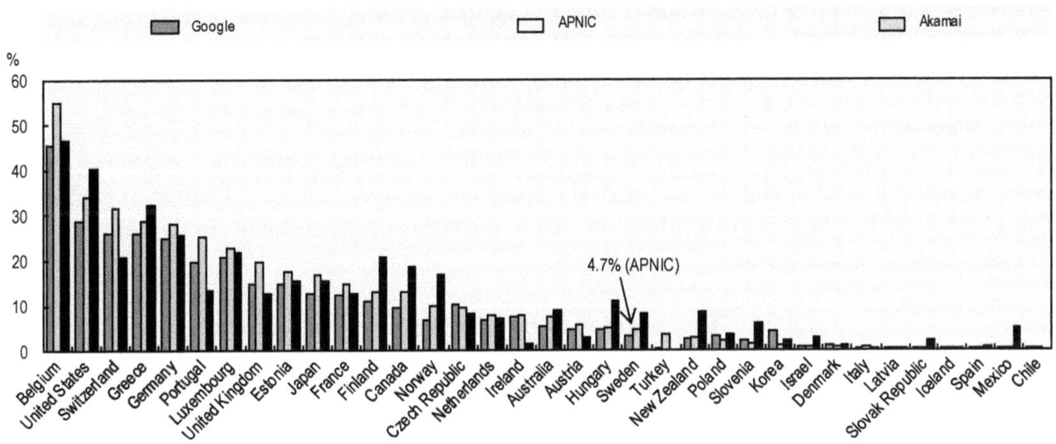

Note: APNIC = Asia Pacific Network Information Centre.

Sources: Google (2016), "Per-country IPv6 adoption", https://www.google.com/intl/en/ipv6/statistics.html#tab=per-country-ipv6-adoption&tab=per-country-ipv6-adoption; APNIC (2017), "IPv6 measurement maps", http://stats.labs.apnic.net/ipv6; Akamai (2016), "State of the Internet IPv6 adoption: Q1 2016 report", https://www.akamai.com/uk/en/our-thinking/state-of-the-internet-report/state-of-the-internet-ipv6-adoption-visualization.jsp.

The specific model used for municipal networks will create different incentives among the three types of players in the broadband market to upgrade network equipment. An approach like the one taken by Stokab, leasing only "dark fibre" (i.e. passive infrastructure), versus the model where municipal networks offer bitstream access (i.e. active infrastructure), may well work better in terms of the incentives of network operators to upgrade equipment to IPv6.

With regards to IPv6 adoption within the country, the PTS has statistics for the deployment of IPv6 in the central government administration, and in local municipalities, as the government's previous Digital Agenda had stated that all central government authorities should have introduced IPv6 by 2013.[21]

Although the Swedish government has not tasked the municipalities with implementing IPv6, there are also statistics of IPv6 adoption by municipalities. These statistics reveal that of the 290 municipalities in Sweden, only 40 have authorities using IPv6 via email, webpages and Domain Name Systems (PTS, 2017b).

Convergence

Fixed broadband services are typically bundled with television services in Sweden. Between 2015 and 2016, television subscriptions via a fibre connection increased by 23%, becoming the main form TV subscription for Swedish people. This contrasts to previous years, where cable was the main technology used to access TV services up until 2015 (PTS, 2017f). Both Telia and Telenor have pay-TV offerings, and although they offer mobile services on a stand-alone basis, they don't usually offer quadruple-play bundles.

By the end of 2016, there were 1 637 000 end user bundled subscriptions in Sweden, out of which most were double play offers (66.2%) or triple-play bundles (33%). The most popular bundle composition was fixed telephony and fixed broadband (almost 36%), and the fixed telephony bundled with fixed broadband and television (32%). The quadruple-play bundle of fixed telephony, broadband, television and mobile telephony remains less than 1% of total bundled offers (Figure 2.20).

The composition of bundles has evolved greatly in Sweden since 2012, when most bundled offers were fixed telephony and broadband (71%); in 2016 this bundle only represented about 36% of bundled subscriptions. Furthermore, in just one year, the double-play bundle of pay-TV and fixed broadband is gaining popularity compared to the fixed telephony and fixed broadband double-play bundle, as the former represented around 13% of bundled subscriptions in 2015, gaining momentum in 2016 with 18.75% of total bundled subscriptions (Figure 2.20).

Figure 2.20. **Composition of bundled services[1] in Sweden**

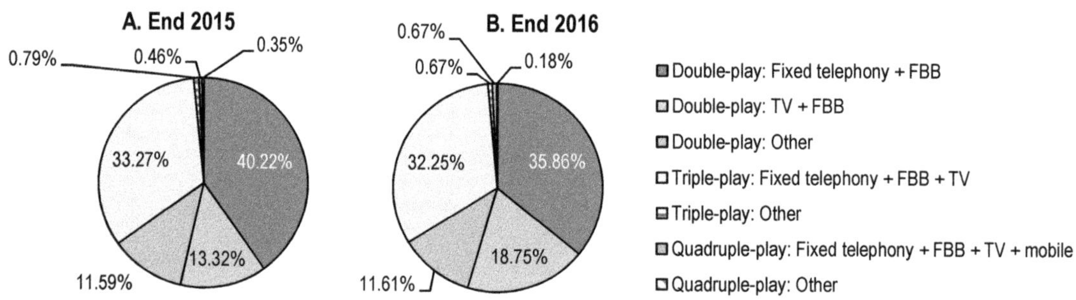

1. Bundled services covers combination offers, which contains two or more services such as fixed and mobile telephony, television or broadband and are offered and marketed as an offer or with a price list for the bundled services.

Note: FBB = fixed broadband.

Source: PTS (2017a), "Assignment in the 700 MHz band", https://www.pts.se/en/english-b/radio/auctions/700.

There are no bundling restrictions on communication services in Sweden, with the caveat that only consumer rules should apply. That is, bundled offers should be transparent and consumers should be treated fairly. In addition, there is no special regulatory treatment or status of video-on-demand services (i.e. streaming) if they are distributed over broadband networks. Some commercial broadcasters even offer services to watch broadcasted content live via the Internet (e.g. SVT play and TV4 provide content over the Internet).[22]

Policy recommendations

As the relationship between citizens and the government, and in general all of the economic activities of society, become increasingly digital, access to fast and reliable broadband connections becomes a necessary condition for Sweden's digital economy.

Connectivity is a building block of the digital transformation, and in this regard in many ways Sweden exhibits a stellar performance in terms of broadband availability, quality and affordability among OECD countries. Sweden is an historical leader in the OECD in mobile broadband penetration, a leader in terms of mobile data usage, and also one of the most developed countries in terms of NGA. For instance, it is the fourth OECD country in terms of fibre as a share of broadband connections. It is also a leader in M2M subscriptions (with the noted caveat that Telenor's foreign M2M SIMs are reported within Sweden though nonetheless highlighting the benefits for serving other markets and supporting exports).

Overall, Sweden is on a solid path to achieve its broadband connectivity targets for 2020. However, some issues still remain, which, if addressed, will further foster the robust deployment of ultra-fast networks in both rural and urban areas, so that by 2025 Sweden can reach its ambitious target of 98% of households and firms with access to 1 Gbps broadband connections.

Although Sweden is on a very positive path to achieve its broadband access goals, areas to continue building upon in terms of connectivity include:

- enhancing co-ordination among national, regional, and local strategies and plans for broadband (fibre) deployment, and increasing the "robustness" of fibre networks
- promoting the deployment of high-speed broadband networks in sparsely populated areas
- spurring the uptake of IPv6.

An additional recommendation to continue enhancing Sweden's current innovative approach in terms of measurement of the digital economy is:

- further develop M2M measurement by introducing a category for subscriptions and data generated by autonomous vehicles.

The specific recommendations regarding each of these opportunity areas are detailed below.

Enhancing policy co-ordination to promote broadband deployment and robustness of fibre networks

The broadband market in Sweden is characterised by more than 500 stakeholders and hundreds of fibre associations (also called "village fibre" networks). There exists a plethora of municipal networks adopting different models in terms of the roles played by infrastructure providers, network operations and service providers. The multiplicity of players in the fibre market is said to have been among the main reasons why Sweden has reached the levels of fibre deployment it has today. Going forward, and with ambitious broadband targets including 1 Gbps connections for all Swedish citizens in mind, potential policy co-ordination issues among different stakeholders at a national, regional and municipal level may become a challenge. This could be the case for digitalisation programmes that require co-ordination among all relevant actors of the different initiatives.

Regarding the robustness of fixed broadband networks, the Swedish National Audit Office published a report on the state of broadband deployment in Sweden pointing out that the risk Sweden faces today is an uneven distribution of "robust" fibre networks (Swedish National Audit Office, 2017). The lack of "robustness" stems from the diversity of players involved in the access network, such as not-profit associations like the village fibre projects, and municipal networks that also engage in operating active parts of the network (i.e. bitstream access).

The Broadband Forum, which has a steering committee headed by the Ministry of Enterprise and Innovation, has served as an important form of co-operation contributing positively to fibre expansion in Sweden. Given the importance of a co-ordinated approach (among several levels of government and among the multiplicity of players in the broadband market), when striving for more ambitious connectivity targets, it is therefore recommended to enhance the role of this forum to promote co-ordination and address issues which arise.

In particular, although there is still no harmonised definition or indicators on what "robust fibre networks" imply, the government should enhance co-ordination among players to improve Swedish fibre networks. The PTS has already taken a number of initiatives in this regard, such as "robust fibre instructions" and the "PTS Operational Safety Regulations", which are steps in the right direction. An additional measure to assist in this respect is to enhance the role of the Broadband Forum in the promotion of robust fibre networks.

Promoting the deployment of high-speed broadband networks in sparsely populated areas

The Broadband Strategy in Sweden is striving for ubiquitous ultra-fast connectivity. At the current state of communication infrastructure in Sweden, there is uneven access to broadband of at least 100 Mbps. For example, at a national level, 68.7% of households have access to this type of broadband connection, whereas only 21.5% of rural households had access to broadband at these speeds in 2016 (European Commission, 2017a).

In addition, Sweden is facing a technology shift, where the incumbent is transitioning parts of the copper network. At present, many households still use copper connections to access fixed broadband (e.g. 869 000 users were connected to fixed broadband through an xDSL by mid-2017). In terms of mobile broadband options, in most cases households have access to 4G (LTE) or other wireless solutions, as Sweden has achieved almost 100% coverage of LTE networks (i.e. meaning that these households have access to 10 Mbps connections). Therefore, in rural areas, Telia has announced that copper technologies will be replaced by mobile technologies. However, the question still remains whether the speeds offered by LTE will be sufficient to compensate households that lose their DSL connections.

The PTS should remain vigilant on how Telia conducts the retirement of its copper network, and ensure that all households that will no longer have DSL connections receive a similar or better technological alternative. This is especially important given the current connectivity targets for 2025 in Sweden.

The government should continue its effort to enhance co-ordination among stakeholders in the administration of the regional funds for rural deployment of broadband (i.e. the European Agricultural Funds for Rural Development and the European Regional Development Fund). In this sense, the establishment of the Broadband Forum was a move in the right direction. The newly created Digitalisation Council could also assist in enhancing co-ordination.

Spurring the uptake of IPv6

The only indicator where Sweden fares extremely poorly, and much worse than the OECD average, is on IPv6 adoption (i.e. around 4% in Sweden compared to 10% for the OECD average). Some stakeholders have pointed out the possibility that the low rate of adoption of IPv6 may be a symptom of larger issues related to the interoperability of fixed networks stemming from the degree of "open access" of these networks. This consideration depends on the different levels of presence in passive and active wholesale participation of infrastructure providers, such as for municipal networks, and the incentives for co-ordination of networks and services. There is a lot of diversity in the municipal network models in Sweden.

The specific model used for municipal networks (i.e. passive infrastructure open access policies compared to bitstream or active infrastructure "open access" policies), may create different incentives to upgrade network equipment among the three types of players in the Swedish broadband market. That is, incentives may depend on the terms of which the network owner grants access on various wholesale levels. For IPv6 adoption to succeed under the current Swedish market conditions, both the ISP and the communication provider of the bitstream access would have to offer the same technical solution. In the cases when an ISP has to use active equipment of a sole provider, the ISP may lack incentives to upgrade equipment. In this sense, fostering competition in the access to infrastructure (with the absence of fibre unbundling) may improve incentives to upgrade and deploy IPv6 equipment.

An approach such as the one taken by Stokab, leasing only "dark fibre" (i.e. passive infrastructure), versus the model where municipal networks offer bitstream access (i.e. active infrastructure), may provide more incentives for network operators to upgrade equipment to IPv6 due to more competition present in the different layers of the network, regardless of ownership. In this sense, the Swedish government should evaluate the incentives that result from municipal networks (or private operators) vertically integrated in two wholesale levels (i.e. passive and active infrastructure layers), and the degree of "open access" of all three layers (i.e. the infrastructure provision, bitstream access and the ISP layer). Incentives to upgrade equipment may vary among networks where the owner of the infrastructure is present only in the passive layer, from those vertically integrated (i.e. present in two downstream markets.

Furthermore, although in 2015 the PTS assessed the geographical definition of broadband markets, the regulator should remain vigilant as to whether there is a concern of lack of competition at the local level in some localities. That is, the PTS should continue ensuring that there is sufficient competition in infrastructure provision within the possibilities of the current SMP framework. Promotion of competition may enhance incentives to upgrade equipment.

Finally, a "focal user" or application can play an important role in facilitating the transition to IPv6, and governments and large companies can sometimes play this role (OECD, 2014b). In this sense, the Swedish government should work as an enabler of the IPv6 transition by establishing government promotion programmes to adjust Internet services for which it has responsibility, by adapting government purchasing and ensuring multi-stakeholder task forces to foster IPv6 deployment.

Further develop M2M measurement

Sweden is a leader in M2M penetration, and is one of the few OECD countries that captures more detailed statistics on M2M, such as revenue and traffic generated by M2M. Ericsson, Volvo and many Swedish companies are engaging in the future of the IoT and 5G and leading the way forward for the rest of the world. The IoT application that is expected to have the most implications in terms of data traffic, and hence, infrastructure requirements, are autonomous vehicles. Sweden, with Volvo, is already leading the way with a massive experiment of 100 autonomous vehicles in Gothenburg.

Given its position of leadership in the IoT and M2M, and taking advantage of the fact that Sweden is already a leader in developing IoT indicators, it is well placed to break out statistics for M2M. More specifically, it could report SIM cards related to connected and automated vehicles as opposed to other M2M applications. This will help policy makers to start measuring an application that may have important implications for communications infrastructure in the near future.

Notes

1. In the *Digital Economy Outlook* questionnaire sent in 2016 (for the 2017 publication), Sweden answered that it had set aside SEK 1.63 billion for 2007-13 and SEK 4.85 billion for 2014-20 to achieve the goals of the Broadband Strategy of 2009 (i.e. 100 Mbps service to 90% of all households and businesses in Sweden by 2020). Using the annual exchange rate of 8.561992 SEK/USD for 2016, these figures are equal to USD 0.19 billion and USD 0.57 billion.

2. Europe's Digital Progress Report-2017 (telecoms chapter) for Sweden mentioned the following: "The Ministry of Enterprise and Innovation notably expects that the 90% coverage target described above will be fulfilled before the initial target date of 2020" (European Commission, 2017d).

3. The Broadband Forum has a steering board headed by the Ministry of Enterprise and Innovation, and all members of this board are appointed by the government. The administrative offices of the forum are within the PTS, as the PTS supports the work of the Broadband Council. The Broadband Council Administrative Office is an autonomous unit placed structurally under the Director General of the PTS, though it reports to the Government Offices of Sweden (www.bredbandivarldsklass.se/Om-Bredbandsforum/Styrgrupp).

4. The countries for which Cisco VNI Mobile Highlights 2016-2017 (Cisco VNI, 2017), includes information for are: Australia, Canada, Chile, France, Germany, Italy, Japan, Korea, Mexico, New Zealand Poland, Spain, Sweden, the United Kingdom and the United States (Cisco VNI, 2017).

5. The RAN consists of the site, mast, antenna, BTS and backhaul. The company managing the site will lease the whole package to an MNO and carry the data to the core network of the MNO. It can use the same radio equipment to broadcast and receive traffic of multiple spectrum license holders.

6. To calculate the number of M2M/embedded mobile cellular subscriptions, the OECD defines M2M on mobile networks as "the number of SIM-cards that are assigned for use in machines and devices (cars, smart meters, and consumer electronics) and are not part of a consumer subscription".

7. This price in USD takes into account the annual exchange rate of 8.56 SEK/USD for the year 2016.

8. See endnote 7.

9. The PTS has pointed out that there are difficulties in comparing numbers between European countries based on the statistics reported to the European Commission since all countries measure coverage in their own way. It states the following: "In general the PTS statistics provide more detailed numbers than average. For example – in Sweden the PTS reports numbers for FTTH (not FTTP) for NGA coverage. The PTS

does not have coverage for FTTP, since that measure is not used in Sweden. In many countries FTTP is measured as having NGA-coverage within 500 metres from the house. The definition of rural areas is not the same in all EU-countries and PTS target quite remote areas in comparison."

10. Sweden holds a similar ranking taking into account that Latvia was not an OECD country in 2012. However, in 2012, Latvia had 45.77% of fibre connections as a percentage of total broadband, thus if it had been an OECD country then, Sweden would have held the exact same ranking (i.e. 4th) after Korea, Japan and Latvia.

11. This price in USD takes into account the annual exchange rate of 8.56 SEK/USD for the year 2016.

12. Stokab, a municipal fibre network owned by the Stockholm City Council, is an "operator-neutral" provider, offers wholesale access to passive fibre infrastructure (i.e. it offers dark fibre on a wholesale only basis). Stokab leases its dark fibre to multiple network providers, who attach their own active equipment on Stokab's passive infrastructure and provide transmission capacity either to end users or to service providers (i.e. ISPs). Stokab's network has 1.25 million kilometres of fibre (a length equivalent to 30 times around the earth). Since the company was established in 1994, its stated goal has been to "build a competition-neutral infrastructure capable of meeting future communication needs, spur economic activity, diversity and freedom of choice, as well as minimizing disruption to the city's streets" (Stokab, 2017). A "competition neutral" network, as the company describes itself, should be understood as pertaining only the retail level (and not the competition in the horizontal level).

13. Although it is difficult to tease out the driver of lower retail prices (i.e. whether it was due to lower costs through the wholesale price effect, or the competition effect of more ISPs being present), both factors are very much linked and create a virtuous circle.

14. The statement refers to the moment of writing of the report. However, the PTS is currently considering other market definitions for future regulation. Please refer to: https://www.pts.se/sv/nyheter/internet/2017/preliminara-forslag-till-marknadsavgransning-pa-bredbandsmarknaderna/.

15. Although the Swedish Competition Act as well as the Treaty on the Functioning of the European Union Articles 101 and 102 are still applicable. In addition, municipalities subject to other laws.

16. See: www.pts.se/sv/Bransch/Telefoni/Konkurrensreglering-SMP.

17. This price takes into account an exchange rate of 0.75 EUR/USD for the year 2014.

18. The PTS provides broadband coverage maps according to speed. See: http://bredbandskartan.pts.se/#.

19. OECD countries agreed to: "Encourage the adoption of the new version of the Internet protocol (IPv6), in particular through its timely adoption by governments as well as large private sector users of IPv4 addresses, in view of the ongoing IPv4 depletion."

20. "Having only commercially launched in September 2016 as the first LTE, all-IP mobile network in India, Reliance Jio Infocomm Limited boosts India past 20% IPv6 capability". See: https://blog.apnic.net/2017/02/07/reliance-jio-boosts-india-past-20-ipv6-capability.

21. See list of authorities using IPv6 at: http://e-tjanster.pts.se/internet/ipv6/Listning.aspx.

22. There are several video-on-demand services available in Sweden (e.g. according to Mediavision, Netflix reported 685 000 subscriptions in 2015 and HBO Nordic 100 000 subscriptions in 2014). In general, over-the-top services in Sweden are not specifically regulated apart from the rules of net neutrality that apply to network operators.

References

Akamai (2017), "State of the Internet: Q1 2017", Vol. 10/1, Akamai, https://www.akamai.com/fr/fr/multimedia/documents/state-of-the-internet/q1-2017-state-of-the-internet-connectivity-report.pdf (accessed 4 December 2017).

Akamai (2016), "State of the Internet IPv6 adoption: Q1 2016 report", Akamai, https://www.akamai.com/uk/en/our-thinking/state-of-the-internet-report/state-of-the-internet-ipv6-adoption-visualization.jsp.

APNIC (2017), "IPv6 measurement maps", http://stats.labs.apnic.net/ipv6 (accessed July 2017).

BEREC (2016), "Challenges and drivers of NGA rollout and infrastructure competition", BoR(16)171, Body of European Regulators for Electronic Communications, Riga, http://berec.europa.eu/eng/document_register/subject_matter/berec/reports/6488-berec-report-challenges-and-drivers-of-nga-rollout-and-infrastructure-competition (accessed 30 March 2018).

Business Sweden (2017a), "Amazon Web Services announces the establishment of a datacenter region in Stockholm", press release, 4 April, The Swedish Trade & Invest Council, Stockholm, https://www.business-sweden.se/en/Invest/industries/Data-Centers-By-Sweden/news-and-downloads/investment-news2/amazon-web-services (accessed 5 April 2018).

Business Sweden (2017b), "Data centers by Sweden", The Swedish Trade & Invest Council, Stockholm, https://www.business-sweden.se/en/invest/industries/data-centers-by-sweden (accessed 21 November 2017).

Carlström, V. (2017), "Volvo just launched the world's most ambitious autonomous driving trial in Gothenburg", 10 January, Business Insider Nordic, http://nordic.businessinsider.com/volvo-just-launched-the-worlds-most-ambitious-autonomous-driving-trial-in-gothenburg-2017-1 (accessed 4 December 2017).

Cisco 6lab (2017), 6lab IPv6 website, http://6lab.cisco.com/stats/cible.php?country=SE&option=all (accessed 12 October 2017).

Cisco VNI (2017), "VNI mobile forecast highlights for Sweden, 2016-2021", Cisco, https://www.cisco.com/assets/sol/sp/vni/forecast_highlights_mobile/#~Country (accessed 10 October 2017).

Ericsson (2016), “Telia and Ericsson demonstrate record-breaking speed and latency in live 5G field trial”, press release, 13 October, Ericcson, Stockholm, https://www.ericsson.com/en/news/2016/10/telia-and-ericsson-demonstrate-record-breaking-speed-and-latency-in-live-5g-field-trial (accessed 4 December 2017).

European Commission (2018), *Digital Agenda Scoreboard Key Indicators*, https://digital-agenda-data.eu/datasets/digital_agenda_scoreboard_key_indicators#download (accessed 9 May 2018).

European Commission (2017a), “Connectivity reports: Digital scoreboard”, https://ec.europa.eu/digital-single-market/en/connectivity (accessed 14 November 2017).

European Commission (2017b), “Country information: Sweden”, webpage, https://ec.europa.eu/digital-single-market/en/country-information-sweden (accessed 14 November 2017).

European Commission (2017c), *Europe's Digital Progress Report 2017*, https://ec.europa.eu/digital-single-market/en/news/europes-digital-progress-report-2017.

European Commission (2017d), “High-speed broadband for more than 400,000 homes in Sweden”, press release, 3 October, European Commission, Brussels, https://ec.europa.eu/commission/news/high-speed-broadband-more-400000-homes-sweden-2017-oct-03_sl (accessed 20 November 2017).

European Commission (2010), “A digital agenda for Europe”, Communication from the Commission to the European Parliament, the Council, the European Economic and Social Committee and the Committee of the Regions, COM(2010)245 final, European Commission, Brussels, https://eur-lex.europa.eu/legal-content/EN/TXT/PDF/?uri=CELEX:52010DC0245&from=EN (accessed 4 April 2018).

Ghosh, M. (7 February 2017), “Reliance Jio boosts India past 20% IPv6 capability”, APNIC blog, https://blog.apnic.net/2017/02/07/reliance-jio-boosts-india-past-20-ipv6-capability (accessed 3 April 2018).

Google (2016), “Per-country IPv6 adoption”, https://www.google.com/intl/en/ipv6/statistics.html#tab=per-country-ipv6-adoption&tab=per-country-ipv6-adoption (accessed July 2017).

Government Offices of Sweden (2017), “Government communication 2017/18:54 Reply on the National Audit Office's report on the government's efforts to meet the broadband policy targets” (in Swedish), Government Offices of Sweden, Stockholm, www.regeringen.se/rattsdokument/skrivelse/2017/11/skr.-20171854.

Government Offices of Sweden (2016), “A completely connected Sweden by 2025: A broadband strategy”, Ministry of Enterprise and Innovation, Stockholm, www.government.se/496173/contentassets/afe9f1cfeaac4e39abcdd3b82d9bee5d/sweden-completely-connected-by-2025-eng.pdf (accessed 14 November 2017).

Ministry of Industry (2016), *State Broadband Infrastructure as a Resource* (in Swedish), Ministry of Industry, Stockholm, www.regeringen.se/48e0c4/contentassets/1b20d1c2460e4c4baedb926efa102121/statens-bredbandsinfrastruktur-som-resurs-sou-20161 (accessed 20 November 2017).

Mölleryd, B. (2015), “Development of high-speed networks and the role of municipal networks”, *OECD Science, Technology and Industry Policy Papers*, No. 26, OECD Publishing, Paris, http://dx.doi.org/10.1787/5jrqdl7rvns3-en.

Norway National Communications Authority (2018), "M2M sales" (in Norwegian), webpage, https://ekomstatistikken.nkom.no/#/statistics/details?servicearea=Mobiltjenester&label=Maskin-til-maskin%20-%20omsetning (accessed 18 April 2018).

NTT East (2017), "Discontinuation of provision of 'FLET'S ADSL' in the 'FLET'S Hikari' offering area" (in Japanese), press release, NTT East Japan, www.ntt-east.co.jp/release/detail/20171130_01.html (accessed 4 December 2017).

OECD (2018a), Broadband Portal, www.oecd.org/sti/broadband/oecdbroadbandportal.htm (accessed 18 April 2018).

OECD (2018b), "Telecommunications database", *OECD Telecommunications and Internet Statistics* (database), http://dx.doi.org/10.1787/data-00170-en (accessed 18 April 2018).

OECD (2018c), Population (indicator), http://dx.doi.org/10.1787/d434f82b-en (accessed 18 April 2018).

OECD (2017a), "Broadband database", *OECD Telecommunications and Internet Statistics* (database), www.oecd.org/sti/broadband/broadband-statistics (accessed October 2017).

OECD (2017b), *OECD Digital Economy Outlook 2017*, OECD Publishing, Paris, http://dx.doi.org/10.1787/9789264276284-en.

OECD (2016), "The Internet of Things: Seizing the Benefits and Addressing the Challenges", *OECD Digital Economy Papers*, No. 252, OECD Publishing, Paris, http://dx.doi.org/10.1787/5jlwvzz8td0n-en.

OECD (2015), *OECD Digital Economy Outlook 2015*, OECD Publishing, Paris, http://dx.doi.org/10.1787/9789264232440-en.

OECD (2014a), "The economics of transition to Internet Protocol version 6 (IPv6)", *OECD Digital Economy Papers*, No. 244, OECD Publishing, Paris, https://www.oecd-ilibrary.org/docserver/5jxt46d07bhc-en.pdf?expires=1522748850&id=id&accname=guest&checksum=15C8655A770DF1C8DAC02FAB5005F6BD (accessed 3 April 2018).

OECD (2014b), "The Internet in transition: The state of the transition to IPv6 in today's Internet and measures to support the continued use of IPv4", *OECD Digital Economy Papers*, No. 234, OECD Publishing, Paris, http://dx.doi.org/10.1787/5jz5sq5d7cq2-en.

OECD (2014c), "Wireless market structures and network sharing", *OECD Digital Economy Papers*, No. 243, OECD Publishing, Paris, http://dx.doi.org/10.1787/5jxt46dzl9r2-en.

OECD (2011), "Next generation access networks and market structure", *OECD Digital Economy Papers*, No. 183, OECD Publishing, Paris, http://dx.doi.org/10.1787/5kg9qgnr866g-en.

OECD (2008), "The Seoul Declaration for the future of the Internet economy", *OECD Digital Economy Papers*, No. 147, OECD Publishing, Paris, http://dx.doi.org/10.1787/230445718605.

PCH (2017), "Internet exchange directory", webpage, Packet Clearing House, https://www.pch.net/ixp/dir#!mt-zoom=%5B1.0674365103262276%2C-0.03975663064950605%2C-0.02356469771396072%5D (accessed 21 November 2017).

Perset, K. (2010), "Internet addressing: Measuring deployment of IPV6", *OECD Digital Economy Papers*, No. 172, OECD Publishing, Paris, http://dx.doi.org/10.1787/5kmh79zp2t8w-en.

PTS (2018), "PTS broadband map", Swedish Post and Telecom Authority, http://bredbandskartan.pts.se/#.

PTS (2017a), "Assignment in the 700 MHz band", https://www.pts.se/en/english-b/radio/auctions/700 (accessed 9 November 2017).

PTS (2017b), "IPv6 map of municipal authorities", Swedish Post and Telecom Authority, https://www.kommunermedipv6.se/maps.php (accessed 21 November 2017).

PTS (2017c), "Key data tables: Statistics Portal PTS", Swedish Post and Telecom Authority, http://sokstat.pts.se/en (accessed 4 December 2017).

PTS (2017d), "PTS launches spectrum plan for 5G tests in Sweden", Swedish Post and Telecom Authority, https://www.pts.se/en-GB/News/Radio/2017/PTS-launches-Spectrum-Plan-for-5G-tests-in-Sweden (accessed 17 November 2017).

PTS (2017e), "PTS orientation plan for spectrum management", webpage, Swedish Post and Telecom Authority, https://www.pts.se/en/news/radio/2017/pts-orientation-plan-for-spectrum-management (accessed 29 March 2018).

PTS (2017f), "Summary of the Swedish telecommunications market 2016", Swedish Post and Telecom Authority, www.statistik.pts.se/media/1071/summary-of-the-swedish-telecommunications-market-2016.pdf (accessed 10 October 2017).

PTS (2017g), "Telecommunication markets in the Nordic and Baltic countries", June, Swedish Post and Telecom Authority, Stockholm, http://statistik.pts.se/en/nordic-baltic-telecom-market/tables/mobile-call-and-data-services/table-1-subscriptions.

PTS (2017h), *The Swedish Telecommunications Market 2016*, Swedish Post and Telecom Authority, Stockholm, http://statistik.pts.se/media/1070/the-swedish-telecommunications-market-2016-final.pdf (accessed 29 March 2018).

PTS (2017i), "Table 1 Key data: The market for electronic communications", *The Swedish Telecommunications Market*, Swedish Post and Telecom Authority, http://statistik.pts.se/en/the-swedish-telecommunications-market/tables/electronic-communications/table-1-key-data (accessed 22 May 2017).

PTS (2006), "PTS spectrum policy", Swedish Post and Telecom Authority, Stockholm, www.pts.se/contentassets/3019229ac3f848b29a59c83f562df91d/spektrumpolicy_eng.pdf (accessed 29 March 2018).

RR Media Group (2017), "Swedish mine trials 5G mobile technology for safety, communications", 28 August, Pandata Corp., https://www.rrmediagroup.com/News/NewsDetails/NewsID/15896 (accessed 4 December 2017).

Sharwood, S. (2017), "Public IPv4 drought: Verizon Wireless to stop handing out static addys", 10 March, *The Register*, https://www.theregister.co.uk/2017/03/10/verizon_running_out_of_ipv4_addresses (accessed 3 April 2018).

Steam (2017), "Steam global traffic map (most recent 7 days)", *Steam Download Statistics*, Valve Corporation, http://store.steampowered.com/stats/content.

SteamSpy (2017), "Summary: Country stats – SteamSpy: All the data and stats about Steam games", https://steamspy.com (accessed 20 November 2017).

Strategy Analytics (2017), "Broadband", *Teligen tariff & benchmarking* (database), https://www.strategyanalytics.com/access-services/service-providers/tariffs---mobile-and-fixed/broadband.

Swedish National Audit Office (2017), "World class broadband? The government's measures to achieve the broadband policy objective", Swedish National Audit Office, Stockholm, https://www.riksrevisionen.se/download/18.78ae827d1605526e94b2e12b/1518435475305/Summary_RiR%202017_13.pdf (accessed 20 November 2017).

Telia (2017a), "5G: Enabling the future – Telia Company", https://www.teliacompany.com/en/about-the-company/archive/gigabit-society (accessed 17 November 2017).

Telia (2017b), "New generation networks: Telia Company", https://www.teliacompany.com/en/about-the-company/archive/gigabit-society (accessed 9 November 2017).

Chapter 3.

Fostering the digital transformations among individuals, firms and in the government

The use of digital technologies by individuals, firms and the government is a core driver of digital transformation. This chapter presents trends in the uptake of digital technologies in Sweden by individuals by geographic location, age, income and education. It analyses the diffusion of digital technologies among firms as well as the skills that workers need to use such tools effectively. It also examines the use of digital technologies by the public sector and the progress in digital public service and open government data. Finally, the chapter discusses policies to enhance the uptake and use of digital technologies in Sweden and provides policy recommendations.

The statistical data for Israel are supplied by and under the responsibility of the relevant Israeli authorities. The use of such data by the OECD is without prejudice to the status of the Golan Heights, East Jerusalem and Israeli settlements in the West Bank under the terms of international law.

The use of digital technologies by individuals, firms and the government is a core driver of the digital transformation. For individuals, digital technologies offer new ways to interact with friends and family, engage with society, and spend and earn. Firms can use digital tools for multiple purposes, ranging from digital market integration to firm reorganisation and data-driven innovation (DDI). Governments and the public sector also leverage digital technologies by making public service delivery more inclusive and effective, building a more efficient data and user-driven digital administration, and fostering economic and societal value creation by opening up government data.

The first section of this chapter presents trends in the uptake of digital technologies by individuals, ranging from simple to more sophisticated Internet uses, by geographic location, age, income and education. It further considers digital security and privacy as barriers to uptake, examines fundamental information-processing and software skills that are needed to use technology effectively, and reviews school performance as an indicator for the acquisition of fundamental skills. Finally, it discusses policies to empower people with the skills that they need to master life in the digital era.

The second section analyses the diffusion of digital technologies among firms as well as the skills that workers need to use such tools effectively. After providing a high-level overview of technology diffusion, it provides a more detailed analysis of the range of uses of digital tools in firms, such as for digital business processes, firm reorganisation and DDI. In relation to different uses, it analyses adequate skills, ranging from generic ICT skills to information and communication technology (ICT) and data specialists and complementary skills. The section finally discusses policies to foster digital technology diffusion among firms, to improve education and training for the skills in demand, and to enhance women's participation in digital occupations.

The third section examines the use of digital technologies by the government and public sector. It focuses on the uptake of digital public services by individuals and businesses, examines progress in opening up government data, and discusses policies to boost both digital public service delivery and open government data. A more comprehensive discussion of these issues can be found in the forthcoming *OECD Digital Government Review of Sweden* (OECD, forthcoming a).

Each section concludes with a summary of the main findings and some policy recommendations.

Use of digital technologies and skills among individuals in Sweden

Individuals in Sweden are fast adopters of digital technologies and intensive Internet users

Individuals in Sweden have come a long way in adopting digital technologies, thanks in part to being "technologically skilled and technology-friendly" (Government Offices of Sweden, 2017b). In 2012, computers were used in almost all households and smartphones in just over half of them; five years later, 85% of households had a smartphone and 69% a tablet. Over this period, smartphones have become the primary device for connecting to the Internet. In 2017, the Internet was used by 76% of individuals via their smartphone, by 67% on a computer and by 31% on a tablet (IIS, 2017). Internet usage rates are very high (Figure 3.1), however, 5% of 16-85 year-olds still have never used the Internet and 3% used it over a year ago (information provided by Statistics Sweden).

Figure 3.1. **Internet usage by individuals, 2017**

Percentage of the population

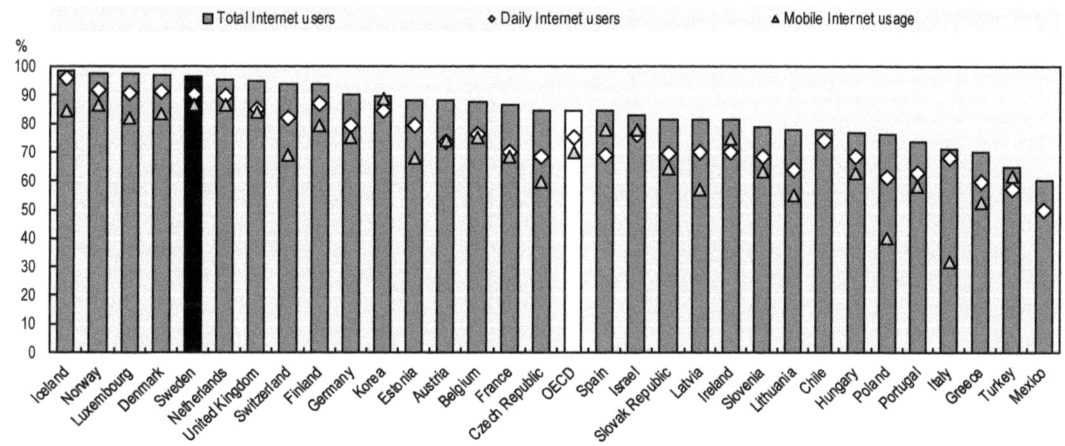

Note: Individuals having used the Internet daily or almost every day over the past three months.

Source: OECD (2018c), *ICT Access and Usage by Households and Individuals* (database), http://oe.cd/hhind.

Most individuals in Sweden not only use the Internet regularly, they also spend an increasing amount of time on line. In 2010, on average, individuals used the Internet 17 hours per week in total, of which 12 hours at home; in 2016, this figure had grown to 24 hours in total and 14 hours at home. On average, 16-25 year-olds spent almost 40 hours while the oldest age group (76+ years) spent only 7 hours per week. Men (16 years and older) spend on average 5 hours more on line per week than women (IIS, 2016). More than nine of the total hours are spent via a mobile phone, which is one hour more than the year before.

Internet usage still varies among different groups of individuals

Important demographic factors that influence Internet usage are age, education, employment and income. The gap between user groups, however, has been decreasing since 2010 (Figure 3.2). The elderly (Panel A) have caught up significantly in sync with retirees (Panel C). Differences between income levels (Panel D) has also decreased, possibly related to lower broadband prices (see Chapter 2). Differences related to education levels (Panel B) have also decreased, but at a slower rate.

Online activities are well diffused, albeit not all and not everywhere

The Internet is used for a variety of online activities, ranging from simple and well-established uses to newer and more sophisticated ones (Figure 3.3). Sweden ranks above the EU28 average on all activities, although some activities are less common, particularly social networking, content creation, software downloads and online sales.

Lower diffusion of some online activities in Sweden can be partly related to weaker uptake in low population density areas (Figure 3.4). The low uptake of e-government services in sparsely populated areas deserves attention (see below), given the large diffusion of other activities in these areas, e.g. e-mail, e-banking and online purchases.

Figure 3.2. **Key factors influencing Internet usage, 2017**

Percentage point difference from average use of all individuals

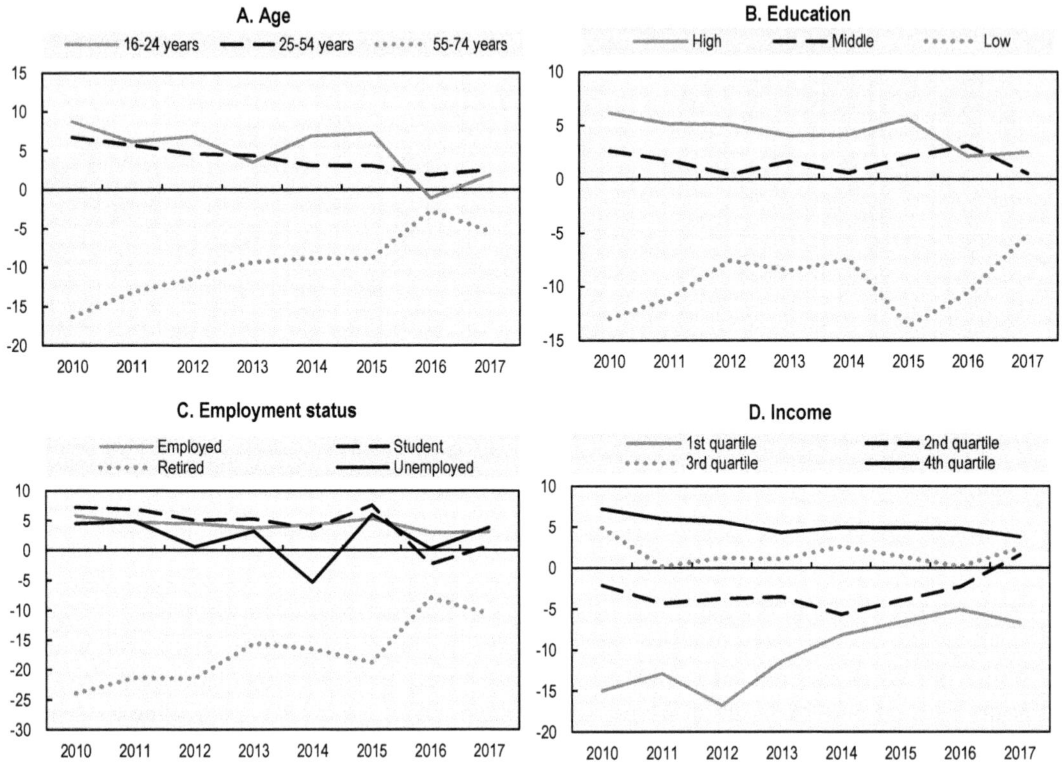

Source: OECD (2018c), *ICT Access and Usage by Households and Individuals* (database), http://oe.cd/hhind.

Figure 3.3. **Diffusion of selected online activities among Internet users, 2017**

Percentage of Internet users performing each activity

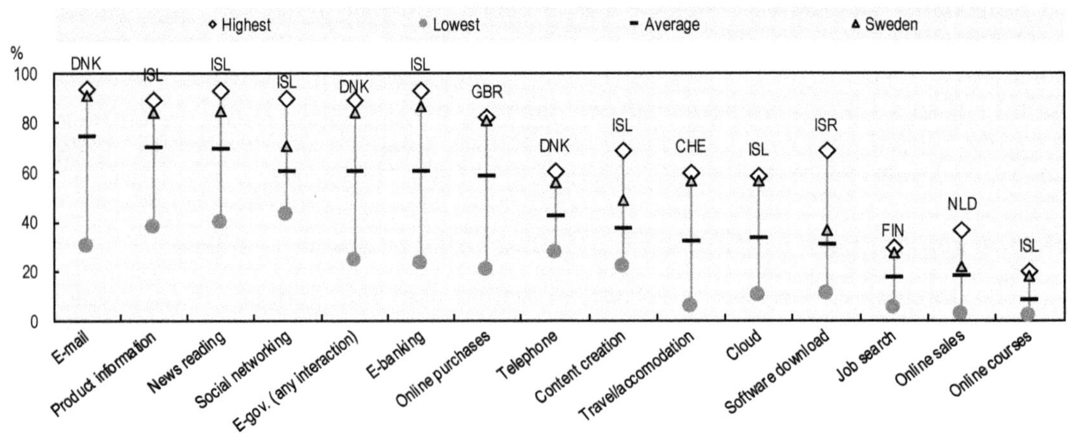

Note: Data for software download refer to 2015.

Source: OECD (2018c), *ICT Access and Usage by Households and Individuals* (database), http://oe.cd/hhind.

Figure 3.4. **Diffusion of selected online activities among Internet users by population density, 2017**

Percentage of Internet users performing each activity

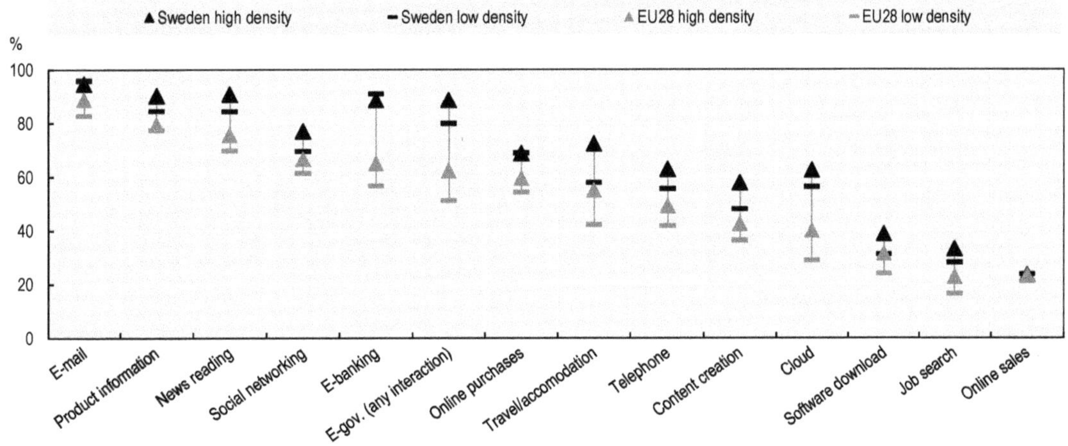

Note: Data on e-government (any interaction) and software download are for 2015.

Source: Eurostat (2018b), *ICT Usage in Households and by Individuals*, http://ec.europa.eu/eurostat/web/digital-economy-and-society/data/database.

The Internet has become the main source of information and news for many individuals in Sweden. In 2016, for the first time, the Internet was ranked higher as a source of information (3.7 on a scale of 5) than TV (3.5), newspaper (3.2) and radio (3.1) (IIS, 2016). In 2017, Google was mentioned by the majority of individuals (57%) as their main online source of information, followed by Wikipedia (31%) and Facebook (10%) (IIS, 2017).

Uptake is held back by digital security and privacy concerns

Another pre-condition to engage in digital and online activities is trust. Two key dimensions affecting trust in and the uptake of digital technologies are digital security and privacy. Uptake requires individuals to trust that usage is secure and to be confident that it does not result in giving away personal data without consent.

In many countries digital security incidents experienced by individuals are not an exception. Such incidents may involve, for example, financial fraud, identity theft or personal data breaches and, in most cases, severely affect the trust of the person concerned. The share of individuals having experienced digital security incidents is over 20% in several countries, including in Sweden (Figure 3.5).

With regards to privacy, individuals are increasingly concerned about the collection, storage and use of their personal data and whether they can access and/or control it (OECD, 2017c). These concerns may be an important barrier to usage, keeping many individuals from carrying out certain online activities. Except for online banking, individuals in Sweden are much more likely to refrain from all other online activities due to security and privacy concerns than the average individual in the EU28 (Figure 3.6). Security and privacy concerns keep close to 50% of individuals from providing personal information for social and professional networking.

Figure 3.5. **Individuals having experienced digital security incidents, 2015 or later**

Percentage of individuals

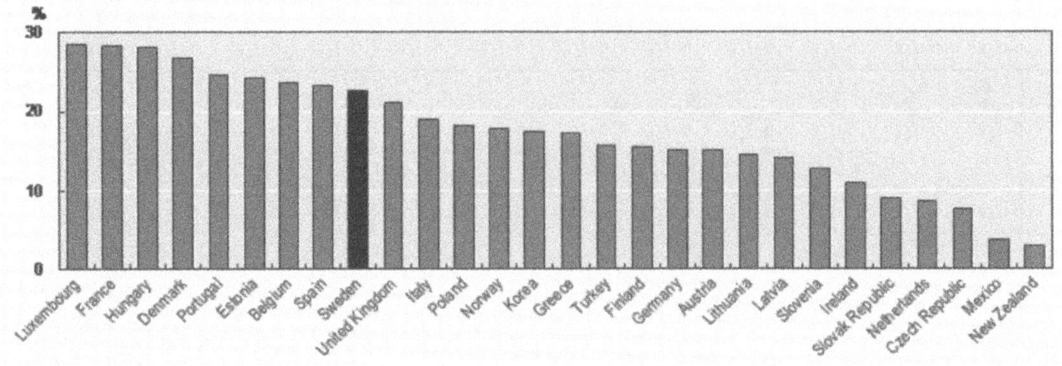

Note: Data for Korea refer to 2016 for all individuals but the breakdown by level of educational attainment refers to 2014. Data for New Zealand and Switzerland refer to 2014. Data for Iceland refer to 2010. Data for Korea, Mexico, New Zealand and Switzerland follow a different methodology.

Source: OECD (2017c), *OECD Digital Economy Outlook 2017*, http://dx.doi.org/10.1787/9789264276284-en.

Figure 3.6. **Security and privacy concerns keeping individuals from carrying out online activities, 2015**

Percentage of individuals

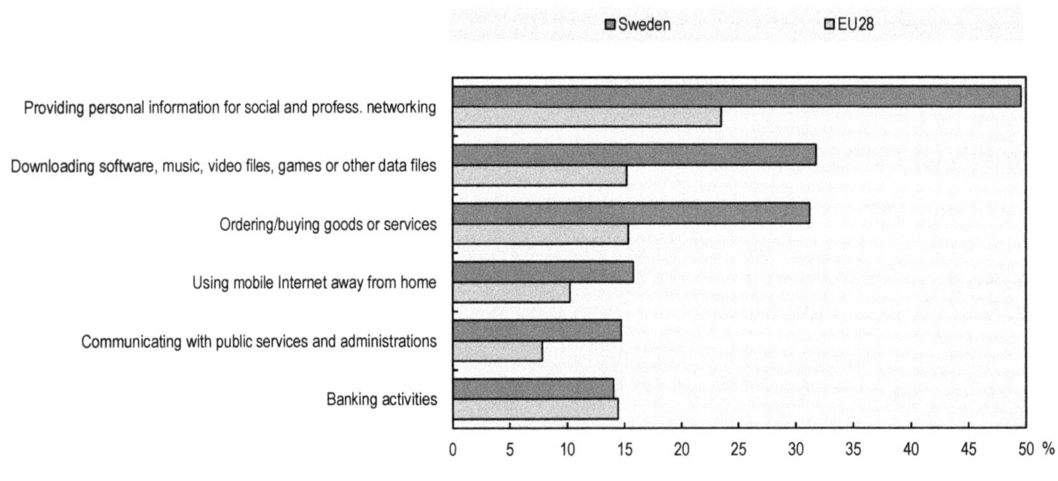

Source: Eurostat (2018b), *ICT Usage in Households and by Individuals*, http://ec.europa.eu/eurostat/web/digital-economy-and-society/data/database.

Some important skills and school performance have room for improvement

In order to fully participate in digital life and society, individuals need the right skills. Compared to the OECD average (10%), Sweden has a low share of adults with no computer experience (1.6%) (OECD, 2016d) However, some information-processing skills are used less frequently in Sweden than in other comparable countries (Figure 3.7). The frequency of use of writing and numeracy skills is close to the OECD average while the frequency of use of ICT skills is lower than in the Netherlands, Germany and Denmark.

Figure 3.7. **Information-processing skills used in everyday life, 2015**

Average use from 1 "never" to 5 "every day"

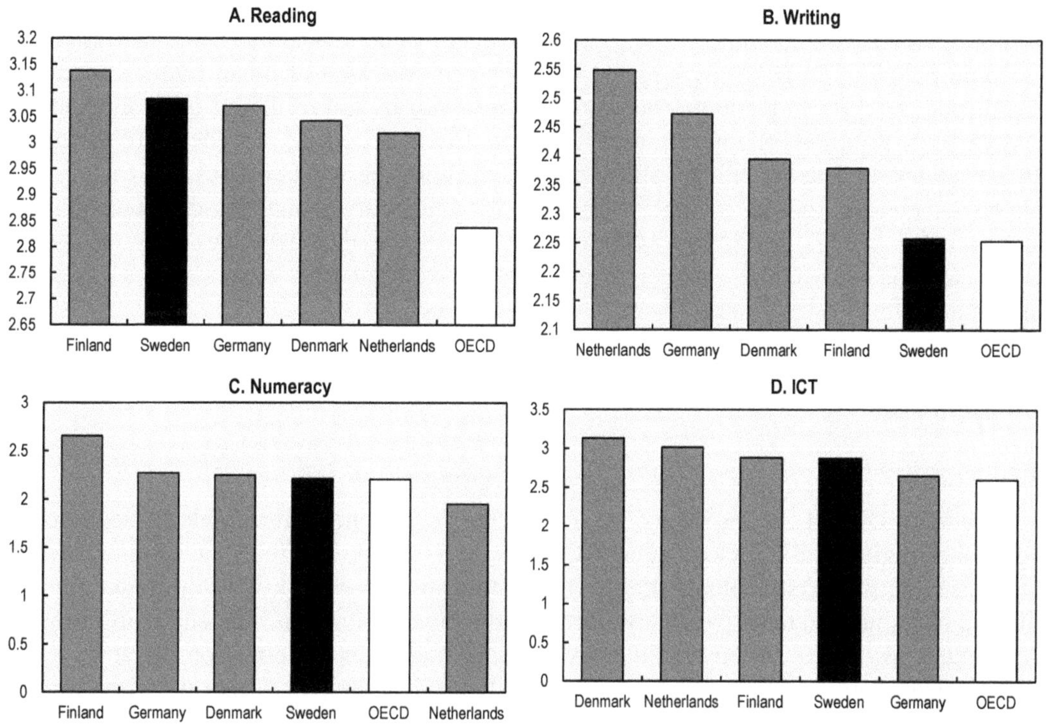

Source: OECD (2017e), *Survey of Adult Skills (PIAAC)*, www.oecd.org/skills/piaac/publicdataandanalysis/#d.en.408927.

On advanced (above basic) software skills, Sweden performs in the midfield of its comparable countries for the share of all individuals (Figure 3.8); however, the shares of young (16-24 years) and elderly (54-74 years) with advanced software skills are only just above the EU28 average.

Figure 3.8. **Advanced software skills, 2017**

Percentage of individuals by age

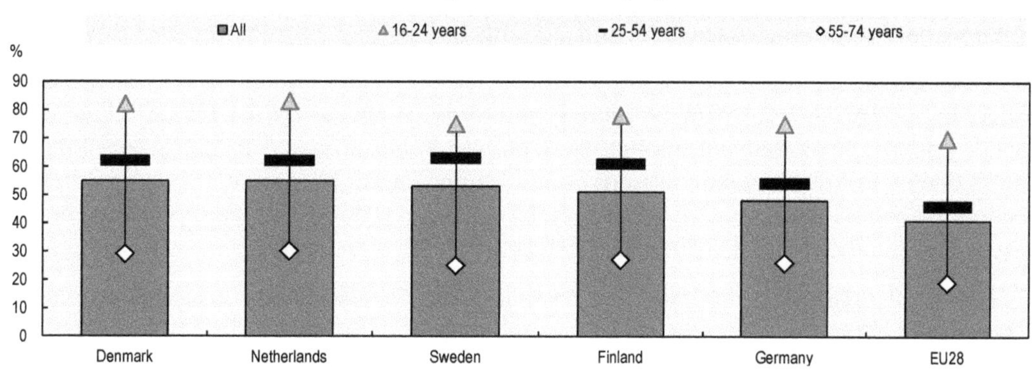

Note: Individuals with advanced (above basic) software skills, as measured in this indicator, performed at least one of the following activities: created a presentation or document integrating text, pictures, tables or charts; used advanced functions of spreadsheet to organise and analyse data (sorting, filtering, using formulas, creating charts); have written a code in a programming language.

Source: Eurostat (2018b), *ICT Usage in Households and by Individuals*, http://ec.europa.eu/eurostat/web/digital-economy-and-society/data/database.

The mixed picture on skills presented above might partly be related to school performance. Over the past decade, the school performance of 15-year-olds, as measured in the Program for International Student Assessment (PISA), has declined in Sweden. From a position well above average in all subjects in 2000 and 2003, Sweden was for the first time below average in all subjects in 2012, ranking 25th of 34 in both mathematics and science and 19th in reading. This trend is confirmed by the results of other international surveys (e.g. Progress in International Reading Literacy Study, Trends in International Mathematics and Science Study) and is consistent with the weaker results of the younger cohorts of Swedish adults in the Programme for the International Assessment of Adult Competencies (PIAAC) Survey (OECD, 2013). While the negative trend in school performance has slowed down over recent years and might have reversed in some areas, performance levels still remain lower than a decade ago.

Policies need to empower everyone with the skills required to succeed in a digital era

Reviewing school reforms to improve the acquisition of fundamental skills

Sweden's Digital Strategy aims to ensure that "everyone will be able to develop and use his/her digital skills" (Government Offices of Sweden, 2017b). The Digital Strategy recognises the important role of the school system in providing all children and students with the skills needed to actively participate in an increasingly digital life and world of work. The strategy also notes that digital literacy includes media and information literacy, such as the knowledge and skills needed to find, analyse, evaluate, and create information in different media and contexts.

Several school reforms have been carried out over the past decade to address Sweden's declining school performance (see below), including reforms aimed at improving digital skills. For example, the 2010 Education Act updated regulations for all levels of education, including pre-school, upper secondary school, the Sámi school and municipal adult education. Focusing on teacher qualifications, the "Boosting the teaching profession" programme (Lärarlyftet), introduced in 2007 and still in place today, provides continuous teacher training, including for mathematics and reading skills. Among different methods being tried to improve writing and numeracy skills, experiments with the "Writing to Learning" method, implemented in several public schools, seem to be successful in making innovative use of digital technologies among teachers and students to improve learning results (Box 3.1).

A key barrier to improving school performance is the low reputation and attractiveness of becoming a teacher in Sweden, already pointed out earlier by the OECD. The ageing teacher cohort shows that not enough students are being attracted to the profession, due, among others, to low economic incentives and limited career progression. In addition, many teachers perceive administrative work they have to carry out as affecting their capacity to deliver high-quality teaching (OECD, 2016a).

The main measure to address this barrier is the "Boosting the teaching profession" programme. This programme includes several suggested actions to be implemented over the course of 2018 to increase the attractiveness of the teaching profession and to improve continuous training offers for teachers: investments of EUR 25.5 million until 2021 to facilitate the uptake of the teaching profession; more places in complementary education programmes and summer courses for teachers; re-prioritisation of funding to teacher training and supplementary education; as well as a strengthening and extension of the "Boost for Teachers" programme with additional funds (MER, 2017b).

Box 3.1. The Writing to Learning method

Writing to Learning (WTL) is an innovative method for integrating ICTs in education. Its overall goal is to leverage the use of digital technology in schools to improve literacy and numeracy skills and to close the gender gap among young students. It involves formative feedback and assessment among students as well as between students and teachers.

The WTL was developed in 2011 and has been tested over several years. A recent assessment of the programme found positive effects. Based on 502 students from 21 classes taught by 23 teachers in 11 public schools in one Swedish city, the assessment included students that passed 8 literacy and 7 numeracy tests. A clear difference was found for both skills between the group of students that used the WTL method compared to the group of students that used a traditional method. For literacy, 92% of students in the WTL group passed all eight tests, compared to 79% of students in the traditional group. For numeracy, 81% passed all seven tests compared to 65% in the traditional group. The use of the WTL method also reduced the gender gap in both literacy and numeracy.

Source: Genlott and Grönlund (2016), "Closing the gaps: Improving literacy and mathematics by ICT-enhanced collaboration", http://dx.doi.org/10.1016/j.compedu.2016.04.004.

More specifically directed at digital skills, a recent reform of curricula and syllabuses in compulsory and upper secondary schools aims at strengthening both programming skills and more general digital and media literacy. This reform: i) introduced programming, especially in engineering and mathematics courses; ii) increased work with digital texts, media and tools to strengthen students' ability to critically evaluate sources; iii) strengthened the teaching of problem-solving skills and of the ability to creatively translate ideas into action using digital technology; and iv) increased the use of digital systems and services in school to foster a better understanding of the impact of digitisation on individuals and society. School principals are requested to implement the reforms within one year from July 2017 (MER, 2017c).

Additional proposed measures for implementation in 2018 include:

- A **read, write, count guarantee**, which would consist of obligatory precautionary measures in primary and lower secondary schools, compulsory schools and special schools for students that need support. Based on an assessment of a student's linguistic and mathematical capabilities, special support will have to be provided to that student in case he/she is not capable of fulfilling minimum requirements. This measure would be implemented through an amendment of the 2010 School Act (COL, 2017a).
- **Compulsory pre-school class** for all children residing in Sweden. Children would enter school one year earlier than today, in the autumn term of the calendar year when the child is six. The school duty in Sweden would thus be extended by one year to ten years. This reform should strengthen the responsibility to prepare children for grade one and be a bridge between pre-school and elementary school. This measure would be implemented through an amendment of the 2010 School Act (COL, 2017b).

Developing digital literacy through better use of digital technologies in schools

Following recent reforms of curricula to better reflect the need for generic ICT skills, and complementing the overarching Digital Strategy, in October 2017 the Ministry of

Education and Research published the National Digitalisation Strategy for the School System. This strategy provides a more comprehensive approach to digital skill development, access to and use of digital technologies, and research and monitoring of digital opportunities for schools (Box 3.2). In a first step to implement the strategy, the central government, together with the Swedish Association of Local Authorities and Regions (SKL in Swedish), is developing concrete initiatives and activities under each objective of the strategy.

Box 3.2. National Digitalisation Strategy for the School System

The National Digitalisation Strategy for the School System focuses on three main areas, within each of which it aims to achieve several objectives by 2022.

1. Digital literacy for everyone in the school system

Objectives:

- all students in Sweden's schools have the opportunity to develop appropriate digital skills
- pre-school managers and school principals should have the ability to strategically lead digital developments
- staff working with children and students should have the skills to choose and use appropriate digital tools in education.

2. Equal access and use

Objectives:

- children, students and staff who work with children and students have access to digital tools based on their needs and circumstances
- adequate infrastructure and technical and educational support are operational
- digital learning resources used in teaching should be appropriate and enable effective use of technologies
- digitalisation will be used to facilitate education and the administration staff's working environment.

3. Research and monitoring of digitisation opportunities

Objectives:

- research on the impact of digitalisation on teaching and learning and support for the development of relevant actions
- follow-up to digitalisation in the school system and support the development of relevant initiatives.

The government is currently working together with the SKL on developing activities under each of the strategy's sub-goals.

Source: MER (2017a), "Nationell digitaliseringsstrategi för skolväsendet", www.regeringen.se/4a9d9a/contentassets/00b3d9118b0144f6bb95302f3e08d11c/nationell-digitaliseringsstrategi-for-skolvasendet.pdf.

Recommendations

This section shows that overall uptake of digital technologies among individuals is well advanced, but also reveals remaining gaps in usage among different groups of individuals, different types of uses and different territories. It further shows that security and privacy concerns are holding back the uptake of certain online activities, and that some important skills and school performance have the potential to be improved. The government may thus consider:

1. **Fostering digital inclusion through policies targeted to groups with lower usage levels of digital technologies,** notably among those in sparsely populated areas and individuals with low levels of education and income, as well as the elderly, retirees and people with special needs. It could also consider measures to enhance trust in digital technologies by addressing individuals' security and privacy concerns.
2. **Empowering people through policies that improve individuals' fundamental skills and digital literacy**, notably writing and numeracy skills and generic ICT skills. Continue reform efforts to improve school performance, increase the attractiveness of the teaching profession, and support effective use of digital tools in schools. Consider creating a comprehensive digital skills strategy (see below).

Diffusion of digital tools and skills among Swedish firms

Despite good performance overall, weaknesses remain in important areas

The use of digital tools is an essential condition for firms to thrive in the digital economy and most of such tools are widely diffused among firms in Sweden (Figure 3.9). Almost all firms have a broadband connection and a website and many use social media. The share of firms using more advanced digital tools (e.g. cloud computing, ERP, e-sales and customer relationship management) is also above the OECD average. However, some important tools such as e-purchases, supply chain management and big data analysis (BDA) are used by fewer firms in Sweden than on average in the OECD. A significant gap also remains between large and small firms for all advanced digital tools, in particular for customer relationship management, cloud computing, social media, e-sales and big data, although small and medium enterprises (SMEs) are expected to benefit more from these tools.

Key digital tools are widely used, but there is room for improvement

A basic condition for firms to participate in the digital economy is access to a broadband connection. Once connected, most firms not only create a website to be visible or to sell on line but many also use social media to promote their brand and products and to communicate directly to and with consumers. Such tools can be considered as basic digital tools. Basic digital tools are used by a large share of firms in Sweden, ahead of the EU28. However, European countries are following suit with higher usage growth (Figure 3.10). SMEs are also catching up, with higher usage growth between 2012 and 2017 than that for large firms.

A next step for many firms is digital market integration. Measured by the share of firms placing and receiving orders over computer networks, more firms in Sweden are digitally integrated into markets than in the EU28. However, European countries are catching up with higher average usage growth than Sweden between 2012 and 2017 (Figure 3.10). Surprisingly, digital market integration increased among small firms, but decreased among large firms. A factor that may support digital market integration in Sweden is the country's dynamically evolving digital payment ecosystem, which includes partnerships between fin-tech start-ups and established banks.

Figure 3.9. **Diffusion of selected digital tools in firms, 2016**

Percentage of all firms, by firm size

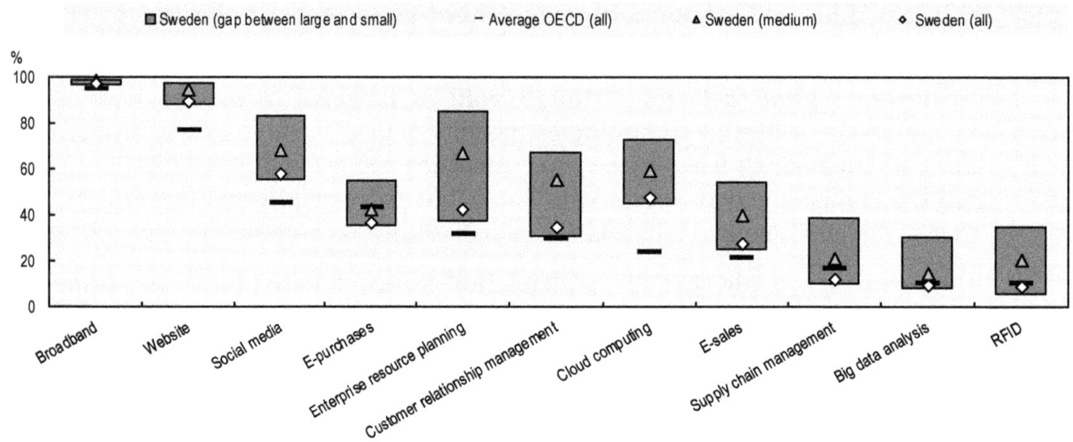

Notes: RFID = radio frequency identification. Large firms = 250 employees and more; medium firms = 50-249 employees; small firms = 10-49 employees. For more details, see Endnote 1.

Source: OECD (2018d), *ICT Access and Usage by Businesses* (database), http://oe.cd/bus.

Figure 3.10. **Key digital tools used by firms**

Percentage of non-financial firms, by firm size

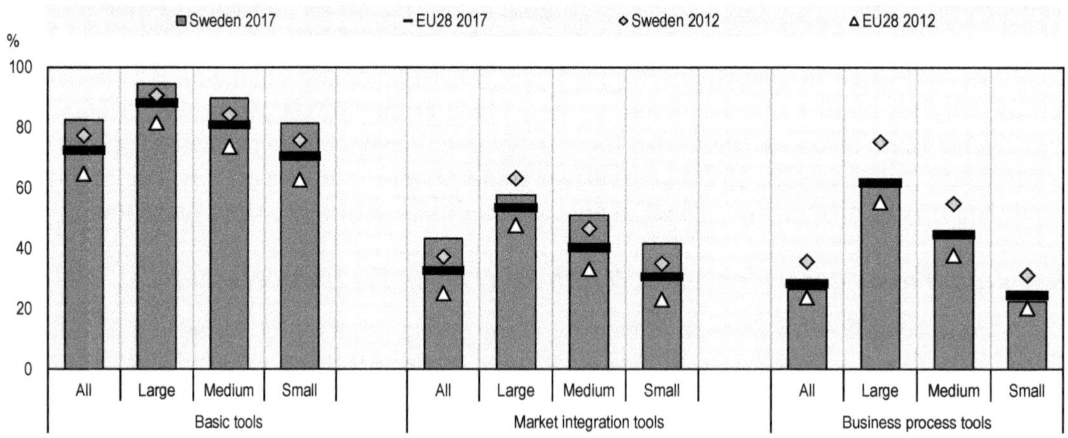

Note: See details in Endnote 2.

Source: OECD (2018d), *ICT Access and Usage by Businesses* (database), http://oe.cd/bus.

Digital tools also play a key role in making business processes more efficient, both internal firm processes as well as exchanges with suppliers and customers. The extent to which business processes are becoming digital can be measured by the use of software for ERP, customer relationship management and supply chain management. Sweden was an early adopter of these tools, but usage declined significantly between 2012 and 2017. Over the same period, average usage in the EU28 increased to being slightly above

Sweden's usage today (Figure 3.10). One explanation for the negative trend in Sweden could be that more and more firms tend to outsource ICT functions and are moving to a next generation of business process software that can be provided as a service over the cloud. This would be in line with high uptake of external ICT services and cloud computing for advanced applications (see below).

Firms' digital maturity varies significantly by sector (Figure 3.11). ICT-using sectors and the ICT sector are the most digitally mature, followed by comparatively high digital maturity of wholesale and retail trade, other services, and manufacturing. Construction, real estate and transport are the least mature.

Figure 3.11. **Digital maturity by sector, 2014**

Digital maturity index

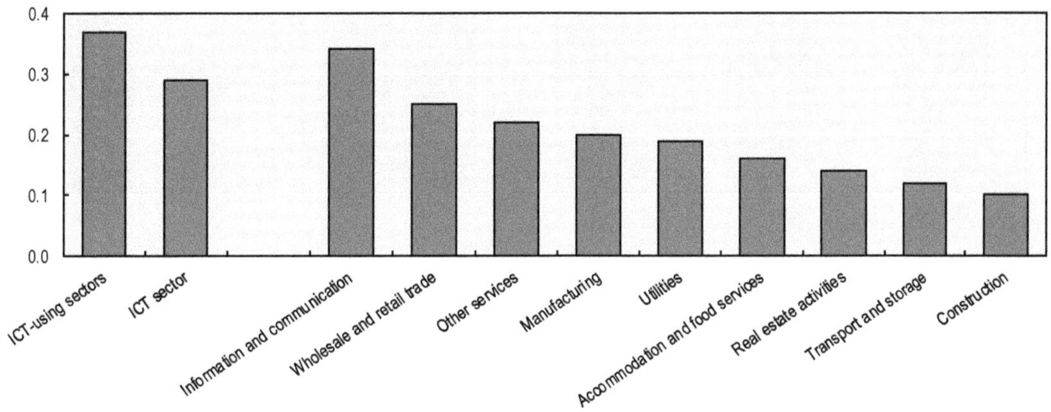

Notes: ICT = information and communication technology. This digital maturity index takes into account firms' use of social media, e-invoices, e-sales, ERP, customer resource management and supply chain management. See source for further details.

Source: Growth Analysis (2017), "Factors affecting the establishment of a testbed: An analysis of Vinnova's 'Environmental Technology Testbeds' program", www.tillvaxtanalys.se/in-english/publications/pm/pm/2017-12-22-factors-affecting-the-establishment-of-a-testbed----an-analysis-of-vinnovas-environmental-technology-testbeds-program.html.

Strong diffusion of digital business organisation tools is matched by high investment in knowledge-based capital

Digital tools also allow firms to reorganise and adopt new business models, which can increase productivity and create new value. Indeed, intensive users of such digital tools, for example ICT service firms, tend to be more productive than other firms (Andrews, Criscuolo and Gal, 2016). But more traditional firms, for example in manufacturing, can leverage external services for ICT functions, including cloud computing, to reallocate resources, e.g. by shifting capital to operating expenditures. For example, tapping into opportunities of the "industrial Internet", General Electric is an intensive user of cloud computing for connecting jet engines, power plants and hospitals (Egan, 2016).

Two important tools that power digital business organisation and new business models are the outsourcing of ICT functions and cloud computing. Sweden ranks above the EU28 average for the share of firms that outsource their ICT functions to an external supplier, with the largest share among comparable countries of medium-sized firms and the second largest share of large firms that outsource ICT functions (Figure 3.12).

In addition to good uptake of ICT outsourcing, cloud computing for advanced applications is widely diffused in Sweden. On average, twice as many firms in Sweden use cloud computing for advanced applications than in the EU28. The dynamic uptake in Sweden is driven to an important extent by large firms as well as by the ICT sector and professional, scientific and technical activities (Figure 3.13).

Figure 3.12. **Outsourcing of ICT functions, 2017**

Percentage of non-financial firms, by firm size

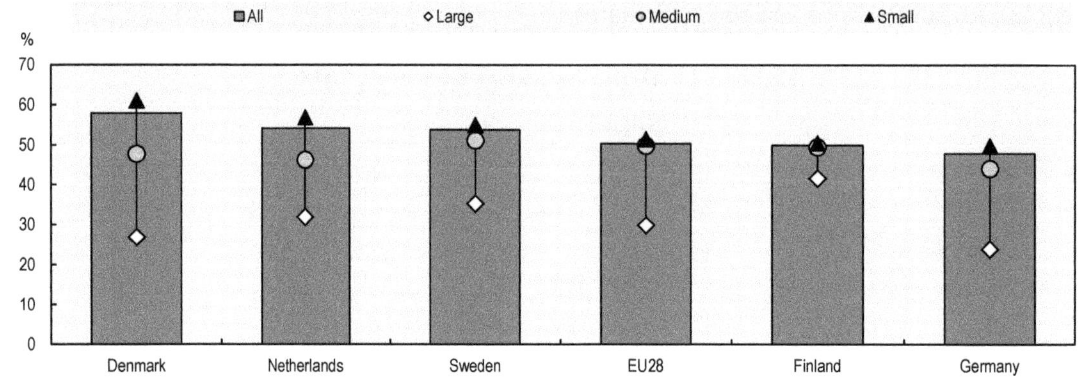

Note: Share of firms in which ICT functions are mainly performed by external suppliers.

Source: Eurostat (2018a), *ICT Usage in Enterprises*, http://ec.europa.eu/eurostat/web/digital-economy-and-society/data/database.

Figure 3.13. **Firms using cloud computing for advanced applications**

Percentage of non-financial firms, by firm size and sector

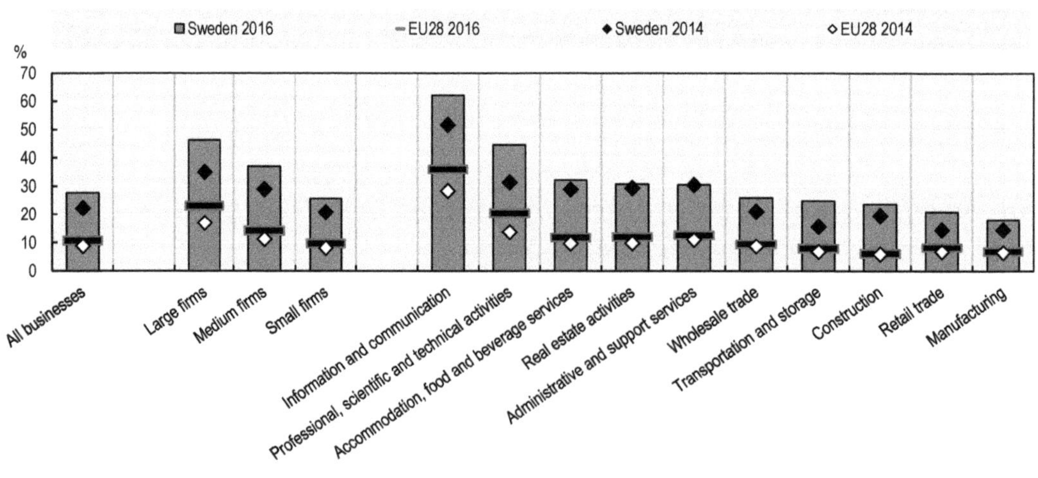

Note: Wholesale and retail trade do not include motor vehicles and motorcycles.

Source: OECD (2018d), *ICT Access and Usage by Businesses* (database), http://oe.cd/bus.

Digitally enabled business organisation and models often require complementary investments in knowledge-based capital, e.g. including software, research and development (R&D), intellectual property, design, and brands (Andrews and Criscuolo, 2013), and most notably organisational capital and management practices (OECD, 2016b). In line with wide diffusion of digital business organisation tools, business investment in knowledge-based capital is high in Sweden, compared to other OECD countries (Figure 3.14).

Figure 3.14. **Business investment in knowledge-based capital, 2015**

Percentage of business sectors' gross value added

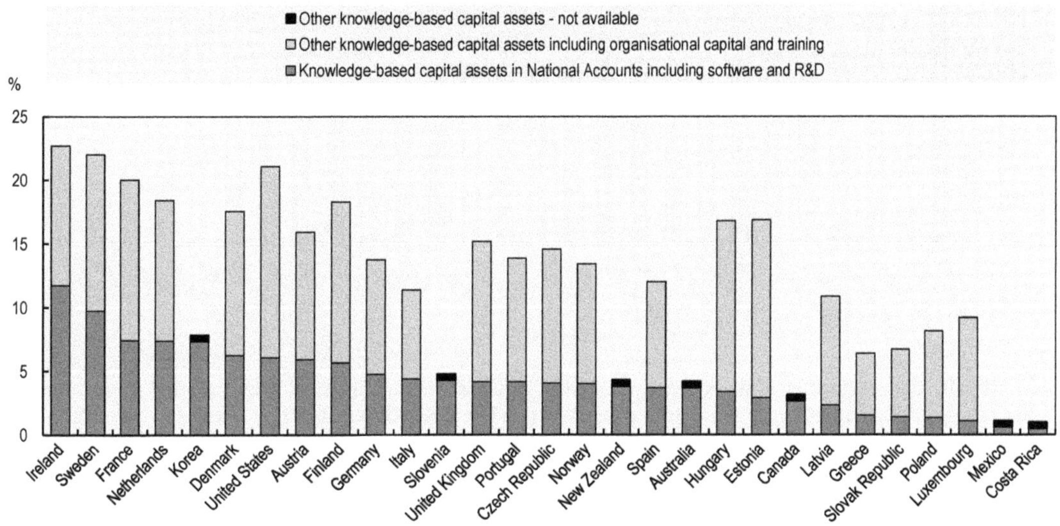

Notes: R& D = research and development. Data, in current prices, refer to the private market sector and follow the definition of INTAN-Invest, i.e. ISIC Rev.4 Divisions 01 to 82 excluding 68 and 72. Intensities are defined as investment over gross value added as sourced from the OECD *System of National Accounts (SNA) Database*. Knowledge-based capital assets in National Accounts are sourced from the *SNA Database* and correspond to the Intellectual Property GFCF. R&D investment by sector for the United States is sourced from the US Bureau of Economic Analysis. Data on other knowledge-based capital assets are sourced from INTAN-Invest and extrapolated, where necessary, using the growth rate of Intellectual Property GFCF from the OECD *SNA Database*. "Other knowledge-based capital assets" include design, new financial products, brands, training and organisational capital.

Sources: Author's calculations based on OECD (2017c), *OECD Science, Technology and Industry Scoreboard 2017: The Digital Transformation*, http://dx.doi.org/10.1787/9789264268821-en; *Annual National Accounts Database*, www.oecd.org/std/na; INTAN-Invest data, www.intan-invest.net; and US Bureau of Economic Analysis data, May 2017.

Organisation capital and management practices are measured by the OECD's High-performance Work Practices (HPWP) Index, which covers work organisation skills and characteristics such as team work, autonomy, task discretion, mentoring, job rotation and applying new learning, as well as management practices including bonus payments, training and flexible working hours. Resonating with the findings above, Sweden also performs high on the HPWP Index (Figure 3.15).

Weak diffusion of big data analysis may thwart data-driven innovation

Innovation is increasingly driven by the use of digital tools and notably by analysis of large datasets. Digital and DDI enables the development of new products, processes, organisational methods, and markets and the improvement of existing ones. DDI can also add value to existing products, for example through data-driven services that complement manufactured goods. As noted by Sweden's Digitalisation Commission, DDI is important for firms to stay competitive against new entrants with data-driven products and business models, such as widely witnessed over the past decade in sectors such as media, publishing, banking, transportation or accommodation (DK, 2015a).

Figure 3.15. **High-performance work practices: Work organisation and management practices**

Percentage of jobs with high HPWP and mean HPWP score, by country

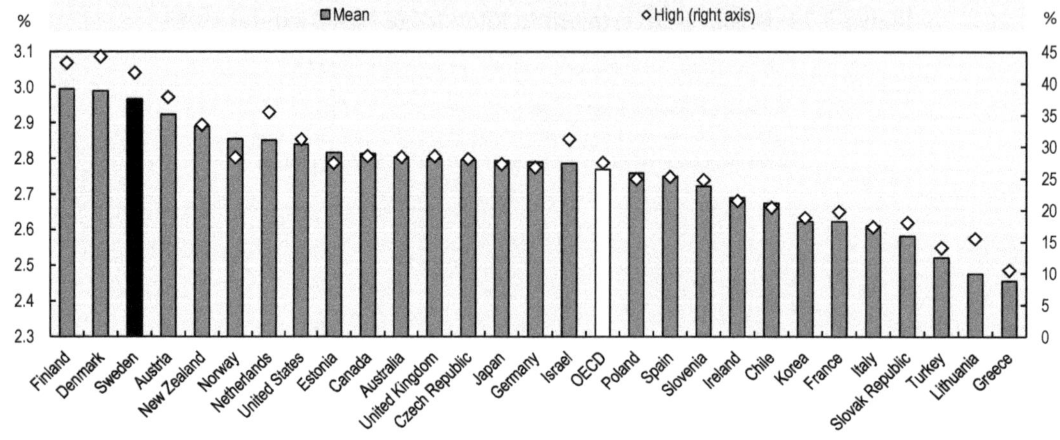

Notes: HPWP: high-performance work practices. This figure reports the mean value of the HPWP indicator and the percentage of individuals in jobs with high HPWP (>p75). The HPWP Index is obtained by summing the scales of all subcomponents as described in OECD (2016d).

Source: OECD (2016d), *Skills Matter: Further Results from the Survey of Adult Skills*, http://dx.doi.org/10.1787/9789264258051-en.

BDA is essential to unleash DDI in firms, and Sweden clearly lags behind in the share of firms using BDA. Uptake is not only sluggish across most sectors, but in particular among medium-sized and small firms (Figure 3.16). In turn, much BDA capacity may be concentrated in fewer large firms and well-performing sectors. The comparatively low share of firms using BDA in the ICT sector is particularly unsettling given the importance of the sector for the Swedish economy and its role as an early adopter and innovator (Vinnova, 2015; OECD, 2017c). Uptake is particularly low for firms that perform BDA with their own employees (Figure 3.17B), while being somewhat higher for firms that perform BDA with an external service provider (Figure 3.17C). This resonates with the strong tendency of Swedish firms to outsource ICT functions and to use cloud computing (see Figures 3.12 and 3.13 above).

Despite good basic digital skills, demand for ICT and data specialists outstrips supply

For digital tools to improve firms' productivity, workers need adequate skills to use these tools effectively. A foundational skill needed for effective use of digital tools is problem-solving proficiency in technology-rich environments, defined as "using digital technology, communication tools and networks to acquire and evaluate information, communicate with others and perform practical tasks". While Sweden performs well on problem-solving proficiency in technology-rich environments, there is still a high share of the elderly (55-65 year-olds) that do not have any computer experience at all or that failed the ICT core test of the OECD Survey of Adult Skills (Figure 3.18).

The use of key digital tools requires ICT skills. In line with good diffusion of most of these tools, ICT skills are widely used at work in Sweden, ranking above the OECD average. However, the comparable countries of Denmark, the Netherlands and Finland are ahead of Sweden (Figure 3.19).

Figure 3.16. **Firms performing big data analysis, 2016**

Percentage of non-financial firms, by firm size and sector

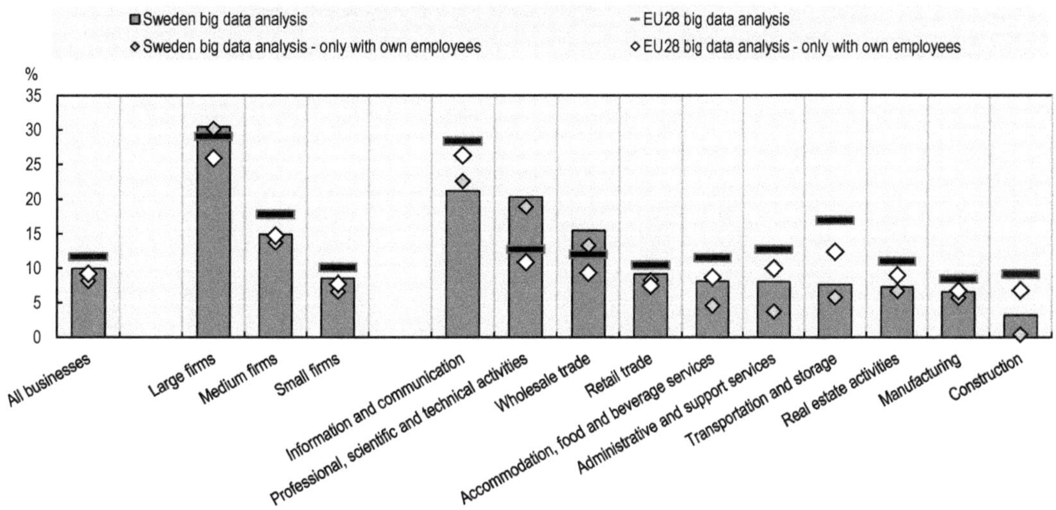

Note: Wholesale and retail trade do not include motor vehicles and motorcycles.

Source: OECD (2018d), *ICT Access and Usage by Businesses* (database), http://oe.cd/bus.

Figure 3.17. **Firms performing big data analysis with own employees and external service providers, 2016**

Percentage of non-financial firms

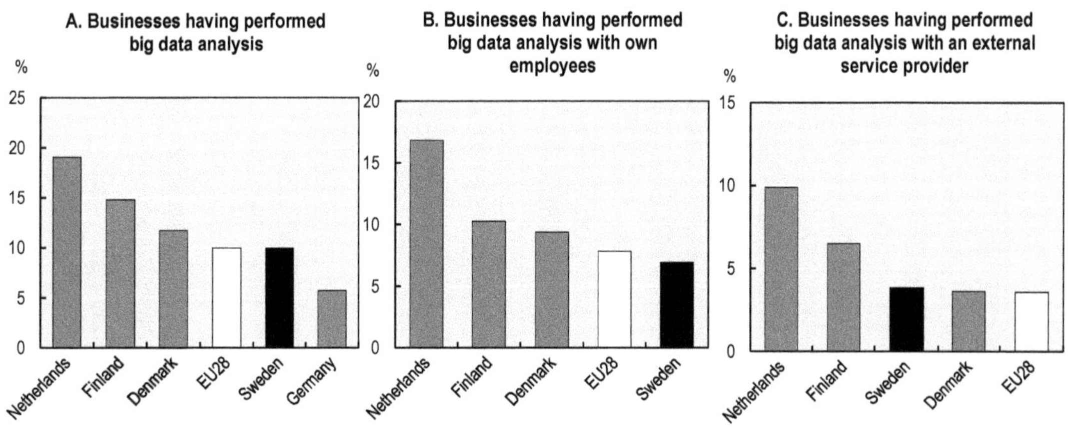

Note: For Germany (DEU) no data available for Panels B or C.

Sources: Eurostat (2018a), *ICT Usage in Enterprises*, http://ec.europa.eu/eurostat/web/digital-economy-and-society/data/database.

Widespread diffusion of digital business organisation tools in Sweden is matched by a high share of ICT specialists, in particular ICT professionals and ICT service managers employed across the economy (Figure 3.20). These professionals are important to effectively implement tools such as advanced cloud computing applications.

Figure 3.18. **Problem-solving proficiency in technology-rich environments, 2015**

Percentage of adults scoring at Level 2 or 3 in digital problem solving or having no computer experience

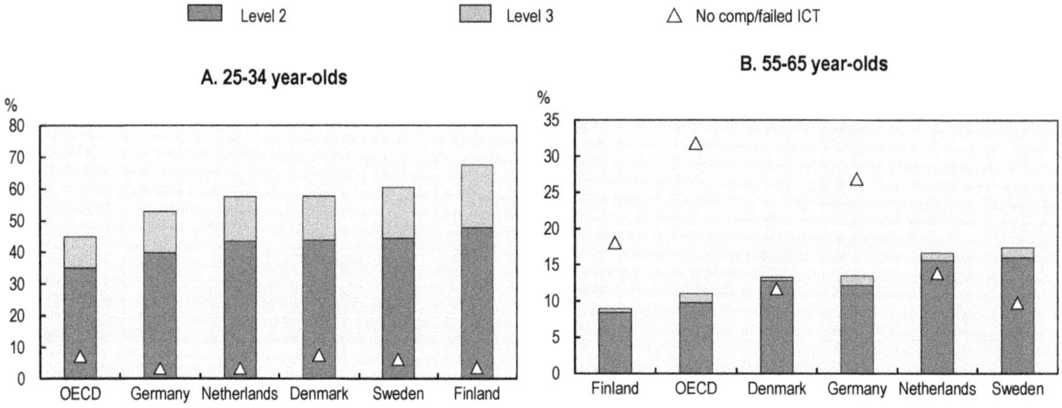

Notes: ICT = information and communication technology. The OECD Survey of Adult Skills defines problem solving in technology-rich environments as "using digital technology, communication tools and networks to acquire and evaluate information, communicate with others and perform practical tasks". Adults in the category "no comp/failed ICT" either had no prior computer experience or had prior computer experience but failed the ICT core test, which assesses the basic ICT skills, such as the capacity to use a mouse or scroll through a webpage, needed to take the computer-based assessment.

Source: OECD (2016d), *Skills Matter: Further Results from the Survey of Adult Skills*, http://dx.doi.org/10.1787/9789264258051-en.

Figure 3.19. **ICT skills used at work, 2015**

Average use from 1 (never) to 5 (every day), working population aged 16-65

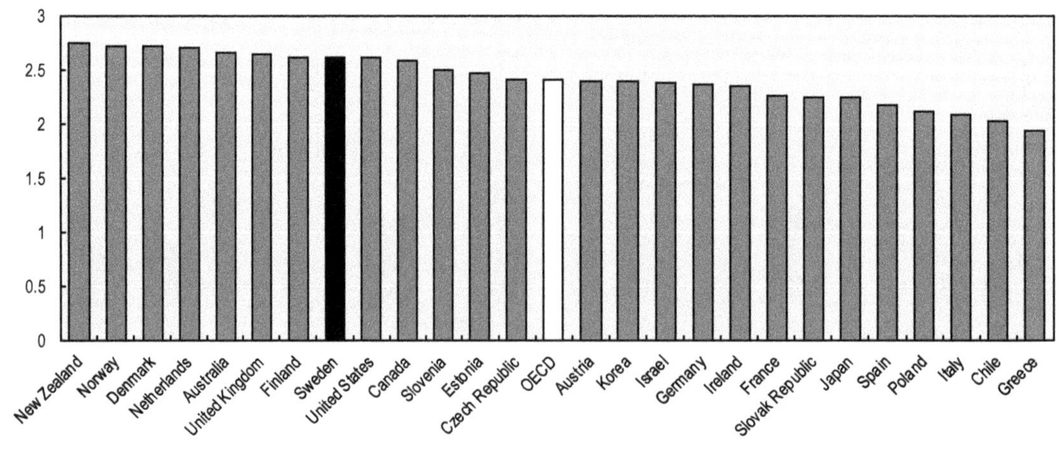

Source: OECD (2016d), *Skills Matter: Further Results from the Survey of Adult Skills*, http://dx.doi.org/10.1787/9789264258051-en.

The strong demand for ICT specialists in Sweden, as indicated in Figure 3.20, is not met by strong supply of related skills. Sweden's share of tertiary graduates in ICTs as a share of all tertiary graduates is below the OECD average (Figure 3.21).

Figure 3.20. **Employment of selected ICT specialists, 2016**

Percentage of total employment, by category

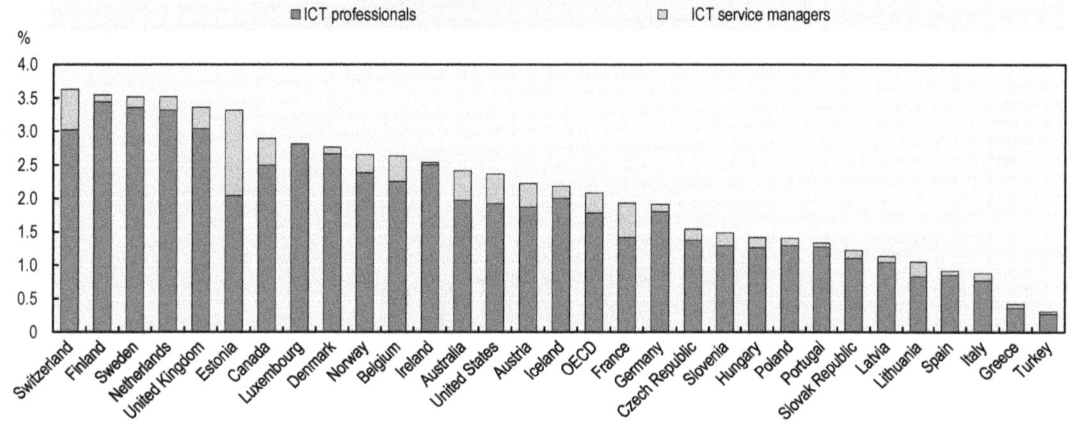

Notes: ICT = information and communication technology. ICT service managers and professionals and ICT professionals correspond to ISCO-08 group 133 and 25, respectively. The OECD aggregate is a weighted average for all countries for which data are available. Data for Canada and the United States refer to 2015.

Source: Based on OECD (2017c), *OECD Digital Economy Outlook 2017*, http://dx.doi.org/10.1787/9789264276284-en.

Figure 3.21. **Tertiary graduates in ICT, 2015**

Percentage of all tertiary graduates

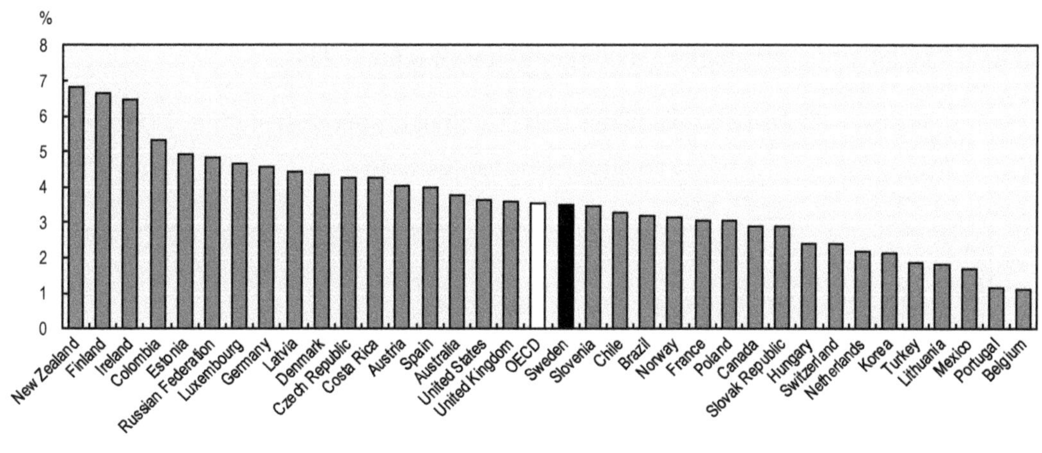

Notes: Graduates at the tertiary level comprise individuals that have obtained a degree at ISCED-11 Levels 5-8. For the Netherlands, data exclude doctoral graduates. For Japan, data are not available because ICTs are included in other fields of study.

Source: OECD (2017d), *OECD Science, Technology and Industry Scoreboard 2017: The Digital Transformation*, http://dx.doi.org/10.1787/9789264268821-en.

In addition, the weak supply of data specialists may contribute to holding back the diffusion of BDA and firms' potential for DDI. Firms with more intensive use of data specialist skills are both more likely to innovate and to have faster productivity growth (OECD, 2015a). Despite the low uptake of BDA in Sweden, the share of data specialists employed in the economy is comparatively high, indicating respective demand (Figure 3.22).

Figure 3.22. **Employment of data specialists**

Percentage of total employment

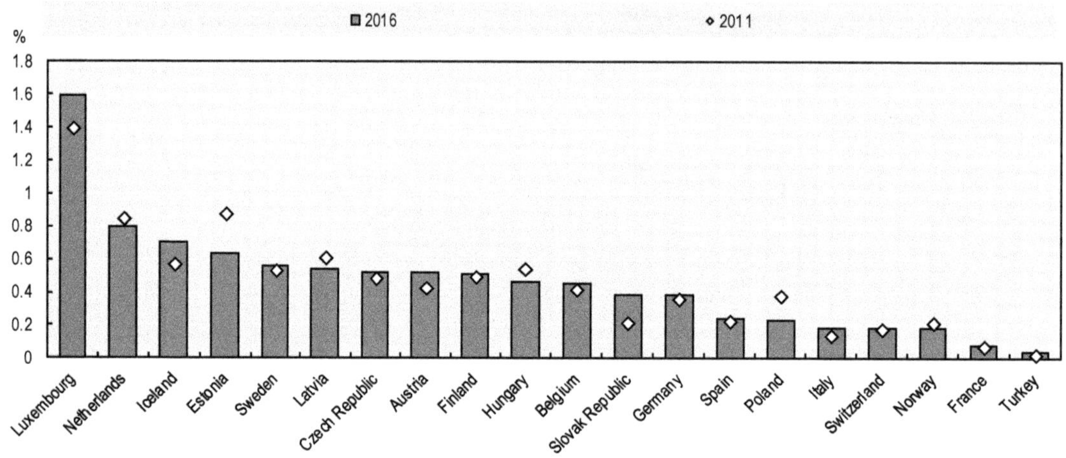

Notes: Data specialists are defined by ISCO-08 codes 212 "Mathematicians, actuaries and statisticians" and 252 "Database and network professionals". Countries for which detailed data are unreliable or not available are not included. For Luxembourg data are for 2015 instead of 2011. For France and Turkey data are for 2014 instead of 2011. For the Netherlands data are for 2013 instead of 2011. For Germany data are for 2012 instead of 2011.

Source: EU Labour Force Survey, November 2017, http://ec.europa.eu/eurostat/web/lfs/data/database.

In view of Sweden's need to boost BDA and of strong demand for data specialists, the current supply of related skills, as measured by the share of tertiary graduates in ICT and data specialist-related studies, is markedly low (Figure 3.23).

Figure 3.23. **Tertiary graduates in ICT and data specialist studies, 2015**

Percentage of all tertiary graduates

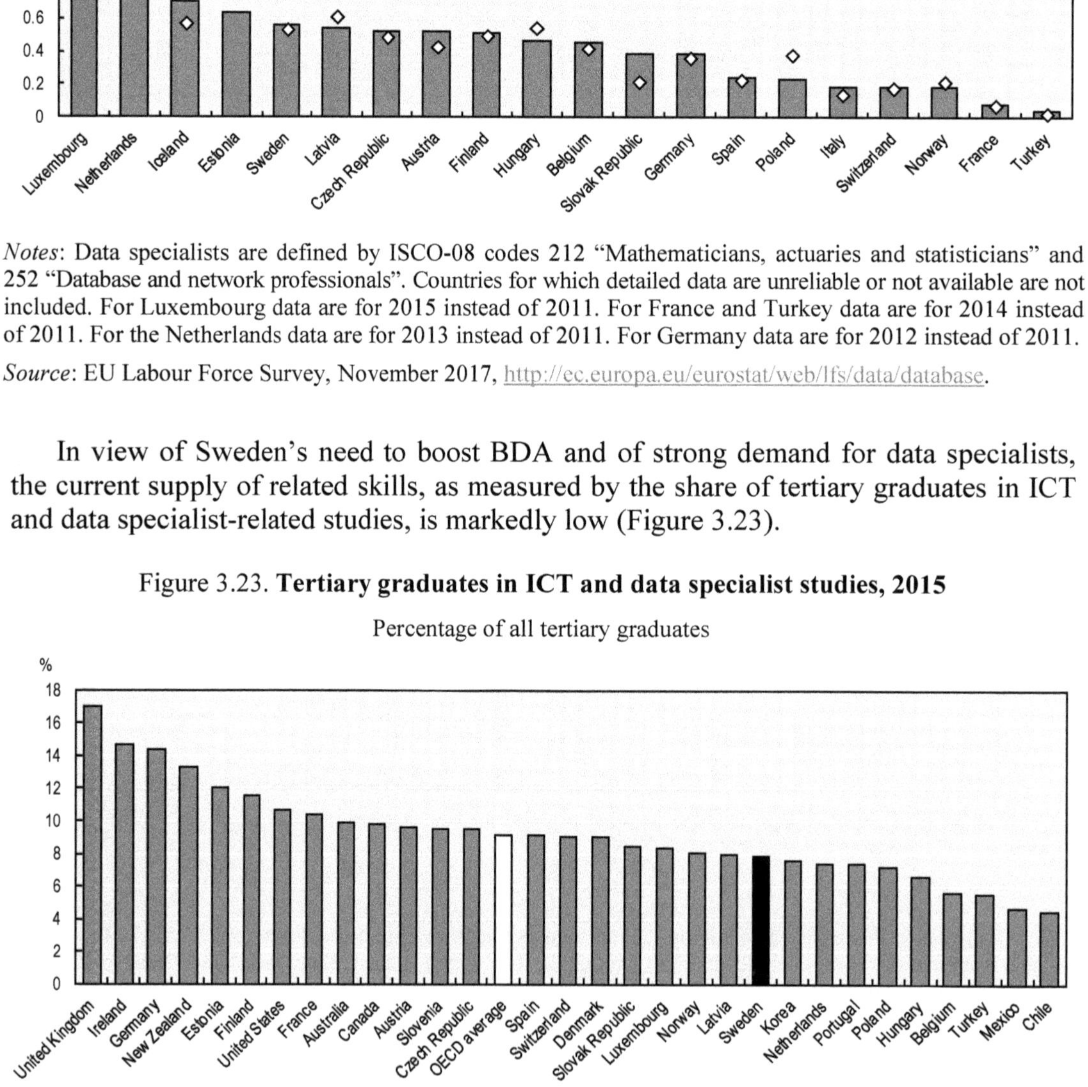

Notes: The fields of studies in this graph include ICTs, natural sciences, mathematics, and statistics. No/insufficient data is available for Greece, Iceland, Israel, Italy and Japan.

Source: Based on OECD (2017a), *Education at a Glance 2017: OECD Indicators*, http://dx.doi.org/10.1787/eag-2017-en.

High demand for both ICT and data specialists and the low supply of related skills documented above also resonates with an above average share of enterprises reporting hard-to-fill vacancies for ICT specialists, an important share of which are data specialists (Figure 3.24).

Figure 3.24. **Firms reporting hard-to-fill vacancies for ICT specialists**

Percentage of all firms

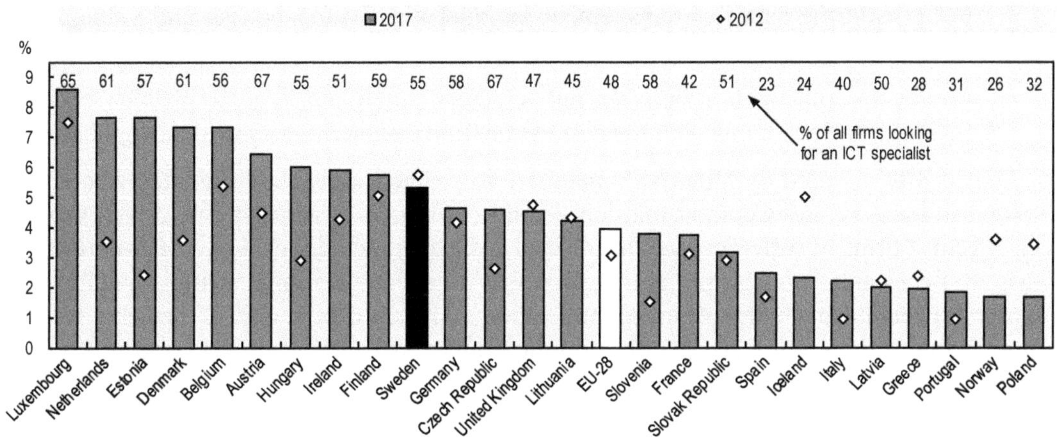

Note: ICT = information and communication technology.

Source: OECD (2017c), *OECD Digital Economy Outlook 2017*, http://dx.doi.org/10.1787/9789264276284-en.

Policies need to strengthen the diffusion of big data analysis and boost skills supply for data-driven innovation

Improving the business environment and targeting measures to strengthen diffusion

A general condition for the diffusion of digital tools among firms is a favourable business environment. The extent to which a business environment is conducive to diffusion of digital tools is affected by policy and structural factors such as product market regulations, employment protection legislation, insolvency regimes and risk capital markets (OECD, forthcoming b). Of particular importance are policies that foster competitive pressures, business dynamism (i.e. rate of churn), resource reallocation, as well as experimentation, notably facilitated by regimes that allow successful firms to scale up and grow while letting less successful ones scale down or exit (Andrews and Criscuolo, 2013).

More specifically, targeted policy measures should be considered to boost technology diffusion, such as is the case in over two-thirds of OECD countries (OECD, 2017c). The overarching goal for such policies in Sweden is provided in the Digital Strategy, which stipulates to "make Sweden the best country in the world in using the possibilities of digitization" (Government Offices of Sweden, 2017b). In addition, the Smart Industry Strategy aims to: i) help firms take advantage of digitisation regardless of the industry, firm size or geographic location; and ii) stimulate the development, deployment and use of digital technology that has high potential to drive industrial transformation. The first objective of the Smart Industry Strategy is being implemented primarily via the "extended digitisation lift" programme (Box 3.2) (Ministry for Enterprise and Innovation, 2016).

The second objective of the Smart Industry Strategy – to stimulate the development, deployment and use of digital technology that has high potential to drive industrial transformation – is being implemented through a range of "digitalisation pilots" that foster collaboration between industry and research (see Chapter 5).

On DDI, the Digital Strategy also highlights the need for building DDI capacity in Sweden, and specifically calls for:

- opening access to research data in open and reusable formats, e.g. from biobank collections, including to contribute to solutions regarding major public health issues
- using real-time data for management, product improvements, risk and vulnerability analysis, and decision support, e.g. for crisis management or transport systems
- improving collaboration between public actors, small and large companies, research institutes and academia with the aim to transform research into practical applications.

DDI is also covered by Vinnova's mandate to promote advanced digital developments in Swedish industry. In its current mission, Vinnova supports a range of data-driven projects with Swedish firms of different sizes in selected industries including trade, construction and transport. Focus areas of these projects include BDA, machine learning, artificial intelligence, augmented reality and encryption, among others. The current round of projects will be supported until the end of 2018 with a public budget of EUR 10 million and up to 50% private co-financing (Vinnova, 2016).

Box 3.3. **The Digilyft programme**

The Digilyft programme is implemented by Sweden's Agency for Economic and Regional Growth with the objective to promote the use of digital tools among SMEs, with a focus on manufacturing and related services.

The programme creates awareness among SMEs about the benefits of using digital tools, notably by organising workshops, including in collaboration with trade unions and business associations. Digilyft furthermore offers targeted coaching and training for firms, for example on digital marketing, including through online learning modules. The Agency for Economic and Regional Growth also provides vouchers to firms proposing a project that makes innovative and strategic use of digital technology. Such a voucher can subsidise up to 50% of the total project value within a limit of EUR 25 000. Firms can spend these funds on either information technology (IT)-related equipment or services.

Return on experience has shown that the firms applying for vouchers are from a large variety of sectors, including areas that are traditionally not prone to using digital technology. Two recurrent themes that firms put forward on their voucher applications are the need to address digital security and privacy issues. On privacy, in particular small firms are searching for support in the implementation of the European Union's General Data Protection Regulation. On security, most firms are lacking a general understanding of how to address digital security from an economic perspective.

Source: Information provided to the OECD during the fact-finding mission in 2017 by the Agency for Economic and Regional Growth.

Increasing ICT skills training to foster diffusion and effective use of digital technologies

Skills are a key asset for diffusion and effective use of digital technologies. A fundamental condition to empower individuals for the digital workplace are sound foundational skills – literacy, numeracy and problem solving; these skills not only enable learning in fast-changing digital environments, but are also the basis for acquiring generic and more advanced ICT skills (OECD, 2016c). As discussed above, reading skills and problem solving in technology-rich environments are widely used in Sweden, while weaknesses remain in writing and in numeracy skills. These weaknesses need to be addressed to fully empower people both for life and for work in the digital era.

An additional condition for diffusion and effective use of digital tools are ICT skills. While the use of ICT skills at work in Sweden is above the OECD average, Sweden still lags behind most of its comparable countries. Recent OECD analysis finds that the uptake of tools such as CRM or cloud computing is significantly related to an increase in workers' ICT skills. The biggest effects on technology diffusion are found to result from the training of low-skilled workers (OECD, forthcoming b). For example, an increase by one standard deviation in the share of low-skilled workers (with low training) that receive training is associated with a 3 percentage points increase in the share of firms adopting CRM or cloud computing systems in knowledge-intensive industries relative to other industries; this compares to only 1.7 percentage points higher adoption from the same increase in training for highly skilled workers (Figure 3.25).

Figure 3.25. **Complementarity between training and technology adoption**

Differential association of training provided to high- and low-skilled workers with the percentage of firms adopting customer relationship management and cloud computing systems

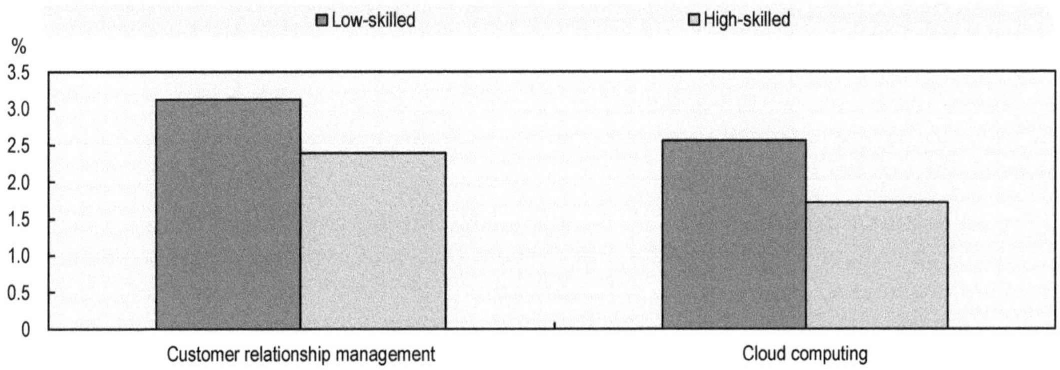

Notes: This figure shows the *ceteris paribus* impact of an increase of a one standard deviation (11% for low-skilled workers, 13% for high-skilled ones) of the percentage of high-/low-skilled workers having participated in formal training on the percentage of firms adopting customer relationship management/cloud computing technologies between industries with a high or low knowledge intensity.

Source: based on OECD (forthcoming b), "Going digital: What determines technology diffusion among firms?".

While the need for training is strategically recognised in Sweden, the share of firms providing training to their workers in Sweden is still lower than in comparable countries. The Digital Strategy and the Smart Industry Strategy both highlight the importance of training and lifelong learning for workers and call for the responsibility of both private and public actors, pointing notably to: i) universities' task to meet digital skill needs of students in view of a changing world of work; ii) better usage of digital education tools in continuous professional training; and iii) employers' responsibility (Government Offices of Sweden, 2017b; Ministry for Enterprise and Innovation, 2016). Figure 3.26 shows that the proportion of Swedish firms providing ICT skills training to their workers is lower than in Finland, Germany and Denmark. In particular, SMEs are lagging behind and may need more support.

Figure 3.26. **Firms providing training to their personnel to develop ICT skills, 2017**

Percentage of non-financial firms

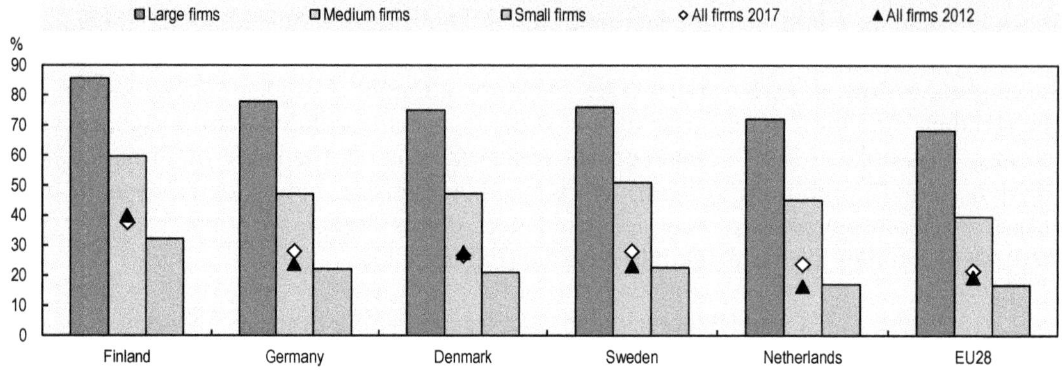

Source: Eurostat (2018a), *ICT Usage in Enterprises*, http://ec.europa.eu/eurostat/web/digital-economy-and-society/data/database.

Recent proposals by the government for new policy measures to improve lifelong learning, to be implemented over the course of 2018, include (Government Offices of Sweden, 2017c; 2017f):

- **Vocational training**. Through the knowledge lift the government plans the creation of more than 90 000 additional permanent places in regional vocational education programmes, high schools, colleges and universities. Total government spending for the knowledge lift is expected to sum up to over EUR 1.2 billion by 2021. Additional investments include EUR 120 million in 2018 to finance 7 750 education enrolments, 1 000 of which are in regional vocational training programmes; EUR 32 million to strengthen the quality and the range of available vocational training programmes; EUR 23 million annually from 2022 onwards to extend vocational training programmes that enable students to continue higher education after upper secondary school.
- **Local centres for lifelong learning**. The government plans to spend EUR 5 million in 2018 and thereafter EUR 7 million annually in the form of a state contribution to municipalities to support the development of local learning centres. These centres should be accessible to students and teachers from different levels of education, including adult education and university, and function as an open learning environment, i.e. a physical site for students to meet and receive study support, including for distance learning.

Many of the policies implemented in other OECD countries to boost diffusion and effective use of digital technologies are focused on awareness raising, skills and training, for example Portugal's "INCoDe.2030", which provides a comprehensive approach to digital literacy and competences, training and employability (Box 3.4).

Other examples include Australia providing "digital business kits" with case studies and tailored advice for digital business management; Switzerland providing information and advice via online portals on themes such as skills (e.g. digital.swiss); and Germany's "Trusted Cloud" training programme that targets SMEs to help firms better understand possible applications of cloud computing (OECD, 2017c).

Box 3.4. Portugal's National Initiative on Digital Competences 2030

Portugal's National Initiative on Digital Competences 2030 (INCoDe.2030) aims to broaden digital literacy, promote employability and professional training in digital technologies, and to raise the national participation in the international R&D network, namely in the production of knowledge in all the areas associated with digital transformation.

INCoDe.2030 aims to make use of existing training infrastructure to improve overall levels of ICT competences. The programme takes a broad view of competences, including digital literacy, information processing, as well as communication and digital content production skills. It also fosters the use of digital technologies and the ability to handle and manipulate data, and considers the need to increase the understanding of advanced communication networks and mobile systems, network hardware and software, and cyber-physical systems like robotics.

INCoDe.2030 includes a range of interventions alongside the promotion of digital competences. It enables citizens to benchmark their level of digital competences and identify knowledge gaps based on the European initiative DigComp2.0. Specific programmes target disenfranchised groups, which get access to free online training. Further elements of the programme include lifelong learning and active labour market programmes for disenfranchised workers to help workers adapt to a dynamic labour market.

Source: Based on OECD (2018b), "Going digital in a multilateral world", www.oecd.org/mcm/documents/C-MIN-2018-6-EN.pdf.

Boosting short- and long-term supply of ICT and data specialists

As discussed above, much potential remains to increase the supply of ICT and data specialists to close the current gap with high demand. This finding is supported by the assumption made in the Smart Industry Strategy that a shortage of workers with appropriate skills is one of the biggest obstacles to the growth of Swedish industry today. ICT specialist skills are also a strategic focus of the Digital Strategy,[3] which points in particular to the importance of technical skills for using and developing digital tools and services. Both strategies call for a closer matching of the education system with employers' digital skill needs by improving and complementing existing collaboration between upper secondary schools, higher education, research and industry (Government Offices of Sweden, 2017b; Ministry for Enterprise and Innovation, 2016), such as practiced in training provided by the Agency for Higher Vocational Education (DK, 2015a).

In addition to offers in public education and training institutions, an effective way of upskilling, notably in the shorter term, is training provided by firms to their employees. With regards to firm-provided ICT specialist training, Sweden has much room to improve, currently ranking above the EU28 average for the share of firms that do not provide any training to develop the ICT specialist skills of their employees (Figure 3.27).

Increasing the supply of ICT and data specialists over the longer term should also be a priority and will require making relevant subjects more attractive to students pursuing a tertiary education. The Smart Industry Strategy draws attention to the need to increase in particular the attractiveness of science and technology studies, pointing to the greater interest of many Swedish students for social issues rather than for mathematics and technology, as well as to the fact that the latter are unpopular also for teacher careers (Ministry for Enterprise and Innovation, 2016). This resonates with the findings from PISA 2015 that among 15-year-old students in Sweden, only 20% expect to be in a science-related career at the age of 30, compared to an OECD average of 25%. Among those Swedish students who expect to pursue a science-related career, only 3% expect it to be in ICTs.

Figure 3.27. **Firms that do not provide any training to develop ICT specialist skills, 2017**

Percentage of non-financial firms

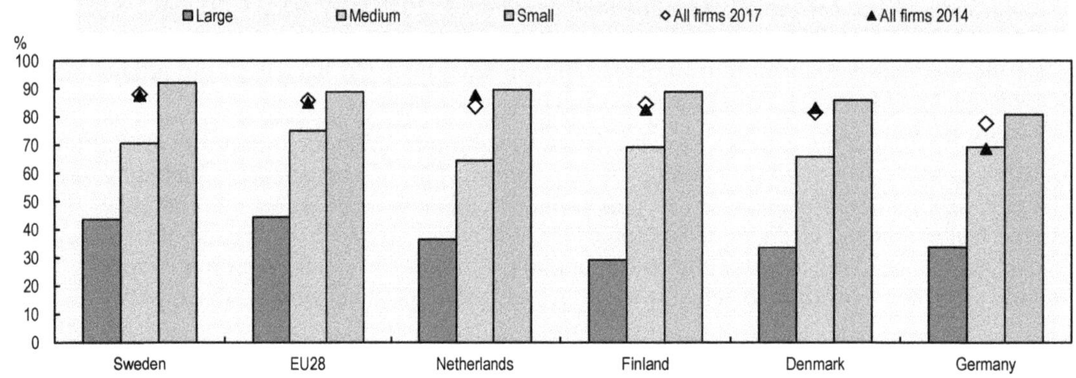

Source: Eurostat (2018a), *ICT Usage in Enterprises*, http://ec.europa.eu/eurostat/web/digital-economy-and-society/data/database.

However, signs for a change in attitude exist, and the government has started to take action. PISA 2015 found that 74% of Swedish students agreed that making an effort in science classes in school will help them in their professional life, which is 12 percentage points more than in 2006 (OECD, 2015b). The government has recently proposed several measures to be implemented over the course of 2018 to foster interest among students with upper secondary education from engineering or natural sciences programmes to participate in engineering studies at university as well as to facilitate the integration of immigrants with an engineering or science background into the Swedish labour market. These measures are planned to be supported with EUR 1.1 million annually in 2018 and 2019, which includes funding of internship opportunities for immigrant engineers (Government Offices of Sweden, 2017g).

Finally, complementary skills are expected to increase in importance with the ongoing digital transformation of organisational forms and business models. Several reports by the Digitalisation Commission have highlighted the importance of complementary skills, such as communication, influencing, leadership and collaboration skills (DK, 2015b; 2016). While neither the Digital Strategy nor the Smart Industry Strategy highlight the importance of such skills, Sweden's good ranking on the High-performance Work Practices Index (discussed earlier) should encourage continued efforts to strengthen school and university graduates' complementary skills relevant for new forms of management and work organisation.

Enhancing women's participation in digitally intensive occupations

Another way to boost the supply of ICT and data specialists would be to increase the share of women in related occupations (DK, 2015b). The overarching goal on gender equality stated by the Digital Strategy is that "women and men should have the same power to shape society and their own lives"; and, more specifically, "women and men, girls and boys, regardless of social background, functional capacity and age, shall be offered the opportunity to access digital information and services from the public and participate in an equal manner in society" (Government Offices of Sweden, 2017b). Already the 2011 IT for Everyone, a digital agenda for Sweden, had the aim to substantially increase the proportion of women in IT-related occupations and women studying in courses with IT specialisations by 2020.

Despite some improvements on gender equality noted in a 2016 evaluation of the Digitalisation Commission, much remains to be done (DK, 2016). Indeed, notwithstanding the long-standing ambitions and efforts of the government, the gender divide remains substantial. While compared to other countries Sweden has a relatively high share of female ICT specialists (2%) as a share of all workers, it is also among the countries with the largest gender difference, with almost 7 percentage points more male than female ICT specialists (Figure 3.28).

Figure 3.28. **ICT specialists by gender, 2016**

Percentage of all male and female workers

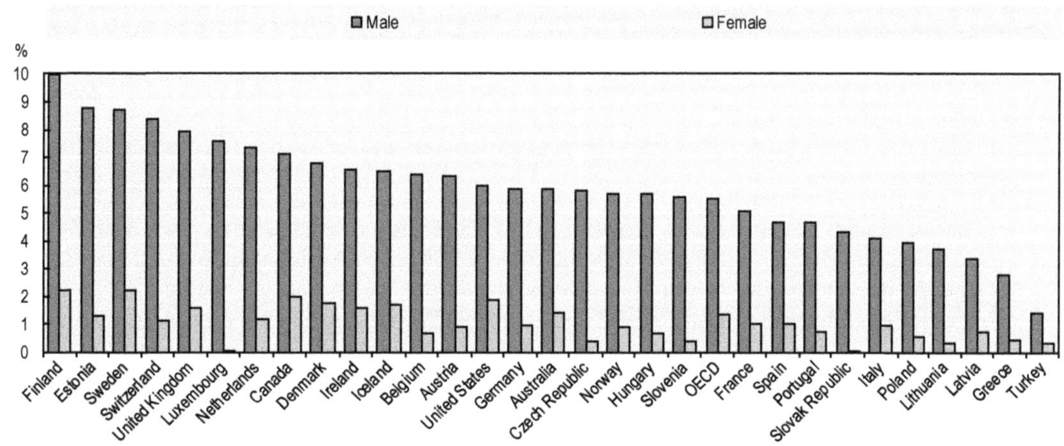

Notes: ICT specialists are defined as those individuals employed in "tasks related to developing, maintaining and operating ICT systems and where ICTs are the main part of their job". The OECD operational definition is based on ISCO-08 and includes groups 133, 215, 25, 35 and 742 (for further details see OECD [2004; 2013]). OECD aggregate is a weighted average for all countries for which data are available. Data for Canada and the United States refer to 2015.

Source: OECD (2017c), *OECD Digital Economy Outlook 2017*, http://dx.doi.org/10.1787/9789264276284-en.

Figure 3.29. **Gender differences in the use of information-processing skills at work, 2015**

Difference between men and women (adjusted)

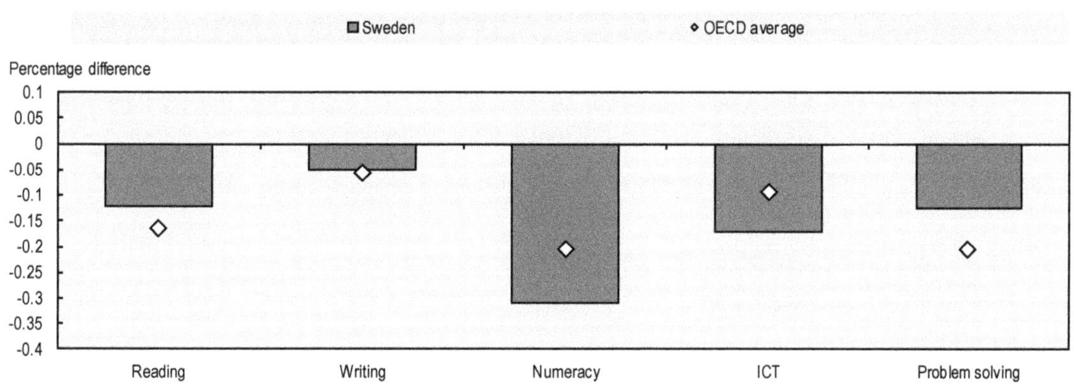

Notes: ICT= information and communication technology. Adjusted estimates are based on OLS regressions including controls for literacy and numeracy proficiency scores, hours worked, and occupation dummies (ISCO 1-digit).

Source: OECD (2017e), *Survey of Adult Skills (PIAAC)*, www.oecd.org/skills/piaac/publicdataandanalysis/#d.en.408927.

The gender divide in ICT specialist occupations resonates with a gender imbalance in information-processing skills used at work (Figure 3.29). Compared to the OECD average, this imbalance is characterised by a pronounced difference between men and women in numeracy and ICT skills used at work, both of which are crucial for acquiring advanced ICT and data specialist skills, and more generally to succeed in digitally intensive occupations.

Both numeracy and ICT skills are acquired to an important extent in education in science, technology, engineering, and mathematics (STEM). Reducing the current gender divide would thus benefit from a focus on STEM education, as can be found in many countries across the OECD (Box 3.5).

Box 3.5. **Examples of countries' efforts to reduce the digital gender divide**

A number of countries have measures to engage women and girls in STEM across education systems, for example:

- The Australian government is investing AUD 13 million over five years from 2016/17 into initiatives focused on women's participation in STEM. The National Innovation and Science Agenda is contributing to ongoing efforts across the Australian government to encourage more girls and women to study STEM and pursue STEM-based and entrepreneurial careers.
- The Japanese government is carrying out the Riko Challenge to inspire women to choose careers in STEM and increase the number of female science and engineering professionals.
- The OECD Mexico initiative, NiñaSTEM PUEDEN, launched in early 2017, invites Mexican women who have prominent careers in science and mathematics to act as mentors to encourage girls to choose STEM subjects. Codigo X in Mexico is a programme to orientate women to disciplines related to STEM and to promote the inclusion of girls and women in ICT sectors.
- Germany launched in 2008 the National Pact for Women in MINT (STEM) Careers to increase women's interest in scientific and technical studies. The initiative brings together politics, business, science and the media to improve the image of STEM-related professions in society.
- In the United States, the Department of Education's programme, Race to the Top, launched in 2009, prioritises improving STEM in the grants it awards to states. The Investing in Innovation programme seeks to increase the number of STEM teachers from groups traditionally under-represented in STEM; and the National Science Foundation awards grants to support the ADVANCE programme, which aims at increasing the participation and advancement of women in academic science and engineering careers.

Source: based on OECD (2018a), "Empowering women in the digital age: Where do we stand?", www.oecd.org/social/empowering-women-in-the-digital-age-brochure.pdf.

Recommendations

This section shows that the diffusion of many digital technologies among Swedish firms is widespread, in particular of basic digital tools, and tools for digital market integration and digital firm organisation. Furthermore, many of the skills needed to make effective use of these tools are widely used.

However, several points merit attention for policy action, in particular: lagging adoption of the most advanced digital tools by SMEs; weak diffusion of BDA among all firms; low supply of ICT and data specialists; and the gender divide among digitally intensive occupations and skills. The government may therefore consider:

1. **Promoting widespread diffusion of advanced digital technologies, in particular among SMEs, with a focus on the diffusion of BDA**, possibly through a national big data strategy. In addition to the existing measures supporting data analytics in selected flagship projects, a wider approach is needed that incentivises firms to use BDA and fosters complementary investment by firms in different sectors and firms of different sizes, and in particular SMEs.
2. **Review training and education policies to boost the supply of ICT and data specialist skills, reduce the gender divide, and anticipate the growing need for complementary skills**. In the short term, incentives for individuals and workplaces should ensure swift training for re- and/or upskilling to boost workers' ICT and data specialist skills, the supply of which should be also enhanced over the longer term though educational institutions. All measures for reskilling and skills supply should be co-ordinated with social partners and industry and contribute to closing the digital gender divide. The need for complementary skills should be considered jointly with other skill needs, possibly in a comprehensive digital skills strategy.

Progress towards digital government in Sweden

The uptake of digital public services is unequally distributed

A key objective of the government's and the public sector's use of digital technologies is to improve public service delivery to citizens and businesses. The Swedish digital government ambitions are high, stating that "state authorities, municipalities and regions should be the best in the world to use digitalisation's opportunities to create a simpler everyday life for individuals and businesses, an efficient public sector with high-quality services, as well as more jobs and increased growth" (Government Offices of Sweden, 2017b).

The government's efforts to implement and improve digital public services over recent years are bearing fruit, as shown in the European Union's 2017 e-government benchmark report, which documents progress in Sweden across almost all of its indicators (European Commission, 2017). Sweden is currently working with the OECD on implementing the OECD's more comprehensive approach to digital government, as outlined in the *OECD Recommendation on Digital Government Strategies* (OECD, 2014; forthcoming a).

However, some basic indicators, such as on the uptake of digital public services by individuals, still show much room for improvement. While overall uptake of different online interactions with public authorities is progressing, among comparable countries, uptake in Sweden is the most unequal, with over a 20 percentage point difference between individuals with high versus those with a low education (education gap) as well as between individuals with a high versus those with a low income (income gap) in all four indicators presented in Figure 3.30 (Panels A-C).

There is also a growing divide in the use of digital public services across areas of different population density. The gap between individuals interacting on line with public authorities in low population density areas versus those in high population density areas has widened significantly over recent years: from just over 2% in Sweden in 2012 to 14% in 2017, that is to the level of the EU28 average gap in 2017 (Figure 3.31). This occurs despite a slight decrease in the difference between urban versus rural areas in general

Internet usage, from 6 percentage points in 2010 to 5 percentage points in 2016. It also occurs despite higher annual average growth in online interactions with public authorities among 55-74 year-olds as compared to 25-54 year-olds, the former of which are more likely to live in sparsely populated areas.

Figure 3.30. **Individuals using the Internet for digital government services**

Percentage of individuals and percentage points

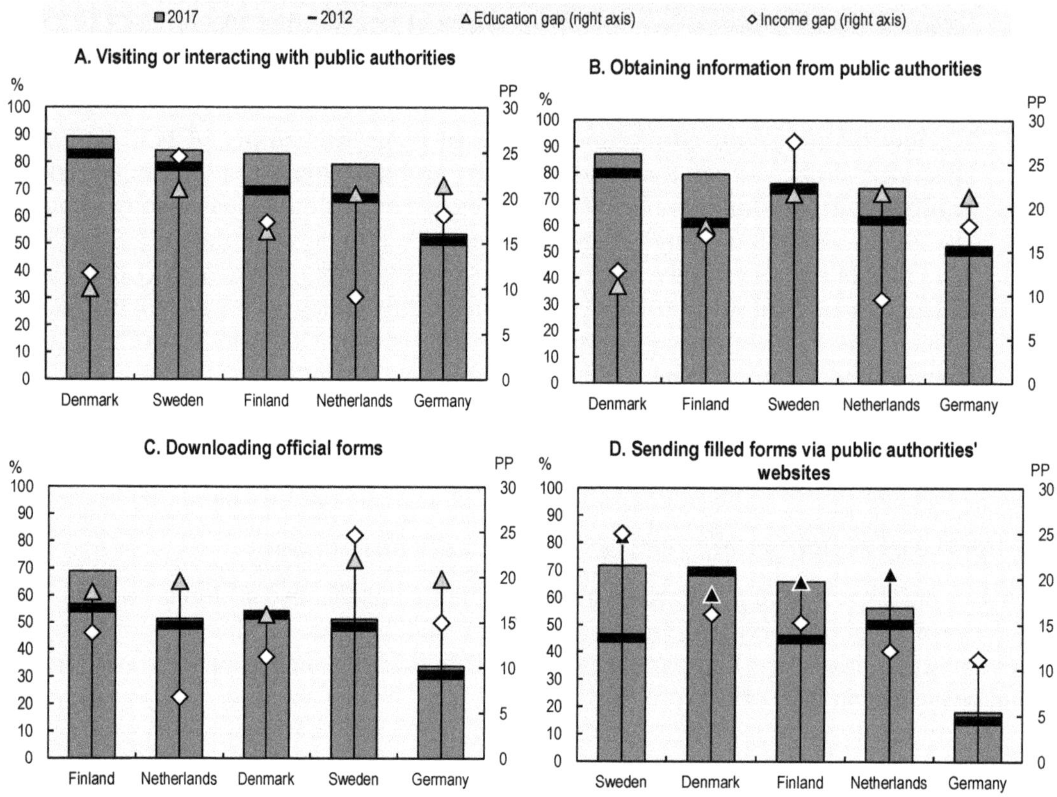

Notes: PP = percentage point. For details see Endnote 4.

Source: OECD (2018c), *ICT Access and Usage by Households and Individuals* (database), http://oe.cd/hhind.

Figure 3.31. **Individuals using the Internet to interact with public authorities by population density**

Percentage point difference between high and low population density areas

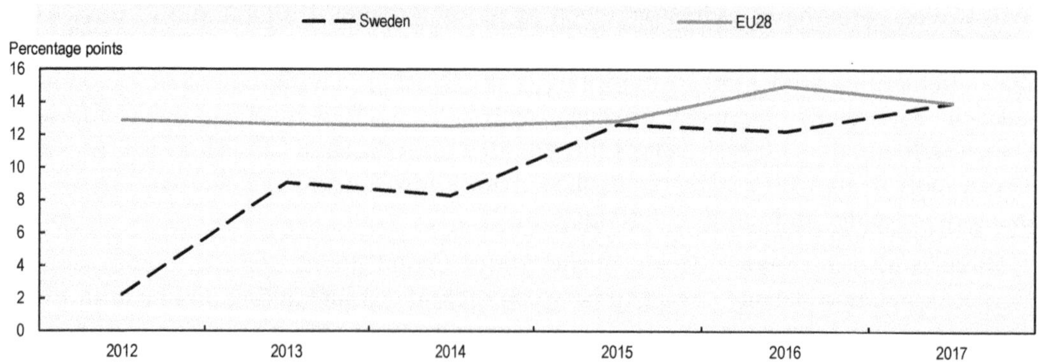

Source: Eurostat (2018b), *ICT Usage in Households and by Individuals*, http://ec.europa.eu/eurostat/web/digital-economy-and-society/data/database.

Digital public services can also boost interactions with firms and reduce costs, for example the burden of firms' annual reporting. While recent comparable data on firms' use of public services is limited, data on firms using the Internet to issue/send invoices to public authorities shows good progress in Sweden compared to the EU28, although not yet at the levels of Finland and Denmark (Figure 3.32).

Figure 3.32. **Firms using the Internet to issue/send invoices to public authorities, 2016**

Percentage of non-financial firms, by firm size

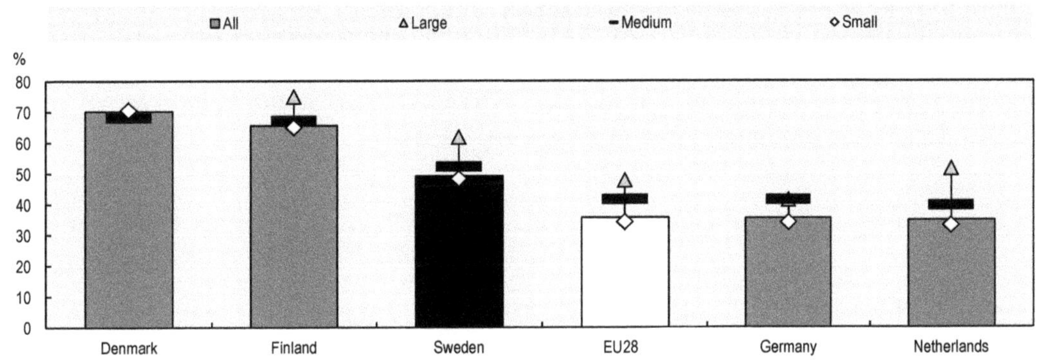

Notes: Includes issuing/sending electronic or paper invoices. All firms = 10 employees and more; large firms = 250 employees and more; medium firms = 50-249 employees; small firms = 10-49 employees.

Source: OECD (2018d), *ICT Access and Usage by Businesses* (database), http://oe.cd/bus.

Much potential remains to improve open government data

Digital technologies enable governments to create new value by opening up government data. While some of this data can be useful within the public sector itself, opening it up to the public promotes innovation among individuals and businesses (DK, 2016). While Sweden has a national open data portal (www.öppnadata.se), operated by the National Archives of Sweden, in comparison to other OECD countries, current efforts on open government data do not seem enough. In 2017, the value of the OECD OURdata (open, useful, reusable government data) Index for Sweden was among the lowest in the OECD (Figure 3.33).

Figure 3.33. **Open, useful, reusable government data, 2017**

OECD OURdata Index

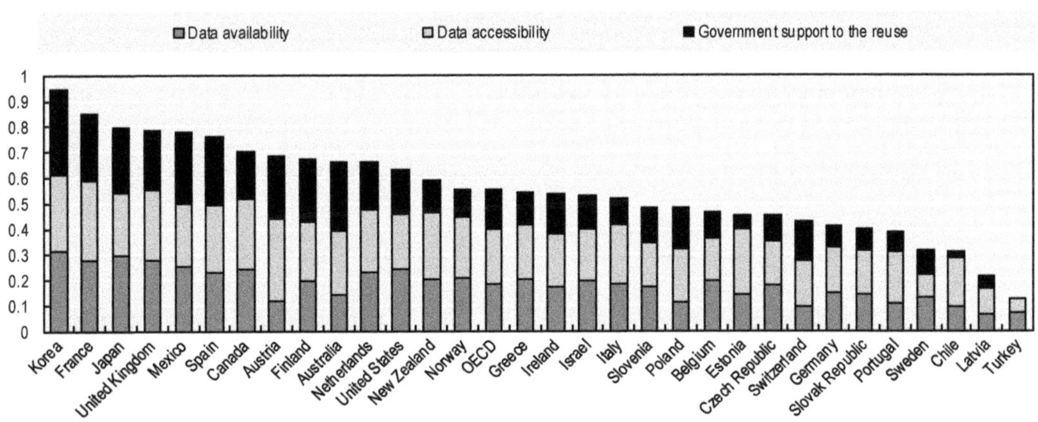

Notes: Data for Hungary, Iceland and Luxembourg are not available. Denmark does not have a central/federal data portal and therefore is not displayed in the index.

Source: OECD (2017b), *Government at a Glance 2017*, http://dx.doi.org/10.1787/gov_glance-2017-en.

Policies need to bolster equal access to digital public services and promote open government data

Making digital public services equally accessible across the country

Sweden's current "Digital First" policy for the digitalisation of the public sector was initiated in 2015 and will run until 2018. The policy aims to strengthen governance and co-ordination and promotes simple transparent, and efficient public management. Its primary goal is to make digital services the main means for the public sector to interact with individuals and companies (Box 3.6). Following the direction of the 2012 national strategy "Bringing the Citizen to the Heart of Government", Digital First is further pursuing the core principle of putting the individual user at the centre of all public services design (Government Offices of Sweden, 2012).

Box 3.6. **Digital First**

Digital First has two main pillars: core actions to speed up the digitalisation of the public sector and targeted initiatives in selected areas.

The core actions of Digital First are:

- improvements of national digital infrastructure, including for municipalities and county councils
- increasing digital maturity in all levels in the public sector
- capacity building for digital innovation, with a focus on open data
- reviews of laws and regulation
- the creation of a new digital government agency.

The new Agency for Digital Government will be operational from 1 September 2018, and will be tasked with co-ordinating and supporting the digitalisation of the public sector, promoting user-driven design, including among municipalities. It will focus, among other things, on developing and managing a national digital infrastructure and will take over several responsibilities that are currently spread across different authorities, such as for open data and e-IDs.

The targeted initiatives implemented under Digital First focused on: i) smart community building processes (housing construction); ii) smarter food chains; iii) smart environmental information; iv) digital enterprise services for restaurants. On the latter, for example, the government is simplifying administrative procedures necessary to start and run a restaurant and plans to extend this initiative to the accommodation sector thereafter – in a joint effort with the SKL.

Source: Government Offices of Sweden (2017a), "Digitalisering av offentlig sektor" (in Swedish), www.regeringen.se/regeringens-politik/digitaliseringspolitik/digital-forvaltning.

Another goal of the Digital First policy is to reduce differences in the availability and quality of digital services across municipalities and regions (Government Offices of Sweden, 2017a). The efforts to reach this goal are undertaken jointly by all levels of government, as stated in a 2015 letter of intent between the central government and the SKL (Government Offices of Sweden, 2015a). Also in 2015, a Council for the Digitization of Public Sweden, with representatives from 11 authorities, municipalities and county councils and a representative of the SKL, was set up to identify strategic issues and challenges to be addressed to increase territorial equality. The council's mandate ends by the end of 2018 (Government Offices of Sweden, 2015b). A key challenge to is to bridge currently often isolated digital systems in different parts of the government and across different levels of government, which requires improving interoperability and adopting common standards, e.g. for e-health services.

An important condition for fostering the use of advanced online activities, including interactions with public authorities, is a simple and secure digital identity (e-ID) (Government Offices of Sweden, 2017b). e-IDs are widely used in Sweden, but the current system faces challenges. In the early 2000s, Sweden opted for a market-based approach to offering e-ID solutions, which led to a scattered ecosystem in which several e-ID issuers are active today and bank-provided e-IDs are the most trusted and used solutions. Steps to improve the current system, including security requirements for e-IDs, are expected to be initiated by the e-ID board (Government Offices of Sweden, 2017d).

Several additional initiatives, budgeted for 2018, aim at advancing the digitalisation of public administrations and improving public services. The 2018 Budget Bill notably includes funds to support open data initiatives over a three-year period and measures to standardise and improve information exchange between public authorities. These measures support the implementation of the "once only" principle, that is to say that data from individuals or businesses will need to be collected once only to be accessible for all relevant agencies and authorities across the public sector (Government Offices of Sweden, 2017h).

Stepping up efforts to use and open up government data

Sweden has worked towards opening up government data for many years, but overall results are still limited. Transposing the European Union's 2003 Directive on the reuse of public sector information (PSI Directive) into domestic legislation, in 2010, Sweden adopted the Reuse of Documents from Public Administration Act (DK, 2016). While this created pressure on authorities to publicise data, a 2015 evaluation of the act's implementation by the State Treasury concluded that much work remains to be done (DK, 2016). Overall results of Sweden's efforts on open government data indeed still have room to be improved, as indicated by Sweden's ranking in the 2017 OECD OURdata Index (Figure 3.34).

Barriers to improving open government data, identified by the OECD (forthcoming a), include the verticality of Sweden's public sector model, characterised by relatively small ministries and strong and independent public agencies; a focus on citizens' right to request public sector information, but not on the proactive role of government agencies to open up government data; fee-based financing models of some agencies selling data; and changing governance and leadership for open data since 2011 (OECD, forthcoming a).

The need for action has been noted by the Digital Strategy, which calls to improve access to and facilitate the reuse of public sector information and government data. The strategy points out in particular the objectives to improve the public sector's capacity to better reuse its own data, within and between authorities; to use public procurement to promote the development, use and implementation of digitally driven innovations; and to use open source solutions, standards and testbeds.

Figure 3.34. **Government support to the reuse of data, 2017**

OURdata Index

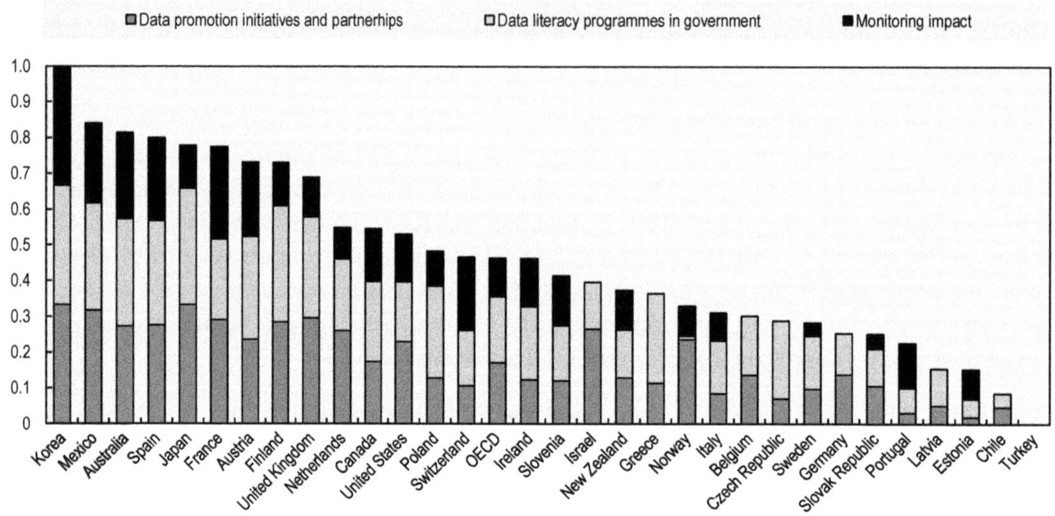

Note: Data for Hungary, Iceland and Luxembourg are not available. Denmark does not have a central/federal data portal and therefore is not displayed in the index.

Source: OECD (2017b), *Government at a Glance 2017*, http://dx.doi.org/10.1787/gov_glance-2017-en.

Important initiatives to step up the government's efforts to implement some of the above-mentioned objectives of the Digital Strategy include (Government Offices of Sweden, 2017e):

- **Open data availability**. The Swedish Agency for Public Management (Statskontoret) has been tasked with mapping barriers to the reuse of open data. This mission complements the National Archives of Sweden's mission to promote government agencies' efforts to make data available for reuse.
- **Reuse of open data**. The Swedish Growth Agency has been tasked with promoting open and DDI, which is expected to increase the reuse of open data. This mission includes the development of a platform that public actors can use to crowdsource solutions to challenging problems, including from academia and businesses.
- **Data-driven management and innovation**. The central government allocated funding to develop national digital services and to enable free sharing of basic data such as census data, between government agencies with the aim to reduce the cost of billing and redundant storage, as well as better use of data to foster innovation in the public sector.

Recommendations

This section showed that despite progress towards digital government, much remains to be done, in particular with regards to divides between different users of digital public services and to opening up and better using government data. The OECD *Digital Government Review of Sweden: Fostering a Data-Driven Public Sector for Public Value Co-Creation* (OECD, forthcoming a) provides a comprehensive set of recommendations. As part of these recommendations, the government may consider, in particular:

1. **Promoting equal access to digital public services by facilitating usage among lagging groups and territories**. Improving ease of use through user-driven design of services; fully implementing the once only principle; and enhancing interoperability among systems at national, regional and municipal levels, including through a national digital infrastructure and the implementation of common standards.
2. **Continuing to step up efforts to make open government data available and accessible for public reuse and innovation** and for better internal use, including through a national digital infrastructure that supports linked data, harmonised data formats, and better horizontal and vertical integration of data within and outside of the public sector, such as through data partnerships with private actors.

Notes

1. Broadband includes both fixed and mobile connections with an advertised download rate of at least 256 kilobits per second.

   E-purchases and e-sales refer to the purchase and sales of goods or services conducted over computer networks by methods specifically designed for the purpose of receiving or placing orders (i.e. webpages, extranet or electronic data interchange [EDI], but not orders by telephone, fax or manually typed e-mails). Payment and delivery methods are not considered.

   Enterprise resource planning (ERP) systems are software-based tools that can integrate the management of internal and external information flows, from material and human resources to finance, accounting and customer relations. Here, only sharing of information within the firm is considered. Data for ERP relate to the year 2015.

   Cloud computing refers to ICT services used over the Internet as a set of computing resources to access software, computing power, storage capacity and so on.

   Supply-chain management (SCM) refers to the use of automated data exchange (ADE) applications. Data for SCM relate to the year 2015.

   Customer relationship management (CRM) software is a software package used for managing a company's interactions with customers, clients, sales prospects, partners, employees and suppliers. Data for CRM relate to the year 2015.

   Social media refers to applications based on Internet technology or communication platforms for connecting, creating and exchanging content on line with customers, suppliers or partners, or within the enterprise. Social media might include social networks (other than paid adverts), blogs, file-sharing and wiki-type knowledge-sharing tools.

   Radio frequency identification (RFID) is a technology that enables contactless transmission of information via radio waves. RFID can be used for a wide range of purposes, including personal identification or access control, logistics, retail trade and process monitoring in manufacturing. Data for RFID relate to the year 2014.

   Unless otherwise stated, only enterprises with ten or more employees are considered.

Broadband: for Australia, includes "DSL", "fibre to the premises", "cable", "fixed wireless", "mobile wireless", "satellite" and "other". For Canada, it includes all connection groups except dial-up connection.

E-purchases: for Australia, data refer to the proportion of businesses placing/receiving orders over computer networks by methods specifically designed for the purpose (includes webpages, extranet or EDI). It includes any transaction where the commitment to purchase was made via the Internet, including via e-mail. For New Zealand, data exclude orders initiated via EDI-type messages. For Switzerland, data refer to the share of enterprises buying or selling and no recall period mentioned in the question.

E-sales: for Australia, data refer to the proportion of businesses placing/receiving orders over computer networks by methods specifically designed for the purpose (includes webpages, extranet or EDI). This includes any transaction where the commitment to purchase was made via the Internet.

ERP: for Canada, data relate to the year 2013, and for Iceland and Sweden to 2014.

Cloud computing: for Canada, data relate to the year 2012, and to enterprises that have made expenditures on "software as a service (e.g. cloud computing)".

SCM: for Turkey, data relate to the year 2012.

Social media: for Australia, data refer to businesses that had a social media presence, and for Canada to enterprises for which Internet websites offer integration with social media (e.g. Facebook, Twitter, Google+).

RFID: for Japan, Korea and Switzerland, data relate to the year 2015; for Canada, data relate to 2013 and for Turkey to 2011.

For countries in the European Statistical System, sector coverage consists of all activities in manufacturing and non-financial market services, and data on e-purchases and e-sales refer to 2015.

For Australia and New Zealand, data refer respectively to the fiscal year 2014/15 and the fiscal year 2015/16, ending 30 June, instead of 2016. For industrial classification, ANZSIC06 division is used instead of ISIC Rev.4 division. For Australia, data include agriculture, forestry and fishing.

For Canada, the North American Industry Classification System (NAICS) is used instead of ISIC Rev.4, and data refer to 2013 except for cloud computing (2012).

For Iceland, data refer to the year 2014. For Japan, Korea and Switzerland, data refer to the year 2015.

For Japan, JSIC Rev.13 division is used instead of ISIC Rev.4 and data include total businesses with 100 or more employees instead of 10 and more.

For Mexico, data refer to the year 2012. For Switzerland, data refer to the year 2015, website data refer to 2011 instead of 2016, and data for 2015 refer to firms with five or more employees.

For Switzerland, data for the year 2015 relate to businesses with five or more employees instead of ten or more.

2. Basic tools include shares of non-financial firms that have a broadband connection and a website, and that use social media. Data on social media use are for 2013 and 2017. Market integration tools include shares of non-financial firms placing

orders (i.e. making purchases) and receiving orders over computer networks. Business process tools include shares of non-financial firms using software for ERP, CRM and supply chain management (SCM).

3. ICT specialist skills are referred to as "enhanced skills" in the Digital Strategy.

4. Individuals using the Internet for digital government services during the last 12 months. "Education gap" refers to the percentage point difference between the usage the rates of individuals with a high level of educational attainment versus individuals with no or a low level of educational attainment. "Income gap" refers to the percentage point difference between the usage the rates of individuals living in a household with income in the first quartile and individuals living in a household with income in the fourth quartile.

References

Andrews, D. and C. Criscuolo (2013), "Knowledge-based capital, innovation and resource allocation", *OECD, Economics Department Working Papers*, No. 1046, OECD Publishing, Paris, http://dx.doi.org/10.1787/5k46bj546kzs-en.

Andrews, D., C. Criscuolo and P. Gal (2016), "The best vs the rest: The global productivity slowdown, divergence across firms and the role of public policy", *OECD Productivity Working Papers*, No. 5/2016, OECD Publishing, Paris, http://dx.doi.org/10.1787/63629cc9-en.

COL (2017a), "Läsa, skriva, räkna – en åtgärdsgaranti, Regeringen" (in Swedish), Council on Legislation, Stockholm, 17 August, www.regeringen.se/4a3c7a/contentassets/8b3616489504408f89f12036cf2a64e5/lasa-skriva-rakna--en-atgardsgaranti.pdf.

COL (2017b), "Skolstart vid sex års ålder" (in Swedish), Council on Legislation, Stockholm, 3 August, www.regeringen.se/4a25bf/contentassets/1562f389bc444dd6bffb9584f7b21248/skolstart-vid-sex-ars-alder.pdf.

DK (2016), *För digitalisering i tiden* (in Swedish), Statens Offentliga Untredningar (SOU) 2016:89, Digitaliseringskommissionen, Stockholm, www.regeringen.se/4af25c/contentassets/f7d07b214e2c459eb5757cea206e6701/sou-2016_89_webb.pdf.

DK (2015a), *Digitaliseringens transformerande kraft* (in Swedish), SOU 2015:91, Digitaliseringskommissionen, Stockholm, www.regeringen.se/4add1a/contentassets/b69dac4f05d44e8d836cdd91a5a7401b/digitaliseringens-transformerande-kraft--vagval-for-framtiden-sou-201591 (accessed 28 November 2017).

DK (2015b), *Gör Sverige i framtiden – digital kompetens* (in Swedish), SOU 2015:28, Digitaliseringskommissionen, Stockholm, www.regeringen.se/49bbaa/contentassets/e0acd9a7659d4c138c6666d2d5e21605/gor-sverige-i-framtiden--digital-kompetens-sou-201528 (accessed 28 November 2017).

Egan, M. (11 July 2016), "GE And Microsoft join forces in the industrial data cloud", General Electric Insights blog, www.ge.com/reports/ge-microsoft-join-forces-give-industrial-cloud-power (accessed 28 November 2017).

European Commission (2017), "Egovernment in Sweden", European Commission, https://joinup.ec.europa.eu/sites/default/files/inline-files/eGovernment_in_Sweden_March_2017_v2_00.pdf.

Eurostat (2018a), *ICT Usage in Enterprises*, http://ec.europa.eu/eurostat/web/digital-economy-and-society/data/database (accessed in March 2018).

Eurostat (2018b), *ICT Usage in Households and by Individuals*, http://ec.europa.eu/eurostat/web/digital-economy-and-society/data/database (accessed in March 2018).

Genlott, A.A. and Å. Grönlund (2016), "Closing the gaps: Improving literacy and mathematics by ICT-enhanced collaboration", *Computers & Education*, Vol. 99/2016, pp. 68-80, http://dx.doi.org/10.1016/j.compedu.2016.04.004.

Government Offices of Sweden (2017a), "Digitalisering av offentlig sektor" (in Swedish), webpage, www.regeringen.se/regeringens-politik/digitaliseringspolitik/digital-forvaltning (accessed 28 November 2017).

Government Offices of Sweden (2017b), "För ett hållbart digitaliserat Sverige – en digitaliseringsstrateg" (in Swedish), Regeringskansliet, Stockholm, www.regeringen.se/49adea/contentassets/5429e024be6847fc907b786ab954228f/digitaliseringsstrategin_slutlig_170518-2.pdf.

Government Offices of Sweden (2017c), "Lärcentrum för livslångt lärande i hela landet" (in Swedish), webpage, www.regeringen.se/artiklar/2017/09/larcentra-for-livslangt-larande-i-hela-landet (accessed 28 November 2017).

Government Offices of Sweden (2017d), "Ökad och breddad användning av e-legitimationer" (in Swedish), www.regeringen.se/pressmeddelanden/2017/10/okad-och-breddad-anvandning-av-e-legitimationer (accessed 28 November 2017).

Government Offices of Sweden (2017e), "Regeringen vill snabba på arbetet med öppna data", www.regeringen.se/debattartiklar/2017/05/regeringen-vill-snabba-pa-arbetet-med-oppna-data (accessed 28 November 2017).

Government Offices of Sweden (2017f), "Satsningar inom utbildningsområdet i budgetpropositionen för 2018" (in Swedish), webpage, www.regeringen.se/artiklar/2017/09/satsningar-inom-utbildningsdepartementets-ansvarsomraden-i-budgetpropositionen-for-2018 (accessed 16 April 2018).

Government Offices of Sweden (2017g), "Satsningar inom utbildningsområdet" (in Swedish), webpage, www.regeringen.se/artiklar/2016/09/satsningar-inom-utbildningsomradet (accessed 28 November 2017).

Government Offices of Sweden (2017h), "Stora satsningar på digitalisering av den offentliga sektorn i höstbudgeten" (in Swedish), www.regeringen.se/artiklar/2017/09/stora-satsningar-pa-digitalisering-av-den-offentliga-sektorn-i-hostbudgeten (accessed 28 November 2017).

Government Offices of Sweden (2015a), "Godkännande och undertecknande av avsiktsförklaring mellan staten och Sveriges Kommuner och Landsting för en digital förnyelse av det offentliga Sverige" (in Swedish), www.regeringen.se/49948d/contentassets/7aca65dd753d4242b4916572a632d007/beslut-om-bemyndigande-att-underteckna-en-avsiktsforklaring-med-skl-om-digital-fornyelse.pdf.

Government Offices of Sweden (2015b), "Regeringen tillsätter råd för digitaliseringen av det offentliga Sverige" (in Swedish), press release, 9 December, www.regeringen.se/pressmeddelanden/2015/12/regeringen-tillsatter-rad-for-digitaliseringen-av-det-offentliga-sverige (accessed 28 November 2017).

Government Offices of Sweden (2012), "Med medborgaren i centrum" (in Swedish), www.regeringen.se/49bbc1/contentassets/24b07f6fd836497cb833d88c36cf51ee/med-medborgaren-i-centrum.-regeringens-strategi-for-en-digitalt-samverkande-statsforvaltning (accessed 28 November 2017).

Growth Analysis (2017), "Digital maturity in Sweden", Policy brief, Swedish Agency for Growth Policy Analysis, Östersund, Sweden.

IIS (2017), *Swedes and the Internet 2017*, Internet Foundation in Sweden, www.soi2017.se (accessed 27 February 2018).

IIS (2016), *Swedes and the Internet*, Internet Foundation in Sweden, www.iis.se (accessed 28 November 2017).

Ministry for Enterprise and Innovation (2016), "Smart industry: A strategy for new industrialization for Sweden", Government Offices of Sweden, www.regeringen.se/49bff2/contentassets/d651a29f7e22474f9b12a385f974f72e/smart-industry.pdf.

MER (2017a), "Nationell digitaliseringsstrategi för skolväsendet" (in Swedish), Ministry of Education and Research, Stockholm, www.regeringen.se/4a9d9a/contentassets/00b3d9118b0144f6bb95302f3e08d11c/nationell-digitaliseringsstrategi-for-skolvasendet.pdf.

MER (2017b), "Stärkt digital kompetens i läroplaner och kursplaner" (in Swedish), webpage, Ministry of Education and Research, www.regeringen.se/pressmeddelanden/2017/03/starkt-digital-kompetens-i-laroplaner-och-kursplaner (accessed 28 November 2017).

MER (2017c), "Utbildningsdepartementets samlade budgetsatsningar 2018" (in Swedish), webpage, Ministry of Education and Research, www.regeringen.se/pressmeddelanden/2017/09/utbildningsdepartementets-samlade-budgetsatsningar-2018 (accessed 28 November 2017).

OECD (forthcoming a), *Digital Government Review of Sweden: Fostering a data-driven public sector for public value co-creation*, OECD Digital Government Studies, OECD Publishing, Paris.

OECD (forthcoming b), "Going digital: What determines technology diffusion among firms?", *OECD Economics Working Paper Series*, OECD Publishing, Paris.

OECD (2018a), "Empowering women in the digital age: Where do we stand?", brochure, OECD, Paris, www.oecd.org/social/empowering-women-in-the-digital-age-brochure.pdf.

OECD (2018b), "Going digital in a multilateral world", OECD interim report to ministers, OECD, Paris, www.oecd.org/mcm/documents/C-MIN-2018-6-EN.pdf.

OECD (2018c), *ICT Access and Usage by Households and Individuals* (database), http://oe.cd/hhind (accessed in March 2018).

OECD (2018d), *ICT Access and Usage by Businesses* (database), http://oe.cd/bus (accessed in March 2018).

OECD (2017a), *Education at a Glance 2017: OECD Indicators*, OECD Publishing, Paris, http://dx.doi.org/10.1787/eag-2017-en.

OECD (2017b), *Government at a Glance 2017*, OECD Publishing, Paris, http://dx.doi.org/10.1787/gov_glance-2017-en.

OECD (2017c), *OECD Digital Economy Outlook 2017*, OECD Publishing, Paris, http://dx.doi.org/10.1787/9789264276284-en.

OECD (2017d), *OECD Science, Technology and Industry Scoreboard 2017: The Digital Transformation*, OECD Publishing, Paris, http://dx.doi.org/10.1787/9789264268821-en.

OECD (2017e), *Survey of Adult Skills (PIAAC)*, database, OECD, Paris, www.oecd.org/skills/piaac/publicdataandanalysis/#d.en.408927 (accessed 28 November 2017).

OECD (2016a), *Getting Skills Right: Sweden*, OECD Publishing, Paris, http://dx.doi.org/10.1787/9789264265479-en.

OECD (2016b), "New skills for the digital economy", *OECD Digital Economy Papers*, No. 258, OECD Publishing, Paris, http://dx.doi.org/10.1787/5jlwnkm2fc9x-en.

OECD (2016c), "Skills for a digital world: 2016 Ministerial Meeting on the Digital Economy background report", *OECD Digital Economy Papers*, No. 250, OECD Publishing, Paris, http://dx.doi.org/10.1787/5jlwz83z3wnw-en.

OECD (2016d), *Skills Matter: Further Results from the Survey of Adult Skills*, OECD Publishing, Paris, http://dx.doi.org/10.1787/9789264258051-en.

OECD (2015a), *Data-Driven Innovation: Big Data for Growth and Well-Being*, OECD Publishing, Paris, http://dx.doi.org/10.1787/9789264229358-en.

OECD (2015b), "Results from PISA 2015: Country note Sweden", OECD, Paris, www.oecd.org/pisa/PISA-2015-Sweden.pdf.

OECD (2014), *Recommendation of the Council on Digital Government Strategies*, OECD, Paris, www.oecd.org/gov/digital-government/Recommendation-digital-government-strategies.pdf.

OECD (2013), *OECD Skills Outlook 2013: First Results from the Survey of Adult Skills*, OECD Publishing, Paris, http://dx.doi.org/10.1787/9789264204256-en.

OECD (2004), "ICT skills and employment", in: *Information Technology Outlook 2004*, OECD Publishing, Paris, http://dx.doi.org/10.1787/it_outlook-2004-8-en.

Vinnova (2016), "Uppdrag att genomföra samverkansprojekt för att utnyttja digitaliseringens potential för ökad konkurrenskraft hos svensk industri", Vinnova, internal document, N2016/02169/IF.

Vinnova (2015), "Slutrapportering "Uppdrag att utföra insatser för att främja digitalisering av svensk industri" (in Swedish), Vinnova, N/2015/6246/IF, www.vinnova.se/contentassets/ecd0206440df49a5aea396f74c90d060/2015-04724-rapp.pdf.

Chapter 4.

Digital security policy

This chapter provides an overarching description and analysis of digital security policy in Sweden. Sweden's 2017 National Cybersecurity Strategy aims to better integrate digital security policy within the broader digital transformation agenda and marks a positive turning point towards a more holistic approach to digital security.

The statistical data for Israel are supplied by and under the responsibility of the relevant Israeli authorities. The use of such data by the OECD is without prejudice to the status of the Golan Heights, East Jerusalem and Israeli settlements in the West Bank under the terms of international law.

This chapter provides an overarching description of digital security policy in Sweden and discusses its strengths and limitations from the perspective of the OECD 2015 *Recommendation on Digital Security Risk Management for Economic and Social Prosperity* ("Security Risk Recommendation"). Unless specified otherwise, "digital security" refers to the management of economic and social risks resulting from breaches of availability, integrity and confidentiality (AIC) of information and communication technologies (ICTs) and data. As explained in the first section, some Swedish policy documents are using this expression in a broader manner; other policy documents use other terms such as "cybersecurity" and "information security".

This chapter does not cover policies directly related to criminal law enforcement (i.e. cybercrime) or national security.

Digital security within the Swedish digital strategy

Digital security is not a new policy area in Sweden, but it took a long time to reach a strategic level. The Swedish government expressed interest in digital security policy as early as 2003 by asking a commission of enquiry to make a proposal for an "information security" policy, including recommendations as to how Sweden should implement the 2002 OECD *Guidelines on the Security of Information Systems and Networks*. On the basis of the commission's 2005 report, the Swedish Emergency Management Agency adopted an action plan in 2008 covering information security in organisations, skills, information-sharing collaboration and response, and communication security and security in products and systems (Swedish Emergency Management Agency, 2008). In 2010, the successor of the Emergency Management Agency, the Swedish Civil Contingencies Agency (MSB) developed a Strategy for Information Security 2010-2015 (MSB, 2010) followed by a new action plan in 2012 (MSB, 2012a). Both documents were developed in consultation with the agencies of the Cooperation Group for Information Security (SAMFI) formed in 2003 (further described below). The strategy recognised that "information security is everyone's business" and aimed to provide a common understanding of digital security in the society. However, neither the strategy nor the action plans were adopted by the government: they reflected the views of independent[1] agencies with the highest stakes on digital security.

It was only in 2017 that the first high-level strategic policy documents addressing digital security were adopted by the government: the Digital Strategy for Sustainable Digital Transformation ("Digital Strategy"), which includes a section on digital security, and the National Cybersecurity Strategy, adopted a few weeks later.

The Digital Strategy is a first step towards approaching digital security as a strategic economic and social policy challenge

The overarching objective of the Digital Strategy released in May 2017 is to make Sweden the world leader in harnessing the opportunities of the digital transformation. Digital security is one of the five strategic goals for achieving this objective, together with digital skills, digital innovation, digital leadership and digital infrastructure.

According to the "digital security" strategic goal, Sweden should provide "the best conditions for everyone to safely take part, take responsibility for and trust in digital society". This strategic goal is broken down into six "important areas":

1. **Digital identity**. Although a large part of the Swedish population has an electronic identity (e-ID) (see below), the strategy aims to ensure that everyone in Sweden can use simple and secure digital credentials, including across borders.

2. **High security requirements** to identify and prevent vulnerabilities and handle incidents. This requires awareness of information and cybersecurity and of how to protect information systems. This area, covered by the Network and Information Security Directive (NIS Directive) (European Union, 2016), is addressed in Sweden's 2017 National Cybersecurity Strategy.
3. **Privacy in the digital society**. The use of personal data is often crucial to streamline and develop both public and the private services. However, the right to privacy is essential to maintain confidence, security and trust in the digital environment. Sweden has the potential to lead with respect to privacy-friendly technologies.
4. **Preserving democracy in digital environments**. Opportunities to spread threats, hatred, extremist propaganda and deliberate dissemination of false information increase. Freedom of expression must be given very wide limits. However, strong action is required against criminal acts, whether online or offline.
5. **A secure and mobile labour market**. Digitalisation fundamentally changes the labour market, including the nature of the work and working environment. Close dialogue between the government and social partners to ensure continuous adaptation to social development, in line with the Swedish model, is essential.
6. **Functioning digital markets and secure consumers**. Digital markets must always be a safe and legal place for consumers, businesses and rights owners. Regulatory and supervisory authorities should maintain effective consumer protection and competition on equal terms.

The Digital Strategy uses the term "digital security" differently from the OECD. The "digital security" strategic goal brings together under one umbrella the policy domains that Sweden views as requiring some protection for digital transformation to be sustainable: identities, systems and networks, privacy, democracy, workers, and consumers. Thus the term "security" in this context can be understood as "social security", that is, the part of the social contract that addresses the need for collective protection against uncertainty, such as loss of job (secure workers), scam (secure consumers) or misinformation by foreign influence (secure citizens). In contrast, the OECD defines "digital security" as the management of economic and social risks resulting from breaches of AIC of ICTs and data. Therefore, only two of the six "important areas" listed above relate directly to AIC and the others have a lower degree of relationship with it, from relatively high (privacy protection) to relatively low (secure and mobile labour market).

In fact, the Swedish term used in the strategy for the expression "digital security" is not "*säkerhet*", such as in "*informationssäkerhet*" (information security) or "*cybersäkerhet*" (cybersecurity), but "*trygghet*".[2] The distinction between *säkerhet* and *trygghet* is subtle: English-Swedish dictionaries translate *trygghet* into "security" but the meaning of *trygghet* might be closer to "safety" than "security", in the sense of relating to people, as suggested by the use of "social *trygghet*" to mean "social security".

Despite the unusual use of the term "digital security", which might be a translation artefact, the Swedish strategy's grouping of issues has the merit of considering digital security (in the OECD sense of AIC-related risk) as an economic and social challenge related to the digital transformation. However, it may suggest that the uncertainty created by potential breaches of AIC requires primarily collective solutions analogous to the collective protection provided by the welfare state. In other words, it may imply that digital security does not require action at the individual level because society, through some form of collective protection, will take care of it. This would be inconsistent with the principle that all stakeholders should take responsibility for the management of digital security risk, according to their role, ability to act and the context, formulated in the OECD 2015 Security Risk Recommendation.

The fact that these documents do not use the terms "digital security" in the same manner as the OECD is not an issue: many countries use different terms to refer to this area. However, the apparent terminological inconsistencies across Swedish policy documents are more troubling. In particular, the differences between the overall "digital security" goal ("digital *trygghet*"), the notions of "high security requirements" ("*Höga krav på säkerhet*") as one of this goal's important areas, and of "information and cyber security" ("*informations- och cybersäkerhet*") as used in the title of the national cybersecurity strategy (see below) are indeed relatively unclear to the non-expert.

One way to clarify the "digital security" strategic goal of Sweden's Digital Strategy would be to call it "digital trust", which would be consistent with all the "important areas" it covers. The title "higher security requirements" important area could be aligned with the title of the National Cybersecurity Strategy, i.e. "information and cybersecurity", or it could be changed to "digital security", if consistency with the OECD is sought.

The "high security requirement" important area of the "digital security" strategic goal is addressed in more detail in Sweden's "National Strategy for the Society's Information and Cyber Security", translated as the "National Cybersecurity Strategy", which was adopted one month after the Digital Strategy, suggesting that both strategies have been developed in parallel and through relatively separate tracks rather than in full synergy, which may explain terminological misalignments.

In sum, the inclusion of digital security (as understood by the OECD) in the Digital Strategy seems to indicate that Sweden has made a first step towards approaching digital security as an economic and social issue. Sweden has, however, not yet developed a clear vision of what this means and implies, nor of how digital security fits within the broader framework of the digital transformation. Terminological inconsistencies reveal more than branding issues. They suggest that Sweden understands many aspects of digital security but addresses them as separate pieces rather than through an integrated and holistic approach (Box 4.1). The Digital Strategy represents a first step towards bringing together the different dimensions of digital security, but further work is needed to devise a truly holistic and unified vision.

Nevertheless, with this first effort to bring digital security to the strategic level, Sweden is likely to be in a situation similar to that of other countries whose first strategy was a necessary first step to develop a real high-level holistic vision a few years later (e.g. Australia, Canada, France, the Netherlands and the United Kingdom). The Netherlands, for example, adopted a "National Cyber Security Strategy 2" in 2013 only two years after the first version. It took other countries a few more years to update their frameworks. In all cases, the second strategy was always much more sophisticated, visionary and holistic than the initial one which, *a posteriori*, looked like a necessary stage in a learning curve towards more strategic thinking.

While Sweden started late in this process, it aims at integrating digital security within a strategy for the digital transformation of Sweden. This is more challenging conceptually and from a governmental co-ordination perspective, but it also has more potential for effectively integrating the economic and social dimension of digital security into the fabric of the digital transformation.

Box 4.1. Digital security, cybersecurity, information security, cyberdefence, cybercrime: The need to simplify terminology

The multiplication of terms related to digital security in Swedish policy documents is an illustration of a maturing policy-making process. Sweden is not the only country in this situation as, unfortunately, there is no universally agreed terminology to capture the different facets of digital security in every context.

In its 2015 *Recommendation on Digital Security Risk Management for Economic and Social Prosperity*, the OECD uses the term "digital security" rather than "cybersecurity". OECD countries considered that "cybersecurity" was already used by different actors as a broad concept that did not reflect the multifaceted nature of this area. More generally, they favoured "digital" over "cyber" as the latter was used in certain circles as a synonym of "cyberwarfare", "cyberdefence" or "cyberinfluence". Furthermore, "cyber" is absent from economic circles, which more generally stick to the digital semantic: digital economy, digital transformation, digitalisation, etc. "Digital" facilitates the recognition of "digital security" as an economic issue by policy makers and business leaders. "Information security" was left aside as a technical management primarily reflecting the view of the technical community (e.g. ISO/IEC 27000 "Information Security Management Systems" standards) rather than business leadership's perspective. It also carries ambiguity in an international context as it has a different scope in countries such as the People's Republic of China and the Russian Federation, which use it also to capture policies against disinformation, influence and information manipulation.

The National Cybersecurity Strategy is focused on information systems and networks rather than economic and social activities

The development and adoption of the National Cybersecurity Strategy follow a series of audit reports by the National Audit Office, which concluded that digital security efforts in several government agencies "fell considerably short of being adequate" (NAO, 2016a; 2016b). The strategy also follows the development of a report by a commission of enquiry which developed proposals for a new digital security strategy focusing on government activities (Government Offices of Sweden, 2015). However, the strategy is broader and aims to: i) "create the long-term conditions for all stakeholders in society to work effectively on digital security"; ii) "raise the level of awareness and knowledge throughout society".

The National Cybersecurity Strategy is based on both the National Security Strategy's objectives of protecting the lives and health of the population, the functioning of society, and the capacity to uphold fundamental values and the Digital Strategy's objectives of becoming the world leader in harnessing the opportunities of the digital transformation. It covers six strategic priorities: i) ensuring a systematic and comprehensive approach in cybersecurity efforts; ii) enhancing network, product and system security; iii) enhancing capability to prevent, detect, and manage cyberattacks and other information technology (IT) incidents; iv) increasing the possibility of preventing and combating cybercrime; v) increasing knowledge and promoting expertise; and vi) enhancing international co-operation.

The scope of the National Cybersecurity Strategy carries some ambiguity. The strategy defines cybersecurity as the set of security measures to preserve the availability, integrity[3] and confidentiality of information. However, the strategy also addresses disinformation and influence campaigns, including to "intentionally disseminate untrue or misleading details in order to influence people's attitudes, standpoints and actions in a certain direction". Disinformation and influence are important issues exacerbated by the digital transformation and can sometimes overlap with digital security, for example when digital security attacks are used to manipulate public opinion. They are, however, different from the management of the economic and social consequences of breaches of AIC, as they involve different policy tools and raise different legal considerations related to freedom of speech, media regulation, etc. Furthermore, the fact that they are addressed in the National Cybersecurity Strategy seems inconsistent with the Digital Strategy, in which disinformation is addressed within the digital security ("*trygghet*") strategic goal, but as a different "important area" related to the "preservation of democracy in digital environments". These inconsistencies suggest that both strategies are not entirely integrated.

Analysis of the National Cybersecurity Strategy confirms that Sweden has not yet developed a clear vision of how digital security fits within the broader economic and social policy framework of the digital transformation. Indeed, the National Cybersecurity Strategy primarily considers digital security from the perspective of ICTs, i.e. focusing on a risk to information systems and networks rather than the economic and social activities that rely on them. This approach is consistent with the 2002 OECD *Guidelines for the Security of Information Systems and Networks* ("Security Guidelines") but not with the *Recommendation on Digital Security Risk Management for Economic and Social Prosperity* that replaced them in 2015. It is essential to understand the difference between these two approaches.

Since the early days of computing and until relatively recently, most stakeholders, including policy makers, approached digital security primarily as a technical issue: they focused on security risk to systems and networks, and so did the OECD with its 2002 *Guidelines for the Security of Information Systems and Networks*. This approach to digital security, which includes technical, human and management aspects, led governments and organisations to increase digital security efforts. In public policy, for example, governments established and strengthened the capacity to respond to digital security incidents through computer emergency response teams (CERTs). They also increased stakeholders' awareness about technical digital security risks (phishing, malware, hackers, identity theft, etc.) and encouraged organisations to adopt standards such as the ISO/IEC 27000 family, a path followed by Sweden.

Progressively however, most economic and social activities have become digital or digital-dependent "by design" and, in parallel, risks continue to increase, elevating the importance of digital security within organisations and at the public policy level. As losses from digital security incidents have become more common, stakeholders' attention has shifted from the technical incidents such as denial of service attacks, ransomware, or personal data breaches to their economic and social consequences to financial and reputational losses, loss of business opportunities and reduced competitiveness resulting from theft of innovation and trade secrets, privacy impact and loss of trust, as well as in some cases, physical assets destruction and, tomorrow, possibly loss of lives (Box 4.2).

In addition, stakeholders have also realised that the security measures put in place to reduce digital security risk can have negative effects on the economic and social activities they are expected to protect: in addition to their financial cost, they can close the digital environment and reduce its dynamism, limiting the opportunities to use ICTs for innovation; they can also increase time-to-market, lower performance and user-friendliness, etc.

While recognising the continued importance of the security of information systems and networks, organisations realised that digital security risk management should primarily focus on economic and social activities rather than on the digital environment that supports them, and that, as a result, it should be led by organisations' business leadership with the support of technical experts rather than the reverse. Managers in charge of realising the economic and social benefits of the digital environment are better placed than technical experts to set the acceptable level of economic and social risk for the organisation (i.e. its "risk appetite") and to assess the consequences of digital security risk on economic and social objectives they have the responsibility to achieve. They are also in a better position to ensure that security measures do not reduce the potential of ICTs to innovate and contribute to competitiveness. But these managers rely on technical experts to understand the risk factors (possible threats, vulnerabilities and incidents) and the options to reduce the risk (i.e. technical security and business continuity measures). Both have to work together, but risk-related decisions and responsibility should be owned by business decision makers and not delegated to technical experts. In fact, risk management should be an integral part of business decision making rather than a separate area. Digital security risk management is no exception.

Box 4.2. Examples of economic and social consequences of digital security incidents

Since robust quantitative data on the cost of digital security incidents are unavailable, policy makers most often rely on anecdotal evidence, which is also rare as most companies do not communicate on the business impact of digital security attacks so as to protect their image. However, the damages from the June 2017 Wannacry and NotPetya ransomware attacks which hit many public and private organisations globally were so high that several publicly traded companies had to disclose financial information as part of their financial transparency obligations requirement. In most cases, the economic consequences were much more important than the technical ICT damages:

- Danish transports and logistics company AP Moller-Maersk: estimated USD 200-300 million losses from business interruption (Palmer, 2017).
- French industrial company Saint-Gobain: EUR 250 million net sales losses and EUR 80 million operating income losses for 2017 (Saint-Gobain, 2017).
- US pharmaceutical company Merck: USD 135 million sales losses and USD 175 million operational expenses for the 3rd quarter 2017, and a similar impact to revenue and expenses expected for the 4th quarter. The temporary production shutdown caused by the attack and higher-than-expected demand at that time forced the company to borrow doses of its Gardasil 9 vaccine from US Centers for Disease Control and Prevention stockpile to fulfil customer orders, reducing the company's 3rd quarter sales by USD 240 million (Merck, 2017; Hufford, 2017).

These examples could be completed by others such as the dismissal of the US retail company Target Store's chief executive officer following a digital security attack in 2014 (Rushe, 2014), or the December 2015 temporary blackout in Ukraine following a sophisticated attack on the country's power grid (Zetter, 2016b). In 2015, an attack reported by the German Federal Office for Security in Information Technology caused "massive" physical damages in a German steel mill (Zetter, 2016a).

Sources: Hufford (2017), "Merck swings to loss as cyberattack hurts sales", MarketWatch, 27 October, www.marketwatch.com/story/merck-swings-to-loss-as-cyberattack-hurts-sales-2017-10-27-134853159; Merck (2017), "Merck announces second-quarter 2017 financial results", www.mrknewsroom.com/news-release/corporate-news/merck-announces-second-quarter-2017-financial-results; Palmer (2017), "Petya ransomware: Cyberattack costs could hit $300m for shipping giant Maersk", www.zdnet.com/article/petya-ransomware-cyber-attack-costs-could-hit-300m-for-shipping-giant-maersk; Rushe (2014), "Target CEO Gregg Steinhafel resigns in wake of customer data breach", www.theguardian.com/business/2014/may/05/target-chief-executive-steps-down-data-breach; Saint-Gobain (2017), "Résultats du 1er semestre 2017", www.saint-gobain.com/sites/sgcom.master/files/cp_vf_resultats_s1_2017_t.pdf; Zetter (2016a), "A cyberattack has caused confirmed physical damage for the second time ever", https://www.wired.com/2015/01/german-steel-mill-hack-destruction; Zetter (2016b), "Inside the cunning, unprecedented hack of Ukraine's power grid", www.wired.com/2016/03/inside-cunning-unprecedented-hack-ukraines-power-grid.

Digital security, which used to be primarily owned by technical experts, should therefore become a business management responsibility. The replacement of the OECD 2002 *Guidelines for the Security of Information Systems and Networks* by the 2015 *Recommendation on Digital Security Risk Management for Economic and Social Prosperity* reflects this evolution at the policy level. This evolution from the security of information systems to the management of digital security risk to economic and social activities is a shift in responsibility which aims to ensure that the assessment and management of opportunities and risks are in the same hands, because they are two sides of the same coin. It implies that organisations' leaders should be responsible for managing digital security risk as much as they are responsible for managing the opportunities offered by the digital technologies. Ultimately, digital security risk is simply one risk among many that business decision makers must own and manage and cannot entirely delegate to technical experts.

An incident in 2017 illustrated the shortcomings of the current approach (Box 4.3). This incident followed others which contributed to raising digital security awareness among the population and the political leadership, such as large co-ordinated denial of service attacks on 20 March 2016 which shut down several national and regional media outlets' websites for at least one hour (Sverige Radio, 2016).

Box 4.3. A digital security risk management failure at the Transport Agency

In July 2017, a newspaper revealed that unauthorised personnel at IBM subsidiaries in Eastern Europe had access to a very large amount of sensitive data as a result of a 2015 outsourcing agreement with the Swedish Transport Agency for the management of vehicle registration and driver's license databases.

A large amount of personal data about Swedish people including the identities of persons working undercover for the police, the security service and the special intelligence unit of the Swedish armed forces, along with details about bridges, roads, ports, the Stockholm subway system and other infrastructures had been exposed (Anderson, 2017). This incident was reported by the press as one of the largest government data breaches in Sweden (The Local, 2017).

Following investigations by the parliament, it appeared that the Director General of the Transports Agency had knowingly bypassed the legal security compliance requirements in an attempt to speed up the outsourcing process. After the publication of this information by the press, this digital security incident turned into a political crisis as the prime minister reshuffled the Cabinet, dismissing the Minister for Infrastructures, responsible for the Transport Agency, and receiving the resignation of the Minister of the Interior, who apparently had been informed about the issue but did not inform the prime minister.

Over the summer parliamentary break, an opposition alliance threatened to launch a no-confidence motion in the parliament against the Minister of Defence, potentially leading to a serious government crisis. Ultimately, the motion failed, but parliamentary investigations were still ongoing at the time of writing.

These incidents followed the 2014 and 2016 National Audit Office reviews of many public sector institutions which underlined "extensive shortcomings" (NAO, 2014) and a level of digital security efforts that "fell considerably short of being adequate", and was "not acceptable" (NAO, 2016a).

Sources: Anderson (2017), "Swedish government scrambles to contain damage from data breach", www.nytimes.com/2017/07/25/world/europe/ibm-sweden-data-outsourcing.html; NAO (2014), "Information security in the civil public administration", https://www.riksrevisionen.se/en/audit-reports/audit-reports/2014/information-security-in-the-civil-public-administration.html; NAO (2016a), "Information security work at nine agencies", www.riksrevisionen.se/en/audit-reports/audit-reports/2016/information-security-work-at-nine-agencies.html; The Local (2017), "Swedish government battles political fallout from transport data leak", www.thelocal.se/20170725/swedish-government-battles-political-fallout-from-transport-data-leak.

Instead of chief executive officers, director generals, board members and business line managers, the approach followed by the 2002 OECD Guidelines and by the 2017 Swedish National Cybersecurity Strategy leads to responsibility for managing digital security risk being owned by those who maintain and operate the digital environment, i.e. chief information officers, chief technology officers, etc. To realise the benefits of the digital transformation, business leaders and decision makers need to undertake a double-sided cultural shift: i) rethink all aspects of their business activities to understand the innovation opportunities that data and digital technologies can unleash to increase their competitiveness, improve their service and grow; and at the same time ii) understand and manage the risk inherently related to digitalising their activities. A leader who does not own, understand and manage the risk related to his/her digital decision is blindly taking it, jeopardising its entire business because digital security risk can quickly contaminate all of the organisation's lines of activities by propagating through networks.

When business decision makers manage both the socio-economic opportunities and the digital security risk related to the use of ICTs, security measures can be appropriately tailored to the economic and social activities of the organisation and viewed as a strategic asset, part of a profit centre, rather than only as a cost centre. Security risk management and security measures can also be integrated into business models and the design of products and services rather than being addressed is isolation, or as an afterthought. In this way they can be turned into a market advantage and contribute to increasing competitiveness. Digital security becomes a driver for innovation, no longer a burden and a constraint.

The economic and social risk management approach promoted by the OECD Security Risk Recommendation is missing from the Swedish National Cybersecurity Strategy. The National Audit Office audit reports include some findings which illustrate a situation in government agencies typical of a digital security approach severed from business decision makers because it is focused primarily on information systems and networks.

For example, the reports note that agencies' leadership, when aware of the digital security risk, has often delegated responsibility to technical staff who do not have the ability to act: government "agency managements have delegated responsibility for information security without ensuring that those responsible have an adequate mandate to carry out their tasks"; "the functions in charge of information security find it hard to contend with core activities that tend to see information security requirements as obstacles"; "it is the IT or security functions that impose security requirements rather than the core organisation"; "the core organisation does not perceive that it has any responsibility for information security, but that this lies somewhere else in the agency, such as the IT or security functions".

The findings of surveys carried out by the MSB and the Swedish Association of Local Authorities and Regions (SKL in Swedish) in 2015 highlight a similar situation, where digital security efforts are disconnected from the leadership of municipalities and are not integrated in their decision making and broader risk management (Box 4.4).

The OECD is currently working to develop comparable indicators to measure digital security risk management practice in businesses. Currently, the lack of such indicators, which is not specific to Sweden, prevents from understanding the extent to which the lack of economic and social digital security risk management is limited to the public administration or cuts across all organisations in Sweden. Nevertheless, the strong focus of the National Cybersecurity Strategy on technical aspects suggests that this is a common issue.

The evolution from a technical to an economic and social digital security risk management approach does not mean that all the efforts accomplished by Sweden over the last 15 years were not useful and should be discontinued. Rather, they form an excellent foundation on which Sweden can lay additional building blocks to strengthen trust and lead in the digital transformation.

Box 4.4. Digital security efforts in municipalities

In 2015, the SKL released aggregated results from the use of a self-assessment tool by 70% of Swedish municipalities and 16 of the 21 Swedish county councils. The same year, 255 out of the 290 Swedish municipalities responded to a questionnaire circulated by the MSB in co-operation with the SKL. They showed that in 2014 (SKL) and 2015 (MSB):

- Municipalities had increasingly focused on the introduction of digital platforms and citizen-oriented services, in comparison with 2012. However, attention to digital security had fallen for most of them and three out of four municipalities still did limited work in this area (SKL).
- While 42% of municipalities' management manifested visible support for digital security efforts, management received systematic reporting on compliance with digital security objectives in only 10% of municipalities (SKL).
- Less than half of the municipalities surveyed had conducted a digital security risk analysis that is consistent with the organisation's other risk management activities, and nine out of ten municipalities had not established criteria for acceptable risk (SKL). Similarly, 41% of municipalities perform a digital security risk assessment, 63% of which do so irregularly (MSB).
- Only three out of ten municipalities had a systematic digital security approach. Forty-one per cent had not designated a digital security function, and for 47% of those that did, the person in charge spent less than 10% of his/her time on digital security. Seventy-one per cent said they did not have enough time to work on digital security (MSB). Only 14% of municipalities had a full-time person or more dedicated to digital security.
- Between half (SKL) and 70% (MSB) of municipalities had adopted a digital security strategy or policy, 25% had created a steering group in this area (SKL). However, 60% had not started to assess risks related to digital services (SKL) and 60% did not monitor compliance and most of those that had done it did so only after incidents had occurred (MSB).
- Between one-third (SKL) and 40% (MSB) of municipalities had a business continuity or contingency plan, leaving two-thirds without assurance that digital service would be available in the event of major operational problem. Existing plans are generally never or only occasionally tested (MSB).
- Only 4% of municipalities had allocated funds to increase the digital security awareness of employees, and 90% had not taken any initiative in this area. Only 5% of municipalities had measured staff's digital security skills. A quarter of municipalities had adopted a framework for digital security training for staff, from one-fifth in 2012 (SKL).

The MSB found no clear correlation between the number of inhabitants per municipality and how well municipal digital security was carried out. There were also no major geographical differences across the results.

Sources: SKL (2015a), "Nordiskt samarbete om informationssäkerhet i kommuner, landsting och regioner promemoria om informationssäkerhet och digitalisering svenska kommuner", https://skl.se/download/18.1ea1a4111513965b0179e6d/1448536942895/NordSec_Rapport%20Svenska%20kommuner%202015.pdf; SKL (2015b), "Nordiskt samarbete om informationssäkerhet i kommuner, landsting och regioner promemoria om informationssäkerhet och digitalisering svenska kommuner 2015", https://skl.se/download/18.1ea1a4111513965b0179e6c/1448536925762/NordSec-Rapport%20Svenska%20Landsting%20och%20Regioner%202015.pdf.

Nevertheless, digitalisation and data-driven innovation, the growing use of artificial intelligence (AI), and reliance on the Internet of Things (IoT) will considerably expand all stakeholders' exposure to digital security risks. As the digital transformation affects all sectors and all stages of value chains, it will increase all stakeholders' digital reliance and exacerbate the need to systematically integrate digital security risk management in every economic and operational decision that implies ICT use.

Concretely, the digital transformation blurs the distinction between ICT-related activities and non-ICT related activities, as illustrated by automated vehicles or smart grids. Digital technologies and data will be at the core of most activities and decision makers will have to understand the risks of using big data, AI, blockchain and other technologies to increase competitiveness, productivity, innovation, etc. It will become hazardous for a decision maker to entirely delegate the security risk to a technical expert who is not responsible for realising the benefits of using ICTs, or to manage the security risk without being informed by these experts in order to take the most appropriate decisions.

This requires a cultural shift whereby the government, as well as economic and social decision makers in public and private organisations, and ultimately all individuals in Sweden, understand and manage the digital security risk of using ICTs just as well as they understand and manage the benefits of digital technologies. From this perspective, digital security risk management not only aims to protect assets, it also aims to increase the likelihood of success, it is part of economic and social decision making as it helps decision makers to take informed choices, prioritise actions and distinguish among alternative courses of action (ISO/IEC, 2009; OECD, 2015).

This cultural shift is likely to take time and, to make progress, the government should set priorities. A good starting point would be to formulate a vision of digital security for prosperity in Sweden and promote it throughout the country, with perhaps economic and social decision makers in public and private organisations as primary target audiences.

Digital security public policies and stakeholders

Digital security in Sweden is addressed by several government bodies in line with their respective mandate. As a general rule, each ministry, government agency, county council and municipality is responsible for addressing digital security in its areas of competence.

Sweden's digital security policy places a major emphasis on crisis management preparedness (also called critical infrastructure protection). As a result, the Ministry of Justice (MoJ), the MSB and the Post and Telecommunications Agency (PTS) play a key role discussed in the first section below. The next section discusses how the implementation of the NIS Directive in Sweden will change the digital security policy landscape. The following section describes other initiatives unrelated to crisis management preparedness, including by the Swedish e-Identification Board, Vinnova and the Swedish Foundation for Strategic Research as well as by the SKL.[4] Digital security activities of municipalities and county councils are important to consider since local self-governments are responsible for the largest operational part of the Swedish welfare state, including for health and education. Finally, the section discusses the overarching governance of digital security from an economic and social perspective in Sweden.

Other government agencies addressing digital security in Sweden focus more exclusively on national security, an area which is beyond the scope of this report. They include the armed forces, the National Defence Radio Establishment, the Swedish Certification Body for IT Security and the Swedish Security Service. For example, since 2014, the military intelligence, security service and defence radio establishment have set up the national Co-operation for Protection against Serious IT Threats in order to analyse and assess digital threats and vulnerabilities related to Sweden's most security-sensitive national interests.

A strong focus on crisis preparedness and the protection of critical infrastructures

Digital security policy in Sweden started as a crisis management and preparedness matter, considered in Sweden as the civilian side of a national defence and security framework. As a result, the most important bodies in charge of digital security policy development and implementation are the MoJ and the MSB. The MoJ defines the high-level policy and prepares legislation; the MSB implements the policy by providing overall support to the society. However, each sectoral agency is responsible for digital security policy in its area of competence. The PTS is the most advanced example. Other sectoral agencies have a limited focus on digital security, but this is likely to change with the implementation of the NIS Directive in Sweden (see next section).

The Ministry of Justice defines digital security crisis management preparedness policy and co-ordinates the development of digital security policy more generally

The MoJ is the main ministry in charge of digital security policy in Sweden. It is responsible for developing digital security policies related to the continuous functioning of society, the prevention of major incidents and the management of crisis preparedness. This role fits within its broader mission in the area of crisis preparedness. The MoJ is responsible for the MSB whose role and activities are described below.

In accordance with the Swedish Constitution, the MoJ's influence over agencies is primarily a matter of co-operation and collaboration with other ministries as the MoJ cannot directly instruct a government agency within another ministry's remit. For example, if the MoJ identifies the need for the telecommunications regulator (the PTS) to enhance its digital security, it needs to first contact the PTS' parent ministry, the Ministry of Entreprise and Innovation, to explore whether a new instruction setting a new target for the PTS should be developed and what it should contain.

The MoJ does not address digital security policy in specific areas covered by other ministries. For example, it does not address digital security for economic and social prosperity, which would fall under the umbrella of the Ministry of Entreprise and Innovation, or digital security-related education, which would be a matter for the Ministry of Education and Research. However, an interdepartmental working group has been set up with several ministries including Enterprise and Innovation, Defense and Foreign Affairs. The group discusses overall digital security issues to achieving equal policy direction in the area of digital security regardless of the departments' responsibilities.

Nevertheless, the MoJ is in charge of developing digital security policy for the Swedish society as a whole and monitoring digital security-related developments. For example, it co-ordinated the development of the 2017 National Cybersecurity Strategy.

Lastly, the MoJ also has a "catch-all" role for digital security in Sweden: it can address all issues pertaining to digital security which do not fall within the responsibility of another ministry.

Like other Swedish ministries, the MoJ is a light structure of 400 civil servants which focuses on public policy making and monitoring. As of May 2018, digital security policy is managed by four full-time and two part-time persons within the MoJ Division for Crisis Preparedness, which is responsible for co-ordination and development for strengthening and monitoring society's emergency preparedness and civil defence (approximately 20 persons). This does not include cybercrime policy, which is addressed by another division.

The MoJ has responsibility for 20 government agencies, from the Swedish police to the prison and probation service. Four of them have a role with respect to digital security: the MSB; the Swedish police authority, which addresses cybercrime law enforcement investigations; the Swedish Security Service (SÄPO), which prevents and detects offences against national security, fights terrorism and protects the central government; and the Data Protection Agency (Datainspektionen).

The Civil Contingencies Agency supports society regarding digital security

The MSB is the main agency with respect to digital security. Overall, it is responsible for issues concerning civil protection, public safety, emergency management and civil defence as long as no other authority has responsibility. This responsibility covers measures taken before, during and after an emergency or crisis.

With respect to digital security, the MSB supports and co-ordinates the digital security efforts in the society and analyses developments in the area. This includes providing advice and support regarding systematic and risk-based digital security to other government agencies, municipalities and businesses. The MSB reports to the MoJ on digital security issues that may require action at different levels and areas of society. The MoJ analyses this information to provide advice to other ministries.

The MSB operates CERT-SE, the Swedish National Computer Security Incident Response Team (CSIRT). As the national CSIRT, CERT-SE addresses government bodies as well as regional authorities, municipalities and businesses (MSB, 2011). It monitors digital security threats and vulnerabilities, disseminates information and warnings, responds to incidents, and participates in efforts to mitigate their consequences. CERT-SE is member of regional and international networks, such as the European Governmental CERTs, the EU CSIRTs Network, TF-CSIRT, and the international Forum of Incident Response and Security Teams (FIRST). Since 2016, a regulation from the MoJ requires government agencies to report serious digital security incidents to the MSB (CERT-SE, 2017). Two hundred fifty incident reports were received in 2016 and 310 reports in 2017. CERT-SE was founded in 2003 at the PTS as the Swedish IT Incident Center, prior to being renamed and transferred to the MSB in 2011. Its staff is increasing, from approximately 20 to 30 people in 2018.

CERT-SE is the only part of the MSB which has operational (i.e. technical) digital security capacity. For its other activities, the MSB acts as a co-ordinator and adviser for other government agencies, municipalities and county councils, as well as companies and organisations, in order to help them meet the standard set by the government. This includes the support and/or co-ordination of several cross-sectoral and sectoral fora and groups as well as the development and publication of various types of guidance information.

Cross-sectoral groups chaired by the MSB include:

- The Cooperation Group on Information Security, which, since 2003, gathers government agencies with a role in information security: the armed forces, Defence Materiel Administration (certification body), Defense Radio Establishment, the telecommunications regulator (PTS), Police Authority and the Security Service. SAMFI meets six times a year to co-operate and exchange digital security-related information, including through specialised working groups. It discusses strategy and regulations, technical questions and standardisation issues, national and international developments in information security, information activities, exercises and education, as well as management and prevention of incidents (MSB, 2014b).

- The Information Security Council (Informationssäkerhetsråd), which gathers since 2009 representatives of significant parts of the public administration, academia, municipalities and industry. The council is the main body that connects the MSB with non-governmental stakeholders. It provides the MSB with information about digital security trends, makes suggestions about its work and helps disseminate information to the rest of society. The MSB's Director General chairs the council, which meets 4 times a year and gathers a maximum of 15 people in their personal expert capacity. Affiliations of members in 2014 included a mix of government agencies (e.g. police, defense, intelligence, regulators), municipality/county councils, university, public and private companies, and the Internet Infrastructure Foundation (IIS).
- Sectoral fora on information sharing in healthcare services, the financial sector and the telecom sector. The MSB also chairs the Media Preparedness Council, the Swedish CERT Forum, the Swedish IT Security Network for PhD Students (SWITS, a research network for PhD students studying in fields related to IT security), the Forum on Information Sharing in SCADA Systems, and the National Centre for Security in Industrial Control Systems (Oehme, 2015).

Unlike broad public-private partnership initiatives such as the British Cybersecurity Information Sharing Partnership or the German UP Kritis, which bring together a wide spectrum of actors involved in digital security across critical sectors, the MSB's co-ordination activities are focused on some key actors. This is, however, likely to evolve with the implementation of the NIS Directive (see below).

The MSB publishes free guides and recommendations regarding systemic and risk-based digital security covering many areas, such as industrial control systems, information security training, toolboxes to organisations, digital security exercises, guidelines for classification modelling, procurement recommendations, guidance for start-ups, etc.[5] It also maintains a website aimed at public sector bodies, companies and non-governmental organisations which gathers methodological and practical information, tools and factsheets about how to systematically manage digital security risk (informationssakerhet.se). This site is a result of the co-operation between the agencies involved in SAMFI. The MSB also carries out awareness-raising initiatives, including in the context of the EU cybersecurity awareness month. It has also allocated research funds, for example to finance a study on the cost of cybersecurity.

The MSB can also issue digital security regulations for government authorities (MSB, 2012b). One example is the 2016 "Regulation about digital security in government agencies" (MSB, 2016), which updates a 2009 regulation and requires government agencies to manage digital security taking into account standards such as ISO/IEC 27001 and 27002, including with respect to risk assessment and business continuity planning. This regulation follows up on reports by the National Audit Office highlighting numerous cases of non-compliance, a survey by the MSB of agencies' digital security (MSB, 2014a) and a 2015 report on "Information and cyber security in Sweden" (Government Offices of Sweden, 2015).

The MSB organises digital security exercises on a regular basis for organisations in essential sectors. The exercise in February 2018 included sectors within the framework of the NIS Directive and the theme was co-operation activities, situational awareness and analysis of consequences.

The MSB's mandate extends beyond the protection of critical infrastructure to support every part of the society. For example, the MSB has issued guidelines for start-ups and small businesses, and provides an e-learning tool on digital security for employees. It also supports research and funds university projects, for instance within the area of economic aspects of threats and incidents. Lastly, the MSB co-ordinates civilian authorities' efforts related to cryptography.

Digital security work at the MSB is carried out by four units: CERT-SE, systematic information security (guidance), analysis and strategic aspects, and critical information infrastructure protection.

Digital security crisis management preparedness in the telecommunications sector is advanced

Other government bodies are responsible for developing and implementing digital security policy in their area of competence and the MSB provides them with support, primarily in relation to crisis management preparedness. This is, for example, the case in the telecommunications sector, under the responsibility of the PTS, which reports to the Ministry of Enterprise and Innovation. Around 20 people are involved in digital security matters at the PTS, including 6 technical staff.

The PTS carries out a number of public-private digital security-related activities to foster higher network security robustness (PTS, 2015). These activities are partially funded by a fee paid by the largest operators (SEK 100 million, or EUR 10 million). The National Telecommunications Coordination Group (NTCG) is an important tool to best manage the funds collected through this fee. The NTCG was created in 2005 as a voluntary co-operation forum to support the restoration of national infrastructures of electronic communications during extraordinary events. Chaired by the PTS, it consists of the ten largest telecommunications operators and Internet service providers (ISPs), the leading distributor of radio and television, the national power grid operator (backbone), the Swedish Transport Agency, and the armed forces. Initially built as a facilitation group with a crisis management focus, it became a venue to also explore how to best manage the funds collected from the operators' annual fee by identifying the most useful initiatives. As a gathering of trusted partners, the NTCG is also the interface with market operators where more sensitive security-related issues are discussed, and sensitive information is shared. It is also a means to preview and discuss secondary legislation prior to its adoption.

The PTS' digital security activities include:

- The "Education and training strategy for crisis preparedness 2017-2021" (PTS, 2017), which includes sectoral and cross-sectoral crisis management training courses for companies, in partnership with other agencies (e.g. energy sector). It also includes exercises for business executives, crisis management and communications staff in the electronic communications sector. So-called "Telö" exercises are carried out every other year to increase the telecommunications sector's preparedness and ability to support the armed forces and civilians in the event of a crisis.
- A system to facilitate the standardised exchange of operational information between electronic communication actors about disturbances caused by emergency or planned interruptions (DIO) (PTS, 2013).
- A free online platform (Ledningskollen)[6] that matches queries from anyone who is planning excavation work with the relevant cable and pipe owners at a

particular location in order to reduce the risk of excavation damage. The platform also lowers cable indication costs for cable and pipe owners and improves co-ordinated digging opportunities. The participation of pipe and cable owners is voluntary. This service has been operational since 2011 across Sweden as a result of a co-operation between the PTS, the state-owned electricity transmission monitoring company Svenska Kraftnät and the Swedish Transport Agency.

- Initial support for the industry programme "Robust Fiber" that aims to create a standard for how a fibre network should be deployed to be robust and reliable. Robust Fiber provides instructions for minimum robustness requirements, certification as well as professional degrees and diplomas.[7]
- Activities to foster the adoption of Domain Name System Security Extensions (DNSSEC) in municipalities and counties in partnership with the IIS. Box 4.5 provides more details about the IIS' DNSSEC initiatives. The .se zone was the first DNSSEC signed top-level domain (TLD) in 2005, and since then the number of signed domains in Sweden has significantly increased thanks to a financial incentive provided by the IIS to registrars (Figure 4.1). The percentage of DNSSEC validated queries in Sweden is one of the three largest in the world, which means that users of .se domains enjoy a high protection against attacks based on forged Domain Name System data, such as Domain Name System (DNS) cache poisoning (Figure 4.2).

Box 4.5. Domain Name System Security Extensions in Sweden

Sweden is one of the leading countries for the adoption of the DNSSEC, a technical protocol that strengthens the security of the DNS. This is the result of an effort led by the Swedish registry responsible for the .se TLD, the IIS and was supported by the government.

With the DNSSEC, users can check that DNS information is correct and was not modified, i.e. that they are communicating with the correct remote system (e.g. website). This requires, however, that domain names are digitally signed in the first place. The IIS was the first registry in the world to sign its TLD (.se) with the DNSSEC (2005) and to offer a complete DNSSEC service (2007). It then convinced important Swedish Internet users such as public authorities, banks, municipalities and counties to sign their domains. It also convinced the largest Swedish ISPs to turn on signature validation on their name servers.

The Post and Telecommunications Agency and the MSB contributed to financing, training and implementing the DNSSEC in municipalities' information systems. Out of 290 municipalities, 231 were granted a total of SEK 10 million (EUR 1 million) to introduce the DNSSEC in 2012-14. The IIS offered a testing tool for municipalities to see on a map which DNSSEC implementation is active, works as expected or generates errors (see https://kommunermeddnssec.se). This tool generated a healthy competition between municipalities.

The number of signed domain names skyrocketed as of 2011 (Figure 4.1) when the IIS offered registrars a yearly discount of SEK 6 for every correctly signed domain name in their portfolio. The IIS also financed an experimental site for naming and shaming non-DNSSEC sites of big organisations and companies (https://dnssec-name-and-shame.com) and continues to actively promote the DNSSEC in Sweden and elsewhere.

Figure 4.1. **Number of DNSSEC signed .se domains by year end and on 1 April 2018**

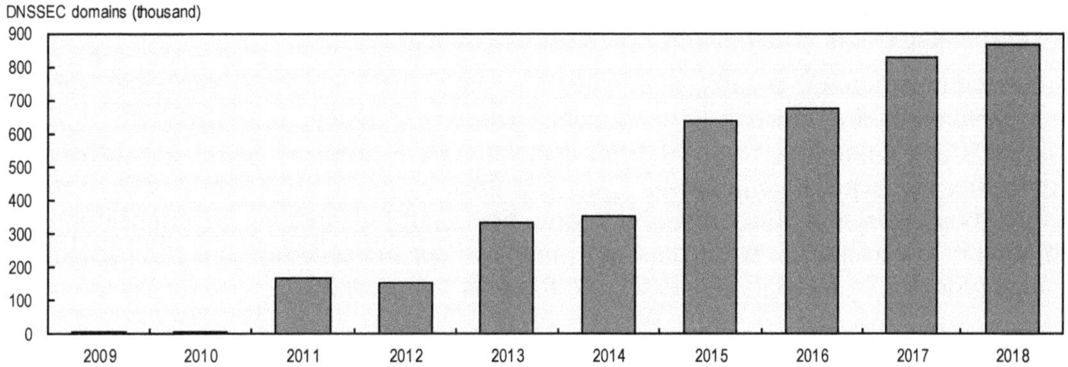

Notes: DNSSEC = Domain Name System Security Extensions. 2018 shows the number of DNSSEC signed .se domains on 1 April 2018.

Source: IIS (2018), "Number of DNSSEC domains per year end and today", www.iis.se/english/domains/domain-statistics/growth/?chart=per-type.

Figure 4.2. **Use of DNSSEC validation, 2018**

Proportion of end users

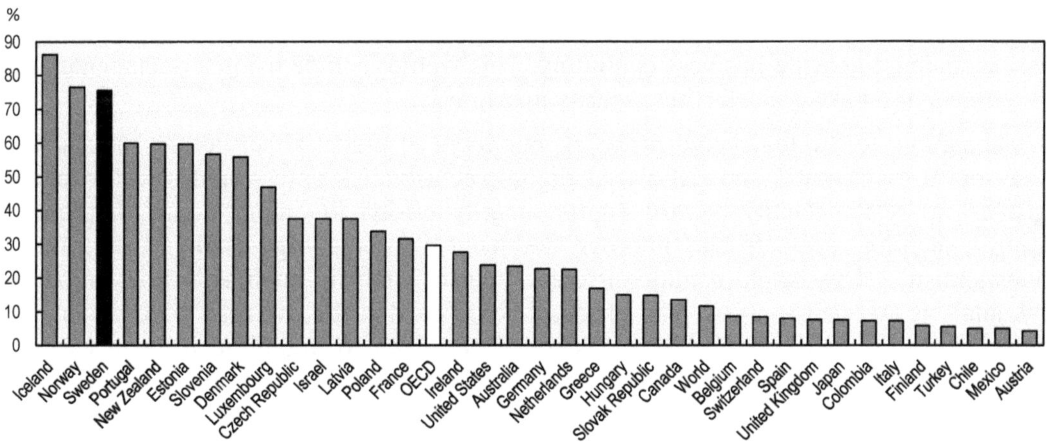

Notes: These statistics reflect the proportion of end users who passed their DNS queries to a DNS resolver that performs the DNSSEC validation from 12 January 2017 to 12 April 2018. It does not reflect the use of the DNSSEC by domain name zone administrators to sign the contents of their DNS zone.

Source: APNIC (2018)," DNSSEC validation rate by country (%)", http://stats.labs.apnic.net/dnssec.

The NIS Directive: A driver for change

This section provides a brief overview of the current (April 2018) plan to transpose the Directive on Security of Network and Information Systems (NIS Directive) in Sweden, with the objective of informing the overall analysis in this chapter. It does not discuss all the aspects covered by the directive.

The NIS Directive is expected to be transposed by EU countries by 10 May 2018. It establishes a framework for enhancing digital security and resilience of essential services, including by requiring that operators of essential services take appropriate and proportionate technical and organisational measures to manage the risks, and by establishing a notification requirement for significant incidents. The directive covers seven sectors, including energy, transport and banking, as well as so-called digital services. It can be viewed as a game changer for digital security in Sweden as its transposition will set clearer requirements for systematic risk management by operators of essential services.

A commission of enquiry nominated in May 2016 developed proposals for the transposition of the directive (Government Offices of Sweden, 2017d). Based on these elements and comments received from stakeholders, a proposal for a new legislation (thereafter the "legislative proposal") was submitted by the MoJ in February 2018 to the Council on Legislation, the body which scrutinises draft bills that the government intends to submit to parliament. A bill has been prepared for consideration by the parliament, with a proposal for legislation to enter into force on 1 August 2018.[8]

The legislative proposal promotes technical risk assessment rather than economic risk management

According to this proposal, the MSB would issue a regulation identifying operators of essential services in line with the NIS Directive. Operators would then examine whether the provision of their service is dependent on networks or information systems and if an incident would cause a significant disruption in the provision of the service, taking into account certain factors, such as the number of users who are dependent on the service in question and sector-specific and cross-sectoral factors included in regulation.

Consistent with the directive, operators of essential services would be required to take appropriate and proportionate technical and organisational measures to manage digital risk, including to ensure business continuity. This would include using a documented risk assessment as a basis for selecting security measures.

According to the legislative proposal, operators of essential services would have to carry out a "systematic and risk-based digital security risk assessment so as to enable business to systematically control digital security efforts in order to plan, implement, control, monitor, evaluate and improve the security of the organisation's information management".[9] This would include different types of analysis, such as business analysis, risk analysis and gap analysis. The proposal confirms that the Swedish government, and in particular the MSB, promotes a risk-based approach to digital security in essential services. Nevertheless, it also confirms that there is no particular emphasis on the need for the risk analysis to be driven by business leadership or to be integrated within the broader entreprise risk management framework of operators of essential services. It addresses risk assessment as a means to select security measures but it does not consider other risk treatment options such as risk acceptance, risk transfer and risk avoidance. In other words, it addresses digital security risk management as a methodology to protect systems and networks in a manner that fits already decided business objectives rather than as an integral part of business decision making. This is consistent with the analysis of the National Cybersecurity Strategy introduced earlier.

The apparent lack of promotion of an economic and social digital security risk management approach in a document such as the legislative proposal might result from its legal nature and from the context of the transposition of the NIS Directive. Guidance documents published by the MSB and discussions with government digital security experts show that there is an understanding of the need for business leadership to integrate digital security risk management in their decision-making processes as promoted by the OECD and explained in the previous section. This is confirmed, for example, by the National Audit Office audit reports and surveys by the MSB and the SKL which show that these bodies are asking the right questions and identify in their findings the same issues as the one pointed out above and in the analysis of the National Cybersecurity Strategy.

This suggests that expertise on what the OECD calls digital security risk management is present in Sweden but that the political and policy leaderships have not yet understood its importance or the need to integrate it more systematically in the economic and social digital culture of the country.

Towards a distributed model of supervision

The directive also requires the establishment of one or more "competent authorities" with the necessary powers and means to assess the compliance of operators of essential services with their obligations and to issue binding instructions to the operators of essential services to remedy the deficiencies identified (Articles 8 and 15). The transposition of the directive will therefore transform the governance of digital security in many EU countries, including Sweden.

As the agency in charge of regulating telecommunications networks, it is not surprising that the PTS is the most advanced sectoral regulator in the area of digital security, and has already established strong co-operation with the MSB in this area. However, the situation with respect to other critical sectors is less clear. With the current governance mechanism, the capacity to develop policies, supervise their application and, if necessary, support the operators of digital infrastructures lies with the government agencies in charge of each sector. However, it seems that sectoral regulators other than the PTS lack the expertise, capacity and perhaps awareness to accomplish this task. In addition, Sweden, like most other countries, faces a general skills shortage for digital security experts.

In deciding upon its governance structure, Sweden faces the following dilemma. While a large percentage of digital security issues are the same across sectors, a small but highly sensitive fraction can be very specific to each sector, for example with respect to industrial devices in the energy and transport sectors, or medical equipment in the health sector. It is important to take into account sector-specific market and regulatory constraints for effective digital security regulation. Should sector-specific digital security regulatory power and expertise be located as close as possible to the digital activity at stake with the risk of spreading resources across sectors and reducing critical mass? Or should they be concentrated in a central position such as the MSB to facilitate a national overview and an overarching operational critical mass, but at the cost of moving the regulation away from the day-to-day reality of the sectoral actors?

The legislative proposal suggests that one supervisory agency in each sector covered by the directive would be competent for monitoring compliance with the rules established by the new law. Concretely, the Energy Agency would be the competent agency for supervising compliance in the energy sector, the PTS for the digital infrastructures sector and digital services, the financial supervisory agency for the banking sector and financial market infrastructures, etc. These agencies would decide on penalty fees for failure to report incidents or taking security measures.

Nevertheless, recognising that the level of digital security knowledge in many sectoral agencies is often quite low, the legislative proposal suggests that the MSB lead a co-operation forum bringing together the agencies to foster uniform supervision and coherent supervisory practices, and prevent an uneven level of digital security in the society. In the context of this forum, the MSB would provide methodological support to sectoral agencies.

In addition to its co-ordination role, the MSB (CERT-SE) would also receive operators' reports of digital security incidents having a significant impact on continuity of service.

The law and additional regulation would set out the factors to be taken into account in assessing whether the incident has such an effect and should be reported. The MSB would issue regulations on mandatory incident reporting and the conditions for voluntary incident reporting. Lastly, the MSB would act as the Swedish national point of contact and represent Sweden in the European Cooperation Group and the CSIRTs Network established by the directive to facilitate cross-border co-operation and communication.

In this framework, it is not anticipated that sectoral competent authorities would acquire operational capacity. CERT-SE would remain the national CSIRT serving essential services operators (i.e. there would be no new domestic sectoral CSIRT) and providing situational awareness, informing the MSB, which would develop a more holistic risk picture.

This distributed supervision model is consistent with Sweden's decentralised model of governance with a strong constitutional principle of separation between ministries, between ministries and agencies, and between agencies. It is not unique in the context of the transposition of the NIS Directive. The United Kingdom, for example, plans to follow a distributed approach where sectoral agencies have responsibility for digital security risk with a strict separation from the National Cyber Security Centre, which will act as a centre of excellence providing them with expert advice and incident response capability (DCMS, 2018). Some other EU countries such as France, however, are following a centralised approach where a single agency (the Agence nationale de la sécurité des systèmes d'information [ANSSI]) is responsible for digital security and co-ordinating with relevant sectoral ministries and agencies. Each country follows an approach that is consistent with its culture and style of government, each with its own pros and cons. Sweden will need to significantly increase the MSB's and sectoral agencies' resources to enhance the level of protection and enable a consistent and uniform level of digital security across essential services. Effective co-ordination will be key to avoid scattering scarce resources and expertise.

A relatively more limited and uncoordinated set of other activities

As noted above, each government agency is responsible for digital security within its area of competence. Digital identity management was identified many years ago as an important area to foster the development of the digital economy, including with respect to payments and e-government. In this area, the Swedish market-led approach is a success story. Other initiatives are relatively modest, and, overall, do not seem co-ordinated and articulated around a common vision and objectives.

Digital identity

Digital identity and electronic authentication play an important role to reduce digital security risks. Sweden has succeeded in creating a favourable environment for a market-based e-ID ecosystem to emerge in order to support the online delivery of public and private sector services (Box 4.6). The main policy goal is that everyone should be able to logon with a user-friendly e-ID. The Swedish e-Identification Board promotes and co-ordinates e-ID and e-signature for public sector e-services. Its goals are to ensure that: i) everyone can access an easy-to-use and secure e-ID; ii) digital services can easily and securely make use of e-ID and e-signatures; iii) public sector use of e-ID and e-signatures is cost-effective. The board reviews Swedish e-ID solutions and provides the market with quality support for secure e-signature service. The Board audits e-ID against a trust level framework based on international standards. Approved e-IDs can use the "Swedish e-ID" logo ("*Svensk e-legitimation*"). The Board, which a public authority under the Ministry of Finance, is the Swedish eIDAS,[10] a node that enables cross-border authentication within the European Union.

Box 4.6. **Digital identity (e-ID) in Sweden**

The Swedish digital or electronic identity (e-ID) system is a success story: most citizens have an e-ID, they made over 1.1 billion transactions in various private and public e-services in 2015 and over 2.5 billion transactions in 2017 (BankID, 2017).

Although e-IDs can be issued by the private and the public sectors, the four operators offering e-ID solutions are private companies: a consortium of 11 banks called BankID has the largest market share (over 7 million users), followed by the telecommunications operator Telia (over 500 000 users), and 2 new entrants: Swedish passports "Svenska Pass" (Gemalto) and Freja eID Plus (Verisec).

Online banking has been the main driver for e-ID adoption in Sweden, explaining why BankID is the market leader with 7.5 million users out of a total Swedish population of 9.9 million. Almost the entire Swedish population aged between 21 and 50 holds a BankID e-ID. The percentage of mobile BankID users has continued to increase, reaching 91.9% users in December 2017: 29.3% users hold a BankID on card and 9.2% on file. BankID is primarily (92%) used for private sector services: Internet and mobile banking (61% of all transactions), payment services (18%), financial services (7%), and other private services (6%). Of the total number of BankID transactions, 6% are made with central government agencies and less than 2% with local government (BankID, 2017). Over 200 government agencies accept e-ID authentication for the delivery of online public services, and half of them also use e-signature. E-ID is used for public sector services such as social insurance, tax, student loans, business registrations and e-health. End users have the freedom to use the e-ID service of their choice, which requires that public services accept all providers on the market that reach the relevant trusted security level.

In 2012, Swedish banks launched Swish, an extremely user-friendly mobile app that enables individuals to make real-time payments to anyone registered in the Swish system (individuals, companies, associations and organisations). It takes a few seconds to create a Swish account with a mobile phone and link it to one's bank account. Then wiring money to another person only requires knowing the person's phone number. A EUR 1.05 transaction fee is borne by the relying party such as a store or business. Over 25 million payments were made in October 2017 using Swish, which only accepts Swedish crowns. Together with a high share of card payments, Swish contributes to the rapid decline of cash in Sweden, with only 20% cash payments in shops in 2014 (Segendorf and Wretman, 2015).

Nevertheless, BankID has experienced technical limitations in the past and does not cover 100% of the population, including migrants and individuals without a bank account. That is why the government is currently exploring the development of a robust public sector alternative to BankID's market dominance. A public sector solution would ensure that everyone can have equal access to authenticated online public service, an important priority in Sweden.

Sources: BankID (2017), "Statistik BankID–användning och innehav – fördjupning", www.bankid.com/assets/bankid/stats/2017/statistik-2017-12.pdf; Segendorf and Wretman (2015), "The Swedish payment market in transformation", www.riksbank.se/Documents/Rapporter/POV/2015/2015_3/rap_pov_artikel_2_151120_eng.pdf.

Innovation and research

In 2015, the Swedish Innovation Agency, Vinnova, analysed Sweden's strengths and challenges in a large range of technological areas, including digital security, in order to develop an action plan to promote the digitalisation of Swedish industry (Vinnova, 2015). The analysis used strategic innovation agendas developed by groups of actors in each area. With respect to digital security, Vinnova's mapping exercise used the "strategic innovation agenda" developed by a coalition gathering the Swedish Security and Defence

Industry Association, academia, research institutes and government agencies (SOFF, 2013). The mapping identified several strengths with respect to enhanced innovation in the area of digital security, such as the presence of major Swedish international companies which represent an attractive and relevant local market for digital security solutions, excellent digital infrastructures and leading security research. The lack of co-ordination between ICT and security as well as the lack of meeting venues were identified as weaknesses. Vinnova's action plan proposed five initiatives, including a "platform of knowledge and problem solving" that covered cybersecurity.

In 2018, the Swedish Foundation for Strategic Research announced a SEK 300 million (EUR 30 million) grant for ten cybersecurity research projects over five years in order to stimulate collaborative interdisciplinary research of relevance to present or future Swedish-based industry and to society (SSF, 2017; 2018). This initiative takes place in concert with the Swedish Government Strategic Partnership Program on Connected Industry, one of the five innovation partnership programmes launched in 2016 to help meet the societal challenges faced by Sweden (Government Offices of Sweden, 2016). The project includes applications involving the IoT, transport, data/telecommunications, power grids, smart cities and buildings, industrial control systems, public administration, healthcare, finance and insurance as well as cloud technologies and virtualised systems. The Swedish Foundation for Strategic Research is a public foundation which supports research in science, engineering and medicine for the purpose of strengthening Sweden's future competitiveness.[11]

Regional growth and activities by municipalities

The Agency for Economic and Regional Growth (Tillväxtverket), under the Ministry of Entreprise and Innovation, promotes economic growth by increasing the competitiveness of companies, facilitating entrepreneurship and creating attractive environments for companies in regions. It has developed information pages about privacy protection and is developing training modules about digital security in partnership with the MSB and the IIS.

The SKL represents municipalities and county councils and supports them in a wide range of areas, including digital security. The SKL recommends that municipalities use the ISO 27001 standard to manage digital security in municipalities and county councils. The SKL's website provides information to help local self-governments address digital security, including advice on digital security and outsourcing, digital identity, cloud computing, and personal data. The SKL developed an online tool to facilitate information classification for system administrators.[12] The SKL's site also points to useful resources compiled by the MSB and other actors. In 2015, the SKL released the results of a survey of municipalities' and county councils' digital security risk management efforts (SKL, 2015a; 2015b).

Towards a more holistic governance framework

Sweden's primary focus on crisis management preparedness and lack of leadership on the economic aspects of digital security prevents it from adopting a more holistic approach to digital security.

Ideally, digital security should be approached holistically as a single policy area. However, the reality is more complex and most governments struggle to find the best governance framework. Digital security is a multifaceted issue that includes technical, economic and social, criminal, as well as national and international security aspects (Figure 4.3).

These facets are interrelated and overlap to a certain extent. However, they can also compete and involve different priorities, actors, cultures and target audiences. They are all important and governments have to address the complex challenge of striking the right balance and ensuring coherence and consistency between them in order to approach this area more holistically. For example, regulation aiming to improve digital resilience of critical infrastructures' operators could inhibit innovation if it does not appropriately balance national security objectives with economic and social prosperity.

Figure 4.3. **Digital security is a multifaceted policy area**

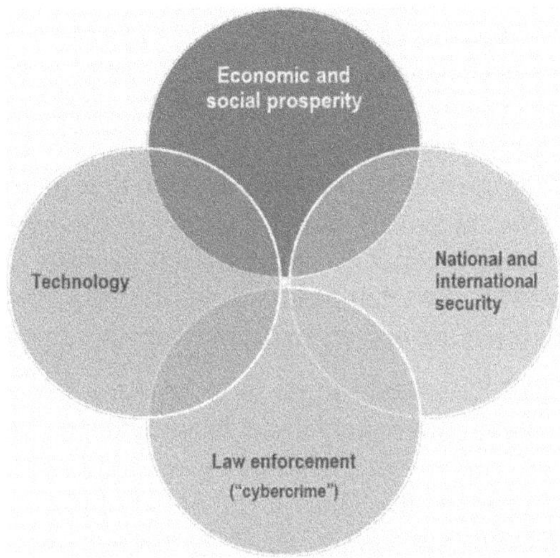

In addition to being multifaceted, digital security also cuts across all sectors affected by the digital transformation (e.g. health, energy, transport, retail, finance, manufacturing, etc.) as well as policy areas. Digital security policies relate to skills policies to fill the digital security skills shortage and enhance security risk management business skills; innovation and research policies; policies to foster the development of a market for digital security products and services; insurance policies; small and medium-sized enterprise (SME) policies; policies to foster trusted public-private partnerships that enable information sharing on threats, vulnerabilities, incidents and good risk management practice; etc. Overall, most strategies related to the digital transformation, sector strategies, as well as technology-specific strategies (e.g. the IoT, AI, big data, etc.) should address digital security to a certain extent.

There is no one-size-fits-all model to digital security governance. Governance arrangements vary and reflect cultures and styles of government. Governments have taken different approaches to establish a policy co-ordination mechanism. For example, Australia, Japan and the United Kingdom have assigned policy co-ordination to the prime minister through the Cabinet Office; France established a national co-ordination agency within a pre-existing co-ordination body under the prime minister (ANSSI); Slovenia plans to establish a "national cyber authority"; the United States has established a "cybersecurity co-ordinator" who reports to the president; Canada, Germany and the Netherlands have placed the main responsibility for digital security under an existing ministry (respectively Public Safety, Interior, and Security and Justice).

In all these cases, there are also different arrangements with respect to how public policy co-ordination is concretely carried out, and where the government operational capacity is located, ranging from within the policy co-ordination agency (France) or ministry (Germany, the Netherlands) to a separate structure (the UK National Cyber Security Centre) or department (the US Department of Homeland Security). In Australia, for example, the Australian Cyber Security Centre is a joint responsibility of the Attorney-

General and the Minister for Defence. Over time, there has been a trend towards bringing together scattered operational bodies and resources to achieve critical mass and generate synergies, and to foster public-private partnerships with businesses across all sectors for information sharing and better situational awareness.

Many countries which developed a "national cybersecurity strategy" at the beginning of the decade have modified their governance arrangement and often also revised their strategy at least once since then to strike a better balance and to bring together scattered operational resources. Several countries have significantly elevated the level at which digital security policy making is being supported and addressed (e.g. prime minister, president). This reflects the increased importance of this area and is consistent with the OECD Security Risk Recommendation which suggests that national strategies should be supported at the highest level of government precisely to facilitate the balancing exercise between economic and social prosperity and national security objectives. Compared to the above-mentioned countries, Sweden has made a first step towards approaching digital security at a strategic level, but it has not yet started to improve its governance framework.

Some voices in Sweden have underlined that the Swedish style of governance with slim and relatively siloed central government and strong independent agencies is particularly challenging with respect to cross-cutting issues such as digital security. Such a governance model is particularly cost-effective for short-term siloed objectives but fails to effectively address longer term cross-cutting issues such as digital security. Some suggest the establishment of a central co-ordination mechanism such as a cybersecurity co-ordinator in the Cabinet Office, who could have an overarching view of all the facets of digital security and balance them most appropriately. The co-ordinator would be supported by an advisory group who would represent different perspectives (Nicander, 2017).

In 2015, a Swedish government report focusing on digital security in the public sector stressed the need to avoid the current fragmentation of digital security arrangements across agencies, municipalities and county councils, an approach which does not scale when the number of stakeholders increases significantly, such as in e-health. The report called for enhanced harmonisation and coherence of digital security across government agencies, encouraged the government to take a holistic approach, and called for a common framework and long-term sustainable national governance model, supported by continuously improved competence for digital security efforts in the public sector.

The authors suggested that such a national model could be eventually extended to public and private organisations. They proposed a governance structure based on a new government authority, the "Information Security Council", consisting of relevant government agencies representatives to enable in-depth co-ordination and facilitate more common systematic risk management. The MSB would lead the council and manage its administration. Policy discussions would be led by the Government Offices (i.e. as opposed to government agencies). The council would include the authorities involved in the existing co-operation group SAMFI (introduced above), as well as authorities and actors not directly involved in the functioning of the public sector, such as sectoral agencies. It would establish working groups to accommodate the various aspects and dynamic nature of the digital transformation. Agencies would be responsible for taking appropriate decisions in their respective areas after consultation with the council, which would not have regulatory capacity. The council would ensure the implementation of the National Cybersecurity Strategy and provide an assessment of the digital security risk level in government agencies. It would develop standards and certification requirements in relation to public procurement (Government Offices of Sweden, 2015).

In December 2017, the government agreed to establish a co-ordination agency for the digitalisation of the public sector that would develop, manage, provide and promote the use of a national digital infrastructure for the public sector. The agency will be responsible for the security of this infrastructure, including key services such as electronic identification, trust services and secure email (Government Offices of Sweden, 2017c). While the details of this agency are still to be determined, it looks like a first step towards bringing together in a central point digital security expertise with respect to public sector electronic services. As an operational technical body, however, it is very different from the 2015 proposal mentioned above which was more focused on digital security co-ordination.

It is clear that Sweden needs a more holistic approach to digital security policy governance, but it is too early to make a realistic detailed recommendation on what it would look like. Sweden would first need to clarify its vision of digital security for prosperity. It is likely that the co-operation process to do so will raise awareness about the cross-cutting nature of digital security.

Policy recommendations

Sweden identified digital security as an important issue as early as 2003. The basic components of digital security policy are in place, with an emphasis on the protection of essential services and critical infrastructure, in particular in the telecommunications sector, both areas where roles and responsibilities are clearly defined. The transposition of the NIS Directive will drive significant improvements by establishing a clearer and more robust framework to strengthen digital security in essential sectors, beyond telecommunications. Other agencies are involved in digital security policy in areas such as innovation and regional growth. However, there does not seem to be a clear co-ordination framework to ensure that such initiatives serve a common vision and objectives. Sweden's market-led digital identity management approach is a success story. Non-governmental stakeholders such as the SKL and the IIS play an important role in promoting digital security.

Sweden should adopt a clear vision of digital security risk management for prosperity to change businesses' and organisations' culture

At the strategic level, the Swedish approach to digital security is characterised by a general focus on the security of information systems and networks rather than on the economic and social activities that rely on them. While strategic documents address many aspects of digital security, they do not yet place a sufficient emphasis on digital security as a business leadership priority and responsibility. They are based on the 2002 OECD Security Guidelines rather than on the 2015 *Recommendation on Digital Security Risk Management* that replaced them.

To become a world leader in harnessing the opportunities of the digital transformation, Sweden must also lead in managing the digital security risk associated with these opportunities. Sweden needs to devise and promote a clearer vision of digital security risk management as an economic and social responsibility for public and private organisations' leaders and decision makers.

Such a vision should promote a cultural shift in organisations, and more broadly across the economy and society. In particular, leaders and decision makers in businesses and other organisations (chief executive officers, board members, business line managers, etc.) should own the responsibility for managing both the opportunities from and the security risks of the digital transformation. They should use digital security risk management as an essential tool to increase the likelihood of success in an increasingly digital-dependent environment, take informed economic and social choices, and prioritise actions. They should integrate digital security risk management into their decision-making processes and rely on technical experts for technical aspects rather than delegate the entire risk management responsibility to them.

The current gap between technical experts and economic decision makers is jeopardising Sweden's efforts to protect essential services against digital security risk. At the operational level, digital security experts (e.g. at the MSB) understand and support the need to tie opportunities and risk management together to effectively protect essential services. But they struggle to get this message across beyond the community of security experts. The current legislative proposal for the transposition of the NIS Directive does not seem to address this important issue. The transposition of the NIS Directive offers a good opportunity to promote a culture of digital security risk management to the leadership of the most important businesses and public bodies in Sweden and to develop enhanced co-operation between ministries and agencies addressing the different facets of digital security (protection and prosperity).

Policy leadership on digital security for prosperity should be clearer and stronger

There is lack of clear policy leadership with respect to the economic aspects of digital security in Sweden. Lack of leadership probably explains why digital security for prosperity is akin to a blind spot, with strategic policy documents that do not yet reflect a vision in this area and economically oriented digital security policy initiatives that are relatively uncoordinated (e.g. research and innovation) or limited (e.g. towards SMEs or in relation to education).

Currently, digital security is primarily a crisis management preparedness matter, an area led by the Ministry of Justice. The MoJ also co-ordinates digital security policy making more broadly. Constitutionally, however, the MoJ cannot address digital security in areas falling under the mandate of other ministries, such as economic prosperity. Clearer and stronger policy leadership on digital security for prosperity would be necessary to develop an economic and social vision of digital security policy for Sweden. Such leadership would strengthen the profile of digital security for prosperity within the broader co-ordination carried out by the MoJ.

Sweden should adopt a more holistic governance, taking stock of the different approaches adopted by other OECD countries

Digital security policy efforts in Sweden are relatively scattered and their co-ordination is partial. Sweden's primary focus on crisis management preparedness and lack of leadership on the economic aspects of digital security prevents it from adopting a more holistic approach to digital security. Other countries' experience shows that leading countries tend to rationalise their governance with stronger co-ordination mechanisms under leadership at the highest level of government. However, there is generally a learning curve towards a balanced governance, and no ideal one-size-fits-all model.

While it is too early to make a realistic detailed recommendation on what an appropriate holistic governance would look like in Sweden, it is clear that the government should strengthen ministerial co-ordination in this area. It is likely this process would raise awareness about the cross-cutting nature of digital security. Proposals made by experts and investigation commissions form a good basis for addressing this issue, as well as comparison with other countries' approaches.

The Digitalisation Council could become a hub for co-operation on digital security

The government should address business and decision makers in the public and private sectors on this issue, and gather all stakeholders to develop a more holistic digital security strategy for prosperity in Sweden (regardless of what it is called).

Nevertheless, because all the facets of digital security are interrelated, it is important that the strategy be developed in co-operation or jointly with other ministries and agencies with a mandate and expertise on digital security, starting with the MoJ. Strong co-operation between ministries and agencies with mutually reinforcing and complementary mandates is essential to foster a holistic approach to digital security policy. The Digitalisation Council might be a useful platform to foster such co-operation, and promote a common vision and more co-ordinated agenda.

Notes

1. All agencies in Sweden are independent from the central government. For more details, see Chapter 1.
2. "Digital *trygghet*" is translated as "digital security" in the government's digital strategy factsheet (Government Offices of Sweden, 2017a) and in the strategy's press release (Government Offices of Sweden, 2017b). English-Swedish dictionaries translate "*trygghet*" as "security".
3. The English translation of the strategy uses the term "authenticity". However, "integrity" seems to be more appropriate since the term used is defined as meaning "that the information is not modified, manipulated or destroyed in an unauthorised manner".
4. This section focuses primarily on government bodies with a strategic digital security policy role. Other bodies may also have a role for digital security. For example, the National Archives of Sweden aims to ensure the integrity of government information in general, and prescribes standards for all government bodies regarding metadata and digital file formats to ensure long-term information availability and usability in e-archives.
5. https://www.msb.se/sv/Forebyggande/Informationssakerhet/Stod-inom-informationssakerhet (in Swedish).
6. www.ledningskollen.se.
7. https://robustfiber.se (in Swedish).
8. Elements in the following sections are based on the legislative proposal (i.e. not the bill) which was available at time of writing.
9. Non-official translation.
10. An eIDAS node enables the participation of a country in the European Union cross-border authentication network established by the EU regulation on electronic identification and trust services for electronic transactions in the internal market (eIDAS) (Regulation 910/2014 of 23 July 2014 on electronic identification).

11. For more details about the Swedish Foundation for Strategic Research, see: www.government.se/government-policy/education-and-research/research-funding-in-sweden and OECD (2016: 69).

12. https://klassa-info.skl.se/page/start (in Swedish).

References

Anderson, C (2017), "Swedish government scrambles to contain damage from data breach", *New York Times*, 25 July, www.nytimes.com/2017/07/25/world/europe/ibm-sweden-data-outsourcing.html (accessed 18 April 2018).

APNIC (2018), "DNSSEC validation rate by country (%)", Asia Pacific Network Information Center, April, http://stats.labs.apnic.net/dnssec.

BankID (2017), "Statistik BankID–användning och innehav – fördjupning" (in Swedish), www.bankid.com/assets/bankid/stats/2017/statistik-2017-12.pdf (accessed 18 April 2018).

CERT-SE (2017), "Vad ska rapporteras?" (in Swedish), webpage, www.cert.se/it-incidentrapportering/vad-ska-rapporteras (accessed 18 April 2018).

DCMS (2018), "Security of network and information systems: Government response to public consultation", January, Department for Digital, Culture, Media and Sport, https://assets.publishing.service.gov.uk/government/uploads/system/uploads/attachment_data/file/677065/NIS_Consultation_Response_-_Government_Policy_Response.pdf (accessed 6 April 2018).

European Union (2016), Directive (EU) 2016/1148 of the European Parliament and of the Council of 6 July 2016 concerning measures for a high common level of security of network and information systems across the Union, European Union, Brussels, http://eur-lex.europa.eu/legal-content/EN/TXT/?uri=uriserv%3AOJ.L_.2016.194.01.0001.01.ENG (accessed 18 April 2018).

Government Offices of Sweden (2017a), "Action on digital transformation", press release, 5 June, www.government.se/press-releases/2017/06/action-on-digital-transformation (accessed 4 April 2018).

Government Offices of Sweden (2017b), "For sustainable digital transformation in Sweden: A digital strategy", Ministry of Enterprise and Innovation, N2017.23, Factsheet, June, www.government.se/information-material/2017/06/fact-sheet-for-sustainable-digital-transformation-in-sweden--a-digital-strategy (accessed 4 April 2018).

Government Offices of Sweden (2017c), "Kommittédirektiv. Inrättande av en myndighet för digitalisering av den offentliga sektorn" (in Swedish), Dir. 2017:117, www.regeringen.se/rattsdokument/kommittedirektiv/2017/12/dir.-2017117 (accessed 11 April 2018).

Government Offices of Sweden (2017d), "Utredning om genomförande av NIS-direktivet överlämnad till inrikesminister Anders Ygeman" (in Swedish), www.regeringen.se/pressmeddelanden/2017/05/utredning-om-genomforande-av-nis-direktivet-overlamnad-till-inrikesminister-anders-ygeman7 (accessed 18 April 2018).

Government Offices of Sweden (2016), "Innovation partnership programmes: Mobilising new ways to meet societal challenges", webpage, Government Offices of Sweden, www.government.se/articles/2016/07/innovation-partnership-programmes--mobilising-new-ways-to-meet-societal-challenges (accessed 18 April 2018).

Government Offices of Sweden (2015), "Informations- och cybersäkerhet i Sverige. Strategi och åtgärder för säker information i staten" (in Swedish), ID-nummer: SOU 2015:23, www.regeringen.se/rattsdokument/statens-offentliga-utredningar/2015/03/sou-201523 (accessed 4 April 2018).

Hufford, A. (2017), "Merck swings to loss as cyberattack hurts sales", MarketWatch, 27 October, www.marketwatch.com/story/merck-swings-to-loss-as-cyberattack-hurts-sales-2017-10-27-134853159 (accessed 18 April 2018).

IIS (2018), "Number of DNSSEC domains per year end and today", www.iis.se/english/domains/domain-statistics/growth/?chart=per-type (accessed 1 April 2018).

ISO/IEC (2009), "ISO 31000:2009: Risk management – Principles and guidelines", International Organization for Standardization, https://www.iso.org/standard/43170.html.

Merck (2017), "Merck announces second-quarter 2017 financial results", press release, 28 July, Merck, www.mrknewsroom.com/news-release/corporate-news/merck-announces-second-quarter-2017-financial-results (accessed 18 April 2018).

MSB (2016), *MSBFS 2016:1 föreskrifter och allmänna råd om statliga myndigheters informationssäkerhet* (in Swedish), Swedish Civil Contingencies Agency, www.msb.se/sv/Om-MSB/Lag-och-ratt/Gallande-regler/Krisberedskap-och-informationssakerhet/MSBFS-20161 (accessed 18 April 2018).

MSB (2014a), *En bild av myndigheternas informationssäkerhetsarbete 2014* (in Swedish), Swedish Civil Contingencies Agency, www.msb.se/sv/Produkter--tjanster/Publikationer/Publikationer-fran-MSB/En-bild-av-myndigheternas-informationssakerhetsarbete-2014 (accessed 18 April 2018).

MSB (2014b), "Samverkansgruppen för informationssäkerhet, SAMFI" (in Swedish), Swedish Civil Contingencies Agency, www.msb.se/Upload/Forebyggande/Informationssakerhet/Faktabad%20SAMFI.pdf (accessed 18 April 2018).

MSB (2012a), *Sweden's Information Security: National Action Plan 2012*, MSB455, Swedish Civil Contingencies Agency, www.msb.se/en/Products/Publications/Publications-from-the-MSB/Swedens-Information-Security---National-Action-Plan-2012 (accessed 3 April 2018).

MSB (2012b), "The MSB and societal information security", February, Swedish Civil Contingencies Agency, www.msb.se/Upload/English/About_MSB_fact/Societal%20information%20security.pdf (accessed 18 April 2018).

MSB (2011), "CERT-SE: Independent and neutral IT security for private and public sectors", June, Swedish Civil Contingencies Agency, www.msb.se/RibData/Filer/pdf/25968.pdf (accessed 18 April 2018).

MSB (2010), *Strategy for Information Security in Sweden 2010-2015*, Swedish Civil Contingencies Agency, https://www.msb.se/RibData/Filer/pdf/25940.PDF.

NAO (2016a), "Information security work at nine agencies", Report No. RiR 2016:8, 26 May, Swedish National Audit Office, www.riksrevisionen.se/en/audit-reports/audit-reports/2016/information-security-work-at-nine-agencies.html (accessed 4 April 2018).

NAO (2016b), "Informationssäkerhetsarbete på nio myndigheter" (in Swedish), Report No. RiR 2016:8, Swedish National Audit Office, https://www.riksrevisionen.se/rapporter/granskningsrapporter/2016/informationssakerhetsarbete-pa-nio-myndigheter.html (accessed 4 April 2018).

NAO (2014), "Information security in the civil public administration", Factsheet. Report No. RIR 2014:23, https://www.riksrevisionen.se/en/audit-reports/audit-reports/2014/information-security-in-the-civil-public-administration.html.

Nicander, L. (2017), "Nu behövs en koordinator för cybersäkerheten", in: Dagens Nyheter, 21 July, www.dn.se/debatt/nu-behovs-en-koordinator-for-cybersakerheten.

OECD (2016), *OECD Reviews of Innovation Policy: Sweden 2016*, OECD Publishing, Paris, http://dx.doi.org/10.1787/9789264250000-en.

OECD (2015), *Digital Security Risk Management for Economic and Social Prosperity. OECD Recommendation and Companion Document*, OECD Publishing, Paris, http://dx.doi.org/10.1787/9789264245471-en.

OECD (2002), *Recommendation of the Council concerning Guidelines for the Security of Information Systems and Networks: Towards a Culture of Security*, OECD, Paris, www.oecd.org/sti/ieconomy/oecdguidelinesforthesecurityofinformationsystemsandnetworkstowardsacultureofsecurity.htm.

Oehme, R. (2015), "Cyber security in Sweden: With focus on National Collaboration Forum and private public partnership", presentation, www.viestintavirasto.fi/attachments/esitykset/Richard_Oehme_Presentation_Fi_2015-11-04.pdf (accessed 18 April 2018).

Palmer, D. (2017), "Petya ransomware: Cyberattack costs could hit $300m for shipping giant Maersk", ZDNet, 16 August, www.zdnet.com/article/petya-ransomware-cyber-attack-costs-could-hit-300m-for-shipping-giant-maersk (accessed 18 April 2018).

PTS (2017), *Utbildnings - och övningsstrategi för krisberedskap 2017 -2021 Sektorn Elektronisk kommunikation* (in Swedish), PTS-ER-2017:02, Swedish Post and Telecom Authority, www.pts.se/globalassets/startpage/dokument/icke-legala-dokument/rapporter/2017/internet/rapport_utbildnings--och-ovningsstrategi-2017-2021_pts-er-2017-02.pdf (accessed 18 April 2018).

PTS (2015), "Safer communications for everyone" (in Swedish), Swedish Post and Telecom Authority, https://www.pts.se/globalassets/startpage/dokument/icke-legala-dokument/faktablad/internet/sv-nat-april-2015.pdf (accessed 18 April 2018).

PTS (2013), "Driftinformation mellan operatörer -för kortare avbrott" (in Swedish), Swedish Post and Telecom Authority, https://diowebb.se/media/57/Faktablad-DIO.pdf (accessed 18 April 2018).

Rushe, D. (2014), "Target CEO Gregg Steinhafel resigns in wake of customer data breach", The Guardian, 5 May, www.theguardian.com/business/2014/may/05/target-chief-executive-steps-down-data-breach (accessed 3 April 2018).

Saint-Gobain (2017), "Résultats du 1er semestre 2017", press release, 27 July, www.saint-gobain.com/sites/sgcom.master/files/cp_vf_resultats_s1_2017_t.pdf (accessed 18 April 2018).

Segendorf, B. and A. Wretman (2015), "The Swedish payment market in transformation", in: *Sveriges Riksbank Economic Review*, No. 2015:3, www.riksbank.se/Documents/Rapporter/POV/2015/2015_3/rap_pov_artikel_2_151120_eng.pdf (accessed 18 April 2018).

SKL (2015a), "Nordiskt samarbete om informationssäkerhet i kommuner, landsting och regioner promemoria om informationssäkerhet och digitalisering svenska kommuner" (in Swedish), Swedish Association of Local Authorities and Regions, Stockholm, https://skl.se/download/18.1ea1a4111513965b0179e6d/1448536942895/NordSec_Rapport%20Svenska%20kommuner%202015.pdf (accessed 5 April 2018).

SKL (2015b), "Nordiskt samarbete om informationssäkerhet i kommuner, landsting och regioner promemoria om informationssäkerhet och digitalisering svenska kommuner 2015" (in Swedish), Swedish Association of Local Authorities and Regions, Stockholm, https://skl.se/download/18.1ea1a4111513965b0179e6c/1448536925762/NordSec-Rapport%20Svenska%20Landsting%20och%20Regioner%202015.pdf (accessed 5 April 2018).

SOFF (2013), "Strategisk Forsknings - och Innovationsagenda: Säkerhet" (in Swedish), Swedish Security & Defence Industry Association, May, http://soff.se/wp-content/uploads/2015/04/fia-sakerhet.pdf (accessed 18 April 2018).

SSF (2018), "300 miljoner till cybersäkerhet –en värdefullinjektion i det digitala samhället" (in Swedish), Swedish Foundation for Strategic Research, Stockholm, https://strategiska.se/app/uploads/pm-ssf-300-miljoner-till-cybersakerhet.pdf (accessed 18 April 2018).

SSF (2017), "SSF call for proposals: Framework grants for research on cybersecurity and information security", Swedish Foundation for Strategic Research, Stockholm, http://strategiska.se/app/uploads/rit17_en.pdf (accessed 18 April 2018).

Sverige Radio (2016), "Online attack hits Swedish media sites", Radio Sweden, 20 March, http://sverigesradio.se/sida/artikel.aspx?programid=2054&artikel=6393804 (accessed 18 April 2018).

Swedish Emergency Management Agency (2008), "Information security in Sweden: Action Plan 2008-2010", Swedish Emergency Management Agency, www.msb.se/Upload/Produkter_tjanster/Publikationer/KBM/Information%20Security%20in%20Sweden.pdf (accessed 3 April 2018).

The Local (2017), "Swedish government battles political fallout from transport data leak", The Local, 25 July, www.thelocal.se/20170725/swedish-government-battles-political-fallout-from-transport-data-leak (accessed 18 April 2018).

Vinnova (2015), "Slutrapportering 'Uppdrag att utföra insatser för att främja digitalisering av svensk industri'" (in Swedish), N/2015/6246/IF, www.vinnova.se/contentassets/ecd0206440df49a5aea396f74c90d060/2015-04724-rapp.pdf (accessed 18 April 2018).

Zetter, K. (2016a), "A cyberattack has caused confirmed physical damage for the second time ever", Wired, https://www.wired.com/2015/01/german-steel-mill-hack-destruction.

Zetter, K. (2016b), "Inside the cunning, unprecedented hack of Ukraine's power grid", Wired, 3 March, www.wired.com/2016/03/inside-cunning-unprecedented-hack-ukraines-power-grid (accessed 3 April 2018).

Chapter 5.

Seizing the opportunities from digitalisation

This chapter focuses on two areas that have acquired a prominent role in the current policy debate about digitalisation: innovation and jobs.

The first section reviews recent innovation performance in Sweden, examines the main policy initiatives in support of research on and diffusion of information and communication technologies (ICTs), and formulates recommendations to foster digital innovation.

The second section examines recent trends in the labour market in Sweden and discusses policies to promote job quality and accompany workers along the digital transformation.

The statistical data for Israel are supplied by and under the responsibility of the relevant Israeli authorities. The use of such data by the OECD is without prejudice to the status of the Golan Heights, East Jerusalem and Israeli settlements in the West Bank under the terms of international law.

The digital transformation cuts across all economic and societal activities, raising opportunities and challenges and calling for adequate policy responses. This chapter focuses on two areas that have acquired a prominent role in the current policy debate about digitalisation: innovation and jobs.

The first section reviews recent innovation performance in Sweden, examines the main policy initiatives in support of research on and diffusion of information and communication technologies (ICTs), and formulates recommendations to foster digital innovation.

The second section examines recent trends in the labour market in Sweden and discusses policies to promote job quality and accompany workers along the digital transformation.

Swedish innovation policies for the digital transformation

Sweden is an international hub of scientific excellence and technological leadership. It is among the global science leaders, both for the number and the quality of its scientific publications. The number of international patents per capita is higher than in most OECD countries (OECD, 2017b). In 2012-15, 43% of all Swedish patents were related to ICT, the fourth largest share worldwide after the People's Republic of China (hereafter "China"), Korea and Finland (Figure 5.1).

Figure 5.1. **ICT-related patents**

As a percentage of total IP5 patent families owned by economies

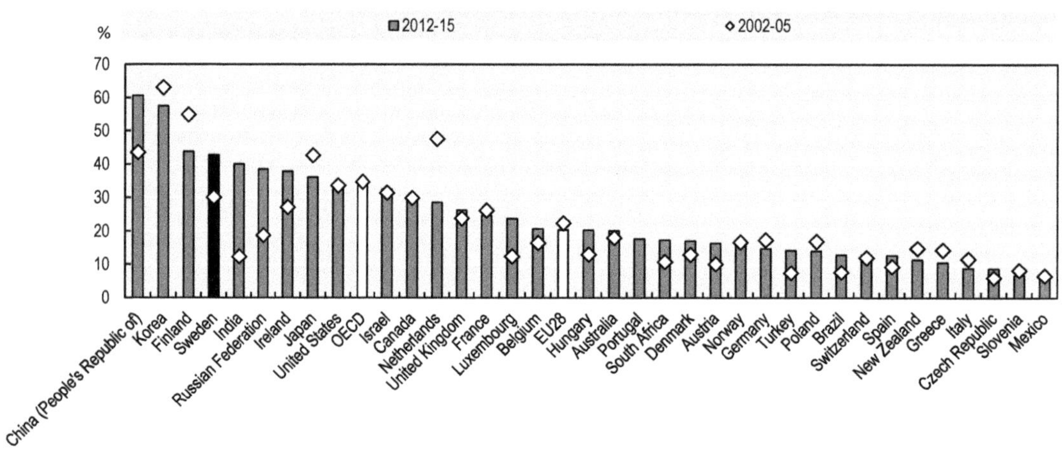

Source: OECD (2017b), *OECD Science, Technology and Industry Scoreboard 2017: The Digital Transformation*, http://dx.doi.org/10.1787/9789264268821-en.

Sweden also used to have the highest expenditures on research and development (R&D) relative to gross domestic product (GDP) in the world. Since 2000, however, R&D intensity has started to decline, down to 3.3% in 2015 (see Chapter 1). While Sweden still stands at a high level, its research performance is losing ground compared to world innovation leaders (e.g. Israel, Denmark, Korea and Switzerland) and to some emerging economies (e.g. Chinese Taipei and China). One main reason for the relative decline of R&D is that a number of large and international companies increasingly locate research activities in other countries.

In 2013, Sweden had the fifth largest share of R&D expenditures in ICT equipment (20%) among OECD countries, but this was much smaller than the same share in Korea

(50%) and Finland (39%). The share of R&D expenditures in information services (5.3%) was among the lowest in the OECD (Figure 5.2). The telecommunication industry is being particularly hit by these changes in the global R&D landscape, as Swedish firms are finding themselves in direct competition with enterprises from emerging economies, notably China (OECD, 2016d).

Figure 5.2. **R&D expenditure by ICT equipment and information services industries, 2015**

As a percentage of total business enterprise expenditure on R&D

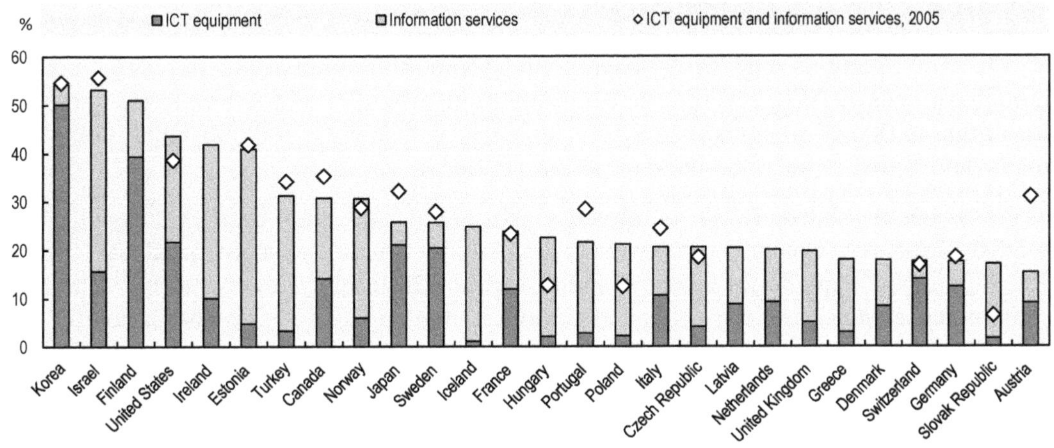

Note: ICT = information and communication technology.

Source: OECD (2017b), *OECD Science, Technology and Industry Scoreboard 2017: The Digital Transformation*, http://dx.doi.org/10.1787/9789264268821-en.

The government's objective is for Sweden to be a world-leading research and innovation country, where high-quality research, education and innovation result in higher welfare and competitiveness and help to meet social challenges.

The Research and Innovation Bill 2017

In 2017, the Research and Innovation Bill "Collaborating for knowledge – for society's challenges and strengthened competitiveness" (Government Offices of Sweden, 2016) sets the orientations for research and innovation policy with a ten-year perspective, focusing in particular on measures in 2017-20. Important cornerstones of the bill include increased basic appropriations to higher education institutions, initiatives in research linked to global societal challenges and increased resources to strengthen Sweden's innovative capacity. The bill provides an increase in the appropriations for research and innovation of over SEK 3 billion (USD 355 million) until 2020.

To achieve these objectives, the bill develops a strategy built around three main policy actions:

1. increase the international attractiveness of Sweden for investment in R&D
2. promote a more efficient and long-term use of resources to enhance the quality of research across the whole country
3. promote a closer collaboration among universities, businesses and society.

Cutting across these three actions, the bill points out the need for a closer and more systematic evaluation of the variety of projects and initiatives supported by Swedish innovation policies.

Digitalisation has a key role in the Research and Innovation Bill 2017 in two respects. First, ICTs are an important technological field of their own; second, digital technologies are an enabler of innovation in other technological fields and a fundamental infrastructure for research activities.

Innovation policies in the ICT field

The ICT sector is one of Sweden's most important industries. In 2015, exports amounted to nearly SEK 140 billion, representing nearly 12% of total exports. There are more than 46 000 companies in the ICT industry, with nearly 200 000 employees. The area is developing rapidly and the competition is fierce.

Government-funded R&D is already substantial and has been increasing. The Swedish Research Council and Swedish Innovation Agency (Vinnova) allocate nearly SEK 900 million annually for research and research infrastructure related to ICT. The field of computer science and electrical and electronic technology alone accounts for nearly 20% of the Research Council's contribution to science and technology (Government Offices of Sweden, 2016). Swedish researchers in computer science can point to their high production of scientific articles that are cited among the leading researchers in the world (OECD, 2017a).

Fifth generation mobile networks (5G) are under development and higher speeds, greater capacity and better connectivity are opening up further opportunities to use mobile technologies in production and consumption. The 2008 Research and Innovation Bill allocated funds for research on information technology (IT) and mobile communication systems to two centres: one at the Royal Institute of Technology, in co-operation with Stockholm University, and the other at the Linköping University, in collaboration with Lund University, the Blekinge Institute of Technology and the University of Halmstad. To support research on the 5G mobile technologies, the 2017 bill has allocated an additional SEK 150 million (USD 18 million) to the centre at the Royal Institute of Technology.

Additional funds have also been allocated for research on machine learning to the Knowledge Cluster in Stockholm, one of the three most prominent centres in the world, and to the Linköping University.

ICT as a fundamental infrastructure for research activities

The digital revolution has profoundly changed the way research is undertaken, universities are organised, interactions between industry and the research community take place. Increased digitisation creates new research opportunities far beyond the ICT technology field.

Modern research generates a massive and rapidly increasing volume of data (so-called big data). The trend towards more data-driven and computation-intensive research has dramatically increased the need for efficient digital infrastructure to process, analyse, store and make data available. In Sweden, this need is particularly strong for major national research infrastructures, such as the Synchrotron Max IV, the National Centre for Life-Science Research and the European Spallation Source.

The 2017 bill provides for an increase in grants to the Research Council in order to support data-driven research. The increase amounted to SEK 20 million (USD 2.4 million) in 2018 and an additional SEK 20 million in 2019.

The allocation to the Swedish University Computer Network (Sunet), a research infrastructure offering affiliated universities and some cultural institutions Internet connections nationally and internationally and related IT services, was also increased through a reallocation of funds from the Research Council.

The bill also takes a strong stance to promote open access to research data. Its goal is that all scientific publications from publicly funded research should be openly accessible immediately after their publication. Likewise, research data used in scientific publications should become openly available. Open access to research outputs is expected to promote high-quality research.

Further to the European Commission's recommendation on access to and preservation of scientific information (European Commission, 2012), the government asked the Research Council to issue national guidelines for open access to research. In addition, the 2017 bill has given the Research Council responsibility for the national co-ordination of the work on open access to research data. To this purpose, the budget of the National Library of Sweden (Kungliga biblioteket) has been increased through a reallocation of funds from the Research Council. This includes further development of the *SwePub*, a national database of the scientific publications available at Swedish universities.

Innovation partnerships programmes

In 2015, the government established the National Innovation Council with the mandate to promote Sweden as a country of innovation and to strengthen its international competitiveness. The council has an advisory role and provides new perspectives on issues of importance in innovation policy, in the short and long run. It is chaired by the prime minister and consists of five ministers and ten external members with backgrounds including in industry and research.

The Innovation Council has identified three areas that are crucial to tackling the great societal challenges of our time: digitalisation, life sciences, and environment and climate. Based on these priority areas, the council has established five innovation partnership programmes (IPPs). The IPPs are meant to encourage and build on many initiatives for research and innovation undertaken in collaboration among industry, academia and the public sector. The five IPPs are: i) next-generation travel and transport; ii) smart cities; iii) circular and bio-based economy; iv) life science; and v) connected industry and new materials. Digitalisation cuts across all five programmes.

The IPPs were launched on 1 June 2016. Each one relies on a partnership group that identifies challenges and opportunities and sets priorities for action. Several groups have been established and a number of concrete partnership projects have been developed.

The IPPs aim to foster synergies among a number of innovation programmes already in place, notably the 17 strategic innovation programmes (SIPs) jointly financed by Vinnova, the Energy Agency and the Research Council (Formas).

The SIPs were the result of an intensive consultation process over 2012-16 among the stakeholders active in a certain innovation area. Their goal is to foster co-operation in areas of strategic importance to Sweden in order to find sustainable solutions to global social challenges and to increase Sweden's competitiveness in the international arena. Businesses, academia and organisations join forces under the umbrella of these programmes to develop the sustainable products and services of the future.

With about SEK 2.11 billion (USD 250 million), "Connected industry and new materials" was the IPP with the largest amount of grants financed by Vinnova in 2017 (Figure 5.3). The other IPPs received between SEK 819 million (life sciences; USD 97 million) and SEK 543 million (circular and bio-based economy; USD 64 million).

Figure 5.3. **Vinnova grants under the innovation partnership programmes, 2017**

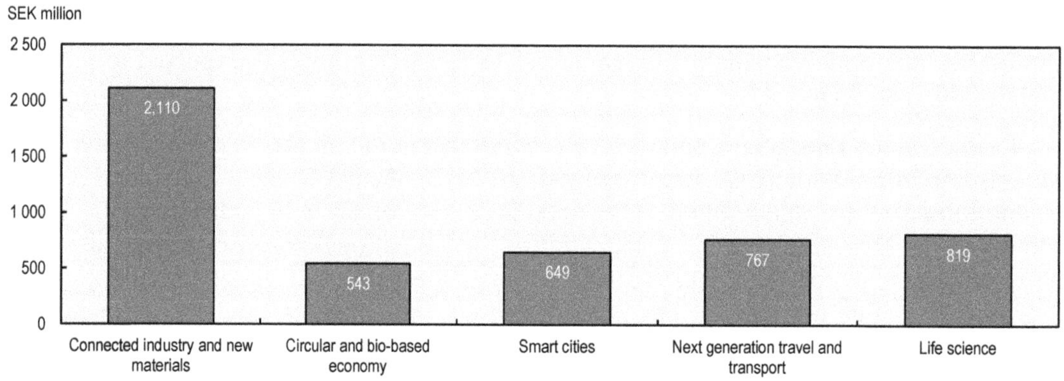

Source: Vinnova (2017), *Annual Report 2017*, https://www.vinnova.se/publikationer/arsredovisning-2017.

A number of programmes under the IPP "Connected industry and new materials" are aimed to support digital innovation.

Process Industrial IT and Automation (PiiA) aims to help grow Swedish process industry by supporting the development of advanced IT and automation solutions. The programme facilitates co-operation between process industry businesses, their suppliers and research partners. The PiiA's goal is that, by 2022, Sweden will be recognised as the world leader for the development and use of innovative and competitive solutions in process industrial IT and automation. The programme consists of four work streams:

1. projects: research, innovation and development projects supporting the digitalisation of the process industry
2. analysis: trends and intelligence within IT and automation
3. innovation: competence and innovation support
4. research: industrial postdoctoral programme to secure that the future competence contributes to the development and use of automation and digitisation in industry.

Smarter Electronics Systems aim to foster cross-border co-operation to develop micro and nano-electronics, photonics, micromechanics, power electronics, and built-in systems in Sweden. Smart electronic systems are increasingly used in technologies to address global challenges, such as renewable energy development, energy production efficiency, energy saving, a long-term sustainable environment and ageing. The programme is carried out in broad collaboration between industry representatives, research institutes and universities.

Produktion2030 aims to make Sweden one of the world's leading countries for sustainable production. The programme focuses on how Swedish industry can strengthen its global competitiveness and create new and attractive jobs. Produktion2030 builds on close co-operation between the Association of Swedish Engineering Industries, the Swedish Production Academy and the Swedish research institutes. Produktion2030 is based on five instruments:

1. projects include research and innovation as well as test and demonstration projects
2. small and medium-sized enterprises (SMEs): it promotes the dissemination of new knowledge and technology to SMEs, through collaboration with local and regional industry clusters and networks
3. education: a national PhD programme Produktion2030 and a portfolio of courses at the master level, with a focus on industrial digitalisation
4. mobility provides financial support for exchange programmes and study visits
5. internationalisation and analysis: contributes to the EU research programmes relevant for the industry and carries out industry analyses through international networks.

The IPP "Next generation travel and transport" consists of four areas where digital innovation plays a key role. In particular, two of these areas focus on the development and use of digital technologies to improve transport and mobility.

The **Strategic vehicle research and innovation programme (FFI)** provides around SEK 1 billion (USD 118 million) per year for R&D activities. Public funds account for about a half of this amount. The programme is a partnership among Volvo, Scania, the Swedish automobile suppliers' association FKG, the Swedish automobile trade association BIL, Vinnova, the Swedish Energy Agency and the Swedish Transport Administration.

The FFI's overarching objectives are to reduce the environmental impact of road transport, reduce the number of people injured and killed in traffic accidents, and strengthen the international competitiveness of the automobile sector.

The programme consists of five permanent sub-programmes and a few strategic initiatives, providing an opportunity to explore a specific area using special funds for a limited time period. Seventy-five per cent of the FFI's budget is allocated to the five sub-programmes and the remainder is earmarked for strategic initiatives.

The five FFI sub-programmes are energy and the environment; road safety and automated vehicles; electronics, software and communication; sustainable production; and efficient and connected transport systems. Current strategic initiatives include: Bicycles and Other Vehicles in a Safe and Smart Cooperation for a Sustainable Future, Automotive Security and Privacy, and Complex Regulation and Machine Learning.

Within the IPP "Next generation travel and transport", **Drive Sweden** hosts a number of projects addressing the challenges related to road safety, infrastructure and legislation. The programme's goal is to develop solutions for "combined mobility as a service", i.e. the ability to purchase a journey from point to point using a variety of means of transport, e.g. autonomous vehicles, public transport, car pools and rental bikes. The programme also includes several projects related to the use of automated vehicles for logistic services and people transportation (Box 5.1).

The SIP MedTech4Health under the IPP "Life science" runs the **Analytic Imaging Diagnostics Arena (AIDA)** programme. AIDA is a national arena for research and innovation around artificial intelligence (AI) for medical imaging diagnostics. Through AIDA, academics, healthcare professionals and industry work together to translate technical advances in AI into clinically useful tools for the benefit of patients.

Medtech4Health enables groups and individuals to become involved with AIDA by applying for technical projects (groups) or clinical fellowships (individuals). Successful applicants can access AIDA's technical infrastructure and human expertise, as well as benefit from a broad exchange with other innovators in the field. Their expenses may be funded by up to 50%. Medtech4Health has SEK 11 million (USD 1.3 million) allocated for AIDA over the period 2017-20. In early 2018, AIDA had nine ongoing projects and four clinical fellowships.

Box 5.1. The "Drive Me" project in Gothenburg

The Gothenburg City Planning Authority is the first in the world to examine the interaction between autonomous vehicles and sustainable, long-term urban planning. The city is exploring the effects and benefits of technology, including the future need for parking facilities, enhanced road safety, accessibility, and implications to the use of public space.

The project is part of two Swedish IPPs, Smart Cities and Next Generation Travel and Transport, and is funded in part by Vinnova within the framework of the public-private partnership Drive Sweden. It will continue through to the end of 2018.

Drive Me is the world's first large-scale pilot project in autonomous driving where 100 self-driving cars are being driven on public roads in Gothenburg.

The ground-breaking project is a joint initiative involving the car maker Volvo, the developer of active safety systems Autoliv, the Chalmers University of Technology, the Lindholmen Science Park for transport-related R&D, and the Swedish Transport Administration. The testbed has required a temporary exception to transport regulation voted by the Swedish parliament following a two-year investigation.

The DriveMe project focuses on a number of areas, including:

- how autonomous vehicles can generate social and economic benefits by improving traffic flows, environment and safety
- infrastructure specifications for autonomous driving
- which traffic situations are appropriate for self-driving vehicles
- the customer's confidence in self-driving vehicles
- how other drivers can be integrated with a self-driving car.

The project started in 2014 with customer surveys, technical advances and the development of user interfaces and cloud-based services. The first pilot cars were launched on the streets of Gothenburg in 2017 and involve local drivers integrating autonomous driving technology into their daily lives.

Source: Test Site Sweden (n.d.), "DriveMe", https://www.testsitesweden.com/en/projects-1/driveme.

Innovation Engines is another programme that is part of Medtech4Health's providing cutting-edge trials for the systematic testing and implementation of new technologies and new work practices (e.g. wireless measurement in hospitals, remote consultations, etc.). To support the Innovation Engines, Medtech4Health has budgeted SEK 10 million (USD 1.18 million) in 2017 and 2018 as well as a further SEK 6 million (USD 0.71 million) each year for 2019 and 2020.

Internet of Things (IoT) Sweden is a SIP under the IPP "Smart cities". The objective of the programme is to promote innovation and adoption of IoT as a tool to address societal challenges, in co-operation with public organisations, businesses and scientists.

The programme works mainly with three different types of activities: seminars and meetings, where IoT opportunities and challenges are identified and discussed; calls for innovation projects, IoT Sweden supports Vinnova in formulating and designing calls for innovation projects in the field of IoT; strategic innovation projects, through analyses and monitoring of the IoT area, IoT Sweden recommends Vinnova to finance a small number of key projects.

Smart Industry: A strategy for new industrialisation in Sweden

In 2016 the Swedish government launched a new industrialisation strategy "Smart Industry" (Ministry of Enterprise and Innovation, 2016). The strategy's vision is that Sweden will be a world leader in the innovative and sustainable industrial production of goods and services. Its goal is that the industrial sector throughout Sweden will increase its competitiveness and participation, primarily in the high-quality segments of global value chains. The strategy set objectives on four focus areas:

1. Industry 4.0: companies in the Swedish industrial sector should be the leaders in the digital transformation and in exploiting the potential of digitalisation.
2. Sustainable production: increased resource efficiency and more sustainable production should contribute to value creation, job creation and competitiveness in the industrial sector.
3. Industrial skills boost: the skill development system in Sweden should meet the skills demand by the industrial sector and promote its long-term development.
4. Testbed Sweden: Sweden should lead research in fields that contribute to strengthening the industrial production of goods and services.

The strategy is supported by an action plan, which is regularly monitored and updated. To support the strategy's implementation, the government has set up an Advisory Board for New Industrialisation, consisting of four members with a wide range of experience and good insight into the conditions and needs of the industrial sector. The Advisory Board monitor the strategy's implementation and regularly submits recommendations for future work.

The strategy is being monitored based on a small set of indicators (employment in different segments of the value chain, productivity, gross investments and R&D investments), which together provide a measure of the capability of the industrial sectors to adapt and innovate according to the strategy's objectives. When appropriate, these indicators are complemented by additional ones to monitor and assess specific areas of the strategy and the action plan.

Some of the projects under the Smart Industry are also part of the IPPs, e.g. Produktion2030, PiiA and IoT Sweden. Other projects of particular interest are related to the development and use of 5G technologies.

PIMM DMA (Pilot for Industrial Mobile communication in Mining, Digitalised Mining Arena) focused on developing a "state-of-the-art" mobile network in a mine and testing a number of applications enabled by mobile communication. The project has shown that cellular-based communication has very good properties, enabling robustness, time performance and low latency for demanding applications. PIMM DMA is expected to lead to the development of new products and services enabling industrial automation, in general, and mining automation, in particular.

Over 2015-17, the **5G-Enabled Manufacturing (5GEM)** project created a pilot production system for world-class industrial manufacturing based on wireless and mobile 5G communication. Fifth generation wireless communication technologies offer new means for Swedish industry to achieve higher productivity, flexibility and competitiveness. The project developed demonstrators for manufacturing system design, deployment, operation and maintenance, which are the key life-cycle phases for competitive and sustainable manufacturing.

As part of the Smart Industry Strategy, Vinnova is investing SEK 10 million (USD 1.18 million) in 2018 on 13 projects to disseminate knowledge on AI, human collaborations with robots and digital security.[1]

New approaches to innovation

In recent years, a number of new approaches to test technological and organisational innovations have emerged in many countries. Current practices include testbeds, sandboxes and policy labs. While there does not seem to be an agreed definition for each of these terms, which are often used interchangeably, the common idea is to set up a separated environment where innovations can be tested in isolation, with the aim to diffuse successful innovations to a larger number of situations and institutions. In a loose sense, testbeds tend to focus more on the technical features of an innovation (i.e. they are similar to a "large-scale" laboratory test); sandboxes look at the interactions among a number of agents implementing or adopting the innovation (e.g. a selection of firms); whereas policy labs focus on the implications of specific innovations on the economy and society and how policies can best address them.

Testbed Sweden

Digitalisation opens new opportunities for simulations, tests and demonstrations in several areas. It also broadens the scope for the collection and analysis of the data generated by these experiments. Test and demonstration environments, referred to as testbeds, are becoming increasingly important for businesses and the public sector as goods and services are developed at a more rapid pace and become increasingly complex.

In January 2016 the Swedish government launched **Testbed Sweden** to encourage new ideas and solutions to be tested in Sweden. The goal of the programme is to create a research and innovation environment more attractive for foreign investors. This requires strengthening co-operation between businesses, regulatory agencies and the public sector. Testbed Sweden includes several different types of tests, mainly implemented through strategic innovation areas, test and demonstration environments, institutions, challenge-driven innovation and collaboration programmes.

Vinnova has been given responsibility for a national co-ordinating mechanism to strengthen test and demonstration activities in Sweden; provide and disseminate information on the hundreds of testbeds available in Sweden; and contribute to make them attractive internationally. A number of testbeds projects are undertaken in the field of digitalisation (Box 5.2).

Box 5.2. Digitalisation testbeds in Sweden

Vinnova is working to strengthen the prospects for testbeds in Sweden. Several testbed projects are undertaken in the field of digitalisation.

3D additive manufacturing

Research in new materials and applications of 3D bio-printing in fields including cancer research. Projects are carried out in collaboration with medical and clinical research teams and industry, in a laboratory and simulated environment.

CRATE

CRATE is an exercise and training facility for the protection of IT systems under realistic conditions. CRATE is also used for research projects and for tests and experiments, in a laboratory, simulated and real environment.

EMC: Testbed for interference resistance of electronics and wireless communication technology

The testbed is used for research, tests, evaluation, and demonstration of electronic disruption resilience and new communications technology. Projects are carried out in a laboratory and simulated environment.

Gamecubator

The testbed's purpose is to provide a creative environment to promote growth in the area of game development and gamification for new and existing companies by means of coaching, infrastructure and tools. Projects are carried out in a real environment.

PrEsEnT

Lapplands Gymnasium – one of Sweden's largest upper secondary school – builds and runs a testbed environment to develop the future of distance teaching via partnerships and smart, inclusive and transparent innovation systems and living labs. Projects are undertaken in a simulated and real environment.

Active Learning

This testbed's purpose is to support teachers to develop more effective teaching approaches using digital tools and content. The project tests, develops, and introduces working methods and tools for active learning, in a simulated and real environment.

"Maker" school

The purpose of this project is to contribute to the development of new subject matter specific methodology based on the creative use of emerging technologies. The project is run in a real environment.

Visualisation Screens (Visualiseringsbordet)

The testbed's purpose is to explore and demonstrate opportunities to visualise and interact with 3D datasets based on large multi-touch screens. Primary areas of use are learning, communication and experiences, and decision making. The project is run in a simulated and real environment.

Source: Vinnova (2018), "Testbeds in Sweden", https://www.vinnova.se/en/m/testbed-sweden/testbeds-in-sweden.

Regulatory sandboxes

Digitalisation is creating opportunities for new business models and reshaping the way firms compete with one another and interact with consumers. Most regulations were established before the development of digitalisation and may not be fit to this new environment. In some cases, regulation may become ineffective and not achieve the goals it was designed for; in others, regulations hamper innovation by preventing the diffusion of new business models or the emergence of new goods and services.

The regulatory sandbox allows businesses to test innovative products, services, business models and delivery mechanisms in the real market, with real consumers. The sandbox seeks to provide firms with the ability to test products and services in a controlled environment, reduced time-to-market at potentially lower cost, support in identifying appropriate consumer protection safeguards to build into new products and services, and better access to finance.

In March 2017, Finansinspektionen (FI), Sweden's Financial Supervisory Authority, received an assignment from the government to map innovations in the financial sector; and review the questions and needs of market participants in relation to the authority's core activities: supervision, authorisation and regulations. The FI is tasked with safeguarding the stability of the financial sector and sound consumer protection but has not been given an explicit assignment to promote innovation.

Innovative activities are initiated either by financial companies or non-financial firms, often start-ups. Companies are experiencing a considerable need for information about rules, processes and principles in order to be able to realise their innovations.

In order to meet this need, the FI has established an Innovation Centre providing information and maintaining a dialogue with companies that conduct innovation-based business (FI, 2017). The objective of the centre is to serve as a single point of contact for companies that are unsure of the rules, processes and principles that apply in the financial sector to their innovations.

At the same time, the Innovation Centre helps the FI to monitor the development of the financial sector since it makes the authority a natural "partner" for businesses when it is unclear how regulations and the FI's processes apply to an innovation. This also helps the FI to develop a more transparent authorisation process, thus contributing to better supervision and stronger consumer protection.

Typically, a regulatory sandbox provides authorisation only for a small set of firms. In Sweden, this mechanism is regarded as problematic for two reasons. First, the selection process can be considered to benefit some companies at the cost of others; second, it may raise conflicts of interest if companies perceive the authority to be standing behind or taking responsibility for certain innovations.

The Innovation Centre, therefore, makes it possible to achieve the main functions of a regulatory sandbox, i.e. a closer and more transparent dialogue between firms and the authority, while avoiding the drawbacks of selecting firms.

Policy labs

Policy labs are dedicated teams, structures or entities focused on designing public policy through innovative methods that involve all stakeholders in the design process (Fuller and Lochard, 2016). Many countries have established policy labs as a tool to enhance co-operation among administrations, authorities and government ministries as well as businesses and citizens.

In Sweden, a number of labs have been founded, such as Co-lab Sweden (working on the inclusion of child and youth immigrants), Experio Lab (addressing challenges to the healthcare system), Trafiklab (a community of developers that aims to disseminate public transport data to various social actors), OpenLab (for social innovation in Stockholm) and Mötesplats Social Innovation (with a focus on social development in Skåne).

Trafiklab is a community where developers can share data and application programming interfaces (APIs) for public transport in Sweden and easily get the information needed to develop new services. Examples of APIs developed through Trafiklab include STHLM Traveling, an application providing travel plans, real-time traffic information and the possibility to buy e-tickets, used by 50 000 people every day and translated into 15 languages. Skutsgruppen is an application offering travellers seats in private buses, boats, cars, bikes, air balloons and public transport throughout Sweden, through co-operation between public transport and the car rental companies. The App Resident makes it easier to travel in public transport, especially for people with cognitive impairment such as attention deficit hyperactivity disorder and autism. The service Keoscreens provides bus travellers in the city centre of Stockholm real-time traffic information directly on screens of the buses.

A policy lab is also active as part of the Drive Sweden programme. The lab aims to help Swedish authorities increase knowledge, stimulate new processes and ultimately create new services, adjust regulations to enable more tests of new mobility technologies and services in real environments in Sweden. The lab focuses on the development of rules for trial and implementation and looks at regulatory issues and policy processes.

The Swedish Tax Agency has also set up a policy lab in order to achieve higher compliance with existing tax rules in the area of the sharing economy. Through the policy lab, the Swedish Tax Agency aims to gain insight about difficulties and incentives for end users to comply with existing taxation rules and develop proposals for changes in the current regulations.

Policy labs are very interesting experiments, but they face high uncertainty due to budget cuts and changes in elected officials. Although policy labs are often intended to spread innovative practices to the public administration and government, in practice such initiatives often remain limited to the community that launched them. Effects on policies seem to be the greatest when a policy lab is initiated by those who will be the potential users of its outputs.

Recommendations on innovation policies for digitalisation in Sweden

Set clearer priorities for digital innovation

Sweden is an international hub of scientific excellence and technological leadership. This vibrant innovation environment also applies to digital technologies. There is a large number of initiatives, publicly funded and in co-operation with business, to foster research in ICT technologies and promote the adoption and development of advanced digital tools for businesses.

While this high dynamism, combined with a bottom-up approach, are very valuable for research and innovation, it would be useful for the government, through its innovation and research agencies, to provide stronger guidance about innovation priorities in the field of digitalisation.

This recommendation is also supported by the assessment of the publication *OECD Reviews of Innovation Policy: Sweden 2016* (OECD, 2016d: 17): "A lack of adequate governance, leadership and strategic vision is at the heart of many of the difficulties encountered in successfully implementing the policy initiatives examined .... Research and innovation policy, governance and co-ordination mechanisms should be transformed to effectively link public research and innovation and address societal challenges".

The establishment of the Innovation Council and the IPPs are a useful step towards setting strategic priorities, streamlining activities and fostering synergies of innovation programmes. There is, however, room for further improvement in this direction.

Scale up the size of programmes for digital innovation

Public funds to research activities related to digitalisation seem to be scattered among a plethora of programmes. The objective and scope of some programmes appear fairly close and, while different approaches to address the same challenges may be an asset for research, too much fragmentation may result in missing economies of scale in research and testing.

Reaching a critical mass is particularly important for innovations related to digitalisation, as challenges and solutions are common to many sectors and industries. By interfacing and co-ordinating the efforts of different industrial sectors, progress in specific technological areas can be attained faster.

As digital solutions often require large investments, it is less costly to develop common test environments that can be shared for different technologies. In addition, the diffusion of successful innovations generated by testbeds may be limited if their scope is too narrow and their replicability on a bigger scale or for a larger community of users unclear (Growth Analysis, 2017).

The publication *OECD Reviews of Innovation Policy: Sweden 2016* made a similar assessment: "Overall, there is insufficient specialisation and concentration of research resources in priority areas. Wise strategic choices coupled with larger centres to exploit the benefits of scale, as well as emphasis on the global positioning of Swedish universities, could help improve their performance" (OECD, 2016d: 16).

Figure 5.4. **Vinnova's funded projects for co-operation in innovation, 2017**

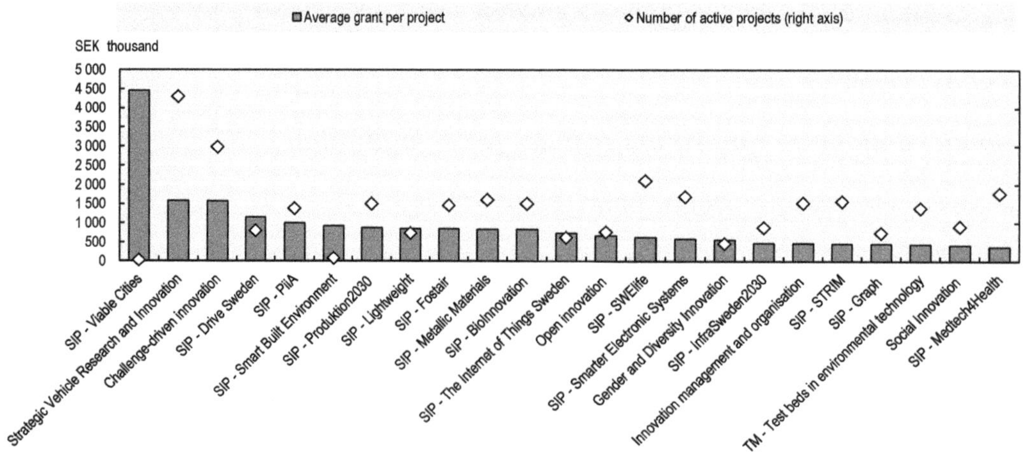

Source: Vinnova (2017), *Annual Report 2017*, https://www.vinnova.se/publikationer/arsredovisning-2017.

As available resources are limited, it is critical to focus on areas of high importance to Sweden and where Swedish firms can gain or sustain a leading position (Vinnova, 2016). Too many projects may result in too little funding for at least some of the projects. For instance, there were over 1 500 projects financed or co-financed by Vinnova in 2017 as part of its strategy to promote co-operation in innovation. However, the average grant for these projects was SEK 881 000 (USD 104 000) (Figure 5.4).

Improve the assessment of innovation policies

The Research and Innovation Bill 2017 points out the need for a closer and more systematic evaluation of the variety of projects and initiatives supported by Swedish innovation policies. Indeed, the OECD's 2016 Review also observed that "there is little evidence" (p. 15) that some of the policies to improve innovation performances in Sweden, e.g. increase in block funding to universities and the establishment of strategic research areas, have produced the expected effects.

A recent review undertaken by the Swedish Agency for Growth Policy Analysis (Deiaco and Tingvall, 2017) concludes that evaluation studies of the effects of innovation policies provide a mixed picture. Different evaluations of the same programme may reach opposite conclusions, with self-assessment based studies resulting in a positive evaluation more often than quantitative studies.

While the assessment of innovation policies is a complex task, it is essential that the large number of programmes active in Sweden are systematically analysed. Support schemes to innovation may lead to unwanted outcomes, such as rent-seeking, picking winners, distortion of competition, excessive administrative costs, bias in investments and tax wedges, only to mention the most common problems.

Strengthening policy labs and regulation sandboxes

Digitalisation is opening up great opportunities for the economy and society, but seizing these opportunities requires innovative ways to design and implement policies and regulations. The complex challenges raised by digitalisation require an ability to work across policy areas and administrative boundaries; involve users, citizens and businesses; and experiment and explore in a more agile, co-creative and open environment.

Furthermore, timely adoption of new digital technologies benefits from a systematic and formal approach, where priorities are set and activities co-ordinated across departments and agencies. The rapid technology evolution, the speed of the digital transformation and its cross-sectorial nature are all factors that policy makers need to consider.

Several policy labs have been established in Sweden in recent years, as in a number of many other countries. While these initiatives are interesting and potentially useful, their effects seem limited by a number of factors, including insufficient political commitment in the long run. The government should take a clear stance in favour of policy labs and include them among its policy tools, particularly in relation to digitalisation.

Regulatory sandboxes provide another useful instrument to ensure co-operation between all stakeholders in the development of new regulations better suited to the digital economy. The successful example of the Innovation Centre launched by the FI, Sweden's Financial Supervisory Authority, points to the opportunity to broaden the traditional mandate of regulatory agencies (supervision, authorisation and regulations) to include support to innovation.

Through regulatory sandboxes, agencies would be able to engage in a closer dialogue with companies that intend to develop new business models based on innovation. This requires a profound change in the culture and the practice of regulatory agencies, but also a clearer mandate by the Swedish government that issues instructions to those agencies.

Labour markets and jobs in the digital economy

The digital transformation is creating job opportunities in new markets and increasing employment in some existing occupations. At the same time, digital technologies enable the production of more goods and services with less labour, thus exposing some workers to the risk of unemployment or lower wages. In addition, digital platforms enable changes in the organisation of work, with implications for the capability of existing policies and programmes to ensure labour market inclusion, job quality and skills development.

To reap the benefits of the adoption of digital technologies, governments, businesses, trade unions and academia will need to address new economic and labour market challenges. This section will focus on policies to accompany workers along the transition to the new jobs enabled by the digital transformation and to help ensure job quality in the digital economy.

Digitalisation and jobs

There is growing concern that digital technologies have contributed to job losses, wage stagnation and rising wage inequality in many OECD countries over the last two decades. Spectacular progress in robotics and AI raises worries that job displacement may continue at an even faster rate in the near future.

Economic history shows that major technological innovations have always been accompanied by extensive transformations in the labour market. Jobs brought about by new technologies are different from the old jobs: they are created in different sectors and different occupations, they involve different tasks and require different skills.

Figure 5.5. **Employment changes by industry in OECD countries, 1995-2015**

Percentage changes

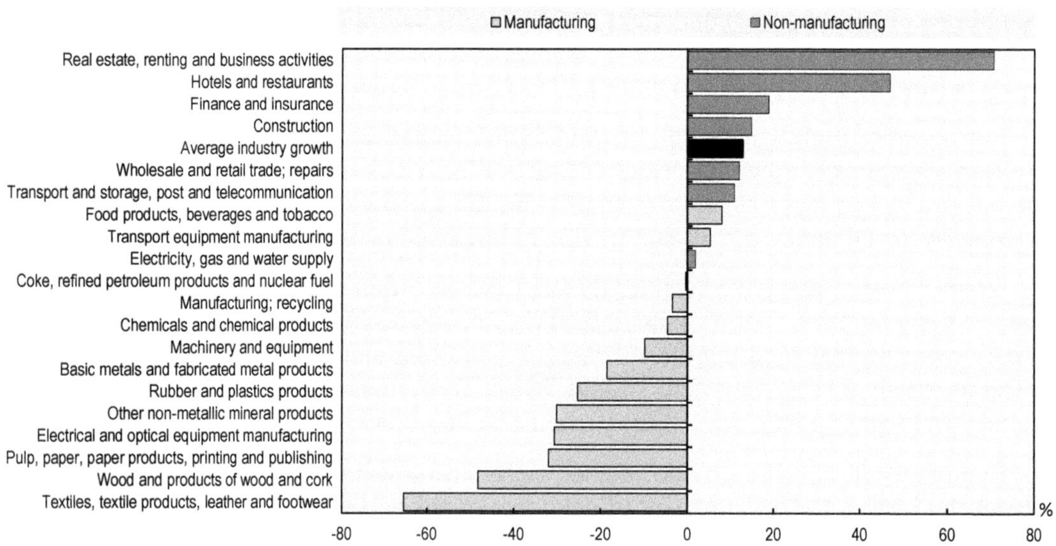

Note: The countries included in this graphic are: Austria, Belgium, Canada, the Czech Republic, Denmark, Finland, France, Germany, Greece, Hungary, Ireland, Italy, the Netherlands, Norway, Portugal, the Slovak Republic, Slovenia, Spain, Sweden, the United Kingdom and the United States.

Source: OECD (2017a), *OECD Employment Outlook 2017*, http://dx.doi.org/10.1787/empl_outlook-2017-en.

In today's digital transformation, employment is decreasing in sectors with more scope for automation and slower growth in demand, such as manufacturing, retail and finance (Figure 5.5). The decrease in employment is more pronounced in routine occupations, both for low- and high-skilled jobs, leading to employment polarisation and the decline in the share of middle-income jobs (OECD, 2016a; 2017a).

In this context, effective labour market policies and institutions are essential to accompany displaced workers along the transition to new jobs and reduce the social costs of this process (OECD, 2016c).

The OECD recently carried out an in-depth review of labour market policies in Sweden (OECD, 2015). Compared to most OECD countries, the Swedish labour market has performed pretty well in recent years. Almost 90% of the displaced workers in Sweden find a new job within a year (Figure 5.6). On average, their wages are lower than they were in their previous job, but the income loss is smaller than in other comparable OECD countries.

The resilience of Swedish employment during the global financial crisis suggests that its labour market policies and institutions are well-equipped to deal with the digital transformation. Sweden's capability to facilitate a smooth transition for workers affected by economic restructuring is mainly the result of two specific features of its labour market institutions: the strong dialogue between the social partners and the active role of the job security councils (JSCs).

Figure 5.6. **Re-employment rates of displaced workers**

Selected OECD countries

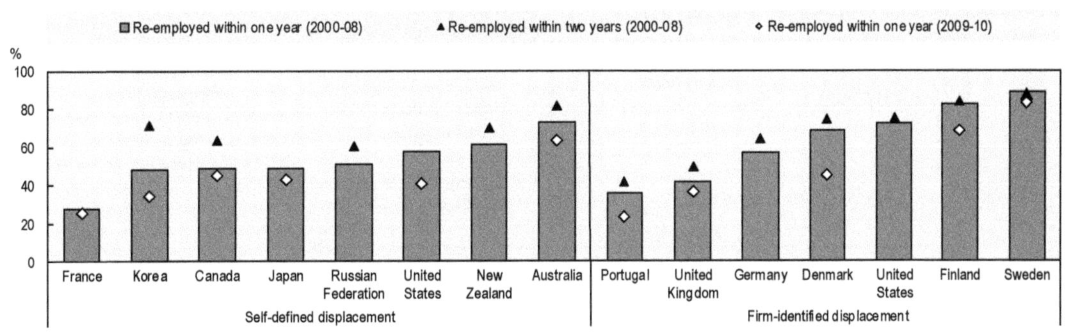

Source: OECD (2015), *Back to Work: Sweden: Improving the Re-employment Prospects of Displaced Workers*, http://dx.doi.org/10.1787/9789264246812-en.

Social partners play a key role in the regulation of the labour market in Sweden through collective agreements (Box 5.3). They also provide comprehensive support for displaced workers in the transition from job to job through the JSCs. These are non-profit foundations, offering advice and consultation to employers as well as transition services and guidance to workers (Box 5.4).

The key feature of the JSCs is that they provide their services before dismissal takes place or at very early stages of the process. Compared to most OECD countries, the notice period in Sweden is longer – up to 12 months for 55-year-olds and above, white-collar workers with at least a 10-year job tenure, which gives the JSCs time to help dismissed workers find a new job.

Box 5.3. Social partners in Sweden

There are three main trade union confederations in Sweden:

1. LO (Trade Union Confederation) – the biggest trade union confederation that covers mainly blue-collar workers.
2. TCO (the Swedish Confederation of Professional Employees) – covers professionals and most white-collar workers.
3. Saco (the Swedish Confederation of Professional Associations) – brings together unions organising civil servants and professional employees.

Collective agreements are made through two main negotiation councils, namely the Federation of Salaried Employees in Industry and Services (PTK) and the Public Employees' Negotiation Council (OFR). These councils play an important role in collective bargaining at branch/sector level.

The PTK negotiates with the Confederation of Swedish Enterprise on pensions and unemployment insurance, comprising 27 national unions from the TCO and Saco and representing 700 000 employees. On the other hand, 14 national unions in the public sector have joined together in the OFR, which is a collaborative body, a forum for dialogue and co-operation where the unions consult and co-operate with each other on common bargaining issues. The unions represent some 560 000 central and local government employees. The OFR is formed by unions from both Saco and the TCO.

Figure 5.7. Social partners in Sweden

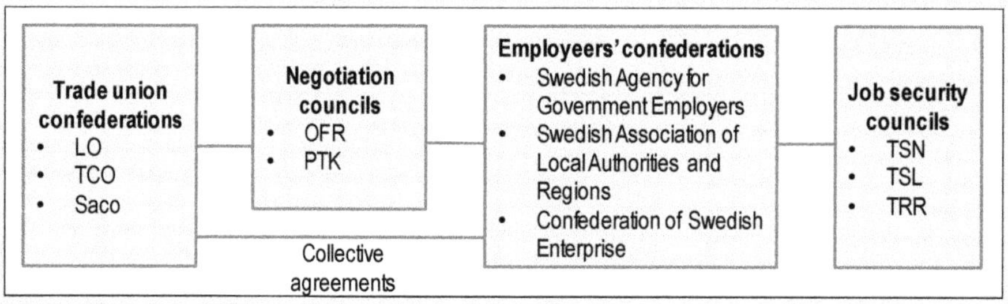

There are approximately ten more JSCs in Sweden. The TSN, the TSL and the TRR are the main ones.

Source: OECD (2015), *Back to Work: Sweden: Improving the Re-employment Prospects of Displaced Workers*, http://dx.doi.org/10.1787/9789264246812-en.

On the government side, the Ministry of Employment has the main responsibility for labour market policy related to displaced workers, acting through the PES. Unlike the JSCs, services provided by the PES come after a dismissal takes place and programmes are not typically tailored to the professional profile of displaced workers. Furthermore, PES services are limited to priority groups, e.g. long-term unemployed, disabled and immigrant workers, while all other groups can benefit from intensive support only after 300 days of unemployment, via the Job and Development Programme.

While the JSCs are very successful, workers with temporary and fixed-term contracts, mainly youth and other vulnerable groups, benefit less from their services, despite the fact that they are more likely to be dismissed. In addition, many of those who qualify for the JSCs support receive only partial services, especially blue-collar workers. Expanding the JSCs' services to all displaced workers remain a major challenge for labour market institutions in Sweden (OECD, 2015).

Box 5.4. Job security councils in Sweden

In Sweden, the labour market is characterised by a high percentage of unionisation and collective bargaining coverage and a unique degree of co-operation between social partners. This is exemplified through the JSCs, a structural mechanism developed by trade unions and employers in the 1970s that operate independently from the government and Public Employment Services (PES). The JSCs are financed by employer contributions based on collective agreements between social partners in specific industries and sectors, with reference to employment protection legislation (EPL).

More than ten JSCs cover almost 80% of the Swedish labour force, including white-collar workers, blue-collar workers and public employees. The JSCs provide transitional services to displaced workers based on their individual circumstances and requirements. They also provide tailored advice and counselling services to both employers and trade union representatives during the earliest stages of restructuring, with the aim of managing voluntary and compulsory redundancies. Crucially, the JSCs provide tailored advice to both employers and trade unions at the very early stages of the unemployment process, often even before workers are officially unemployed. As a result, the majority of re-employment offers to displaced workers are made before the end of the formal redundancy transition period. In 2016, the council responsible for white-collar private sector employees (Trygghetsrådet) was successful in finding new employment opportunities for 88% of laid-off workers.

The JSCs in Sweden are remarkable in their capacity to provide rapid response services in the case of mass layoffs of entire workplaces, but also in terms of extending early intervention measures to individual and small-scale layoffs. This helps workers from all backgrounds and competences transition to new work, regardless of the nature of the previous employment. The JSCs further highlight the role of constructive engagement among all concerned parties, including the individual, trade unions and former employer, while also accommodating the specific needs of displaced workers.

Source: OECD (2015), *Back to Work: Sweden: Improving the Re-employment Prospects of Displaced Workers*, http://dx.doi.org/10.1787/9789264246812-en; TUAC (2018), "The Swedish job security councils: A case study on social partners' led transitions".

Not only the coverage but also the quality and range of services provided vary among the JSCs. For instance, the Early Risk Service, i.e. a set of special anticipatory measures focusing on career planning for all workers who could potentially be affected by displacements, is currently offered by all the JSCs to provide all displaced workers with the same opportunities. Assessing the outcomes of JSC services and promoting the uptake of the most successful ones is another challenge for the social partners system in Sweden.

The current separation between job-search counselling and training – the first being provided by the JSC during the notice period and the second under the PES after dismissal – are likely to weaken the effectiveness of job-transition services. There is room to improve the co-ordination between the JSCs and the PES at an early stage, which currently takes place only for large-scale redundancies, and to increase resources for the training of blue-collar workers.

Finally, the target groups of the PES should be enlarged from disadvantaged groups to all short-term unemployed, particularly blue-collar workers, who have higher employability and could benefit the most from the PES' services (OECD, 2015).

New forms of work in the digital economy

Over the last few years, Internet platforms have emerged as major actors in the digital economy, providing digital marketplaces for information, goods and services. Among them, Internet job platforms are providing new ways to match demand and supply for labour services.

Some job platforms provide a marketplace for low-skill physical tasks, mostly carried out by young people on an occasional basis. Others enable digital services on line, matching demand and supply across different countries and over a wider range of tasks, from low-skill tasks like data entry or administrative support to high-skill ones like programming, legal advice or business consulting (Figure 5.8).

Figure 5.8. **Tasks on platform-mediated jobs**

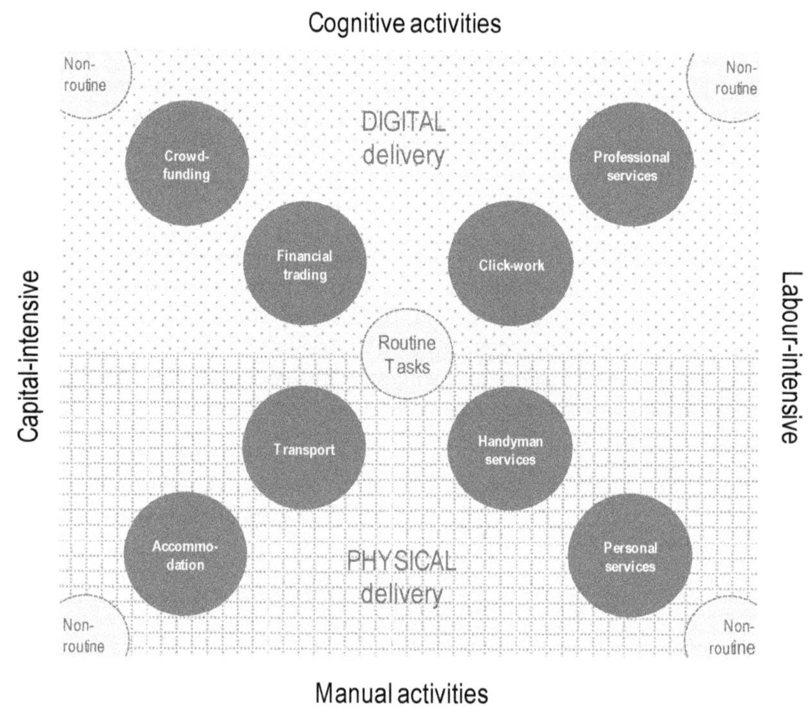

Source: OECD (2016b), "New forms of work in the digital economy", http://dx.doi.org/10.1787/5jlwnklt820x-en.

Internet job platforms have the potential to dramatically change traditional work arrangements and labour market relationships. Some full-time, long-term jobs are being turned into an uneven flow of "on-demand" tasks for a large global pool of "virtual workers". While these changes create opportunities for workers, jobseekers and firms, they also raise major challenges for job quality, taxation and social security.

Platforms have contributed to job creation in a time of economic crisis and may create further job opportunities in lagging regions while mitigating skills shortages in dynamic areas. In addition, the platform economy has reduced transaction costs and enables employers to avoid many regulations and taxes associated with standard employment contracts, which has led many SMEs to use them. The platform economy could also lead to more inclusive labour markets as it removes many barriers to employment faced by certain under-represented groups in the labour market.

The main advantages for platform employers are the access to a larger pool of skills and experience, faster execution of the tasks contracted out and lower costs for hiring, administration and facilities. The risk of losing in-house competences as well as poor control over the process and the quality of the service provided are reported as the main drawbacks.

According to workers, among the main reasons for working via an online platform is the ability to manage working time independently, to choose the place of work and to achieve a better work-life balance (OECD, 2016b). These benefits tend to be higher for certain groups, notably single parents, students and seniors.

The benefits from higher flexibly, however, do not come without costs. Platform-based workers may have to perform many tasks in parallel, working longer hours and under higher stress. Other negative aspects include the information asymmetry between employers and workers, the lack of a reliable dispute resolution system, the possibility of privacy violation, and the lack of support from colleagues and managers. Work satisfaction also tends to be low as tasks are often low-skilled and trivial (Eurofound, 2015).

Under the existing labour market programmes and regulations, platform-based workers are likely to face some of the same problems as those in non-standard work, such as temporary, part-time or short-term jobs. Non-standard workers tend to experience lower wages than standard workers as well as greater job insecurity and earning losses between contracts (OECD, 2014).

The self-employed are more likely to have fewer work-related benefits, in particular for unemployment, work injury, sickness, maternity and retirement. Non-regular workers are also less likely to receive employer-sponsored training in most OECD countries but have a higher probability of becoming unemployed or leaving the labour force (OECD, 2014).

EPL is also lower for non-standard workers. In Sweden, EPL includes heavy notification procedures in case of dismissal, stringent regulation of the order of layoffs in case of redundancy, a relatively broad definition of unfair dismissals and sizeable compensation following such dismissals. However, many of these provisions apply to permanent work contracts only. The gap in EPL between permanent and temporary workers in Sweden is among the highest in the OECD (Figure 5.9).

Figure 5.9. **Gap in the strictness of employment protection legislation between permanent and temporary contracts in OECD countries, 2013**

Scale from 0 (low strictness) to 6 (high strictness)

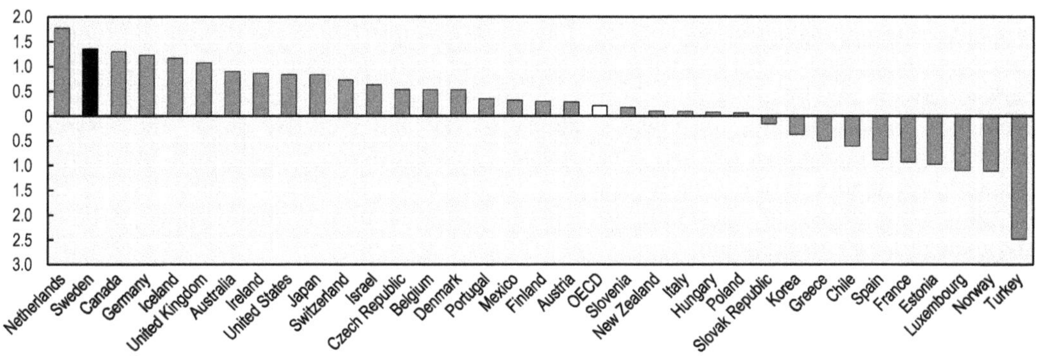

Source: OECD (2015), *Back to Work: Sweden: Improving the Re-employment Prospects of Displaced Workers*, http://dx.doi.org/10.1787/9789264246812-en.

To meet these challenges, governments, employers' organisations and trade unions should improve their capability to detect emerging labour market trends and explore ways of developing existing labour market programmes and safety nets, where eligibility is tied to standard employment models, so as to ensure inclusive growth and job quality.

Box 5.5. A "social partners' platform": A proposal by Unionen

Unionen, Sweden's largest trade union on the private labour market, is developing a novel approach to self-regulating the emerging platform-based labour market, based on the Nordic social partner model.

Existing regulation is designed with "analogue firms" in mind. To increase compliance and lower regulatory transaction costs for platform firms, it is crucial that the relevant regulation and the associated regulatory supervision be more adapted to the digital environment and the algorithms driving these firms. To achieve this, new, highly digital standards of regulation will need to be created.

Unionen proposes creating a platform institution tasked to create digital standards and guidelines for firms wishing to abide by the rules and norms established by society. By centralising this function, rather than relying on a plethora of government agencies to create such standards, relevant expertise can be concentrated, creating the best possible conditions for creating top standards and ease of use. The institution will be owned by the stakeholders, i.e. it will be shared between relevant trade unions and platform firms that have signed collective agreements. Centralised standard creation will also mean that standards are created "closer to the market" than would otherwise be the case.

Further efficiency gains can come from concentrating required expertise in a single institution, in turn continually improving existing standards and the process of creating novel ones. The created standards will be the result of negotiations between platform firms, trade unions and the relevant government agencies. The institution itself may thus be seen as a social compact tasked with adapting existing institutions to a changing labour market.

This will ultimately require the consent of legislators, as individual government agencies would normally be tasked with creating such standards. Given that platform-based firms may arise in a plethora of markets, an uncoordinated regulatory response might produce mixed results. There is also a risk of the developed standards not sufficiently balancing the sometimes shared and fragmented interests of platform firms and labour.

Apart from adapting existing regulation, there are already examples of novel practices possibly requiring regulatory supervision. One such example lies in the design and function of rating and reputation systems, an integral function of many platforms today. By creating trust between parties, and by giving an indication of expected quality, ratings determine the individual provider's, and sometimes the client's, ability to sell and purchase goods and services on platform markets. Ratings are thus also pertinent to wage formation. Ratings and reputations produced on platforms are usually not portable to other platforms, creating lock-in effects. Creating some degree of transferability between platforms may increase labour mobility and stimulate platform competition.

Source: Söderqvist, F. (2017), "A Nordic approach to regulating intermediary online labour platforms", https://doi.org/10.1177/1024258917711375.

The strong "social partners" model in Sweden may provide the space where platforms and trade unions can address these issues. There would be potential gains for all parties.

Platform firms would face lower transaction costs to comply with existing regulations and contribute to shaping regulations that are well-suited to their business model. Trade unions would contribute to setting up effective mechanisms to extend safety nets to platform workers not covered by current labour laws and agreements. Through this process, the government and its regulatory agencies would gain a better understanding of the features specific to a digital environment and be able to assess the effectiveness of existing rules and, when appropriate, design new rules fit to this environment.

In most countries, policy discussions on online platforms have mostly focused on specific sectors so far. Cross-cutting policy issues, such as the ones relating to work, consumer protection, taxation, competition, or privacy and security, should be addressed more systematically. A few countries have started to develop a more comprehensive approach though. The US Federal Trade Commission held a hearing and public consultation earlier in 2016 while the UK government has issued recommendations in response to an independent review of the sharing economy (Department for Business, Innovation & Skills, 2015). In Sweden, Unionen, the largest trade union on the private labour market, has proposed a platform institution tasked to create digital standards and guidelines for firms wishing to abide by the rules and norms established by society (Box 5.5).

A regulatory sandbox on platform-mediated jobs could also help to address some of the issues related to compliance with the current labour market regulations and the opportunity to develop new ones. The Innovation Centre established by the FI, Sweden's Financial Supervisory Authority, would provide a useful model for such a sandbox (see subsection "Regulatory Sandboxes" above).

An Innovation Centre for the labour market could also be established, with the task of providing tailored information and developing a dialogue with job platforms about regulatory obligations and issues. To this purpose, the Ministry of Labour may consider issuing instruction for the National Mediation Office (Medlingsinstitutet) to map innovations in the labour markets and review issues that platforms and trade unions may raise in relation to the agency's core activities: labour disputes, wage formation, and statistics on wages and salaries.

Policy recommendations

Effective labour market policies and institutions are essential to accompany workers during the digital transformation. The Swedish model, based on the strong dialogue between the social partners and the active role of JSCs, seems well-equipped to facilitate a smooth transition for workers affected this transformation. However, there is room to improve the coverage and the quality of the JSCs' and of the PES' services.

Social partners may want to:

- extend the provision of the JSCs' services to all displaced workers, including blue-collar, youth and other vulnerable groups
- promote successful job-transition services, e.g. the Early Risk Service across all JSCs
- improve the co-ordination between the JSCs and the PES at an early stage of the dismissal procedure, in co-ordination with the government
- enlarge the coverage of the PES' services to all short-term unemployed.

In an increasingly integrated global economy, digital technologies are enabling firms to segment work in new ways and to increase the use of temporary labour. Platform-based workers are likely to face some of the same problems as those in non-standard work, such as temporary, part-time or short-term jobs, i.e. lower wages, greater job insecurity and fewer work-related benefits. In Sweden, EPL is well developed but the gap in EPL between permanent and temporary workers is among the highest in the OECD.

As mentioned above, to meet these challenges, governments and social partners should improve their ability to detect emerging labour market trends and explore ways of developing existing labour market programmes and safety nets, in which eligibility is tied to standard employment models, so as to ensure inclusive growth and job quality in the new work organisation enabled by the digital economy:

- Social partners may want to take initiatives to promote the establishment of a negotiation council where job platforms and trade unions may negotiate collective agreements fit to the new forms of work enabled by digitalisation.
- The government may want promote a regulatory sandbox on the labour market, based on the model of the Innovation Centre established by the FI. To this purpose, the Ministry of Labour may consider issuing instructions for the National Mediation Office to map innovations in the labour markets and review issues that platforms and trade unions may have in relation to the agency's core activities.

Note

1. https://www.vinnova.se/en/m/digitalisering-av-industrin.

References

Deiaco E. and P. Tingvall (2017), "Swedish innovation policies: Design, selection and evaluation", paper presented at the 130th Meeting of the OECD Committee on Industry, Innovation and Entrepreneurship, Paris, https://www.researchgate.net/publication/316738521_Swedish_Innovation_Policies_-_Design_Selection_and_Evaluation.

Department for Business, Innovation & Skills (2015), "Sharing economy: Government response to the independent review", Department for Business, Innovation & Skills, London, https://www.gov.uk/government/publications/sharing-economy-government-response-to-the-independent-review.

Eurofound (2015), *New Forms of Employment*, Publications Office of the European Union, Luxembourg, https://www.eurofound.europa.eu/publications/report/2015/working-conditions-labour-market/new-forms-of-employment.

European Commission (2012), Commission Recommendation of 17.7.2012 on access to and preservation of scientific information, C(2012) 4890 final, European Commission, Brussels, https://ec.europa.eu/research/science-society/document_library/pdf_06/recommendation-access-and-preservation-scientific-information_en.pdf.

FI (2017), "FI's role regarding innovation", Finansinspektionen, Stockholm, https://www.fi.se/contentassets/d3cd30fe473d4a7995f0c38209ddb7f1/fintech_report_engny.pdf (accessed 21 April 2018).

Fuller, M. and A. Lochard (2016), *Public Policy Labs in European Union Member States*, Publications Office of the European Union, Luxembourg, http://dx.doi.org/10.2788/799175.

Government Offices of Sweden (2016), "Collaborating for knowledge: For society's challenges and strengthened competitiveness" (in Swedish), Prop. 2016/17: 50, www.regeringen.se/rattsdokument/proposition/2016/11/prop.-20161750.

Growth Analysis (2017), "Factors affecting the establishment of a testbed: An analysis of Vinnova's 'Environmental Technology Testbeds' program", PM 2017:17, Swedish Agency for Growth Policy Analysis, Östersund, Sweden, www.tillvaxtanalys.se/in-english/publications/pm/pm/2017-12-22-factors-affecting-the-establishment-of-a-testbed----an-analysis-of-vinnovas-environmental-technology-testbeds-program.html.

Ministry of Enterprise and Innovation (2016), "Smart industry: A strategy for new industrialisation for Sweden", Government Offices of Sweden, Stockholm, www.regeringen.se/informationsmaterial/2016/05/smart-industry---a-strategy-for-new-industrialisation-for-sweden.

OECD (2017a), *OECD Employment Outlook 2017*, OECD Publishing, Paris, http://dx.doi.org/10.1787/empl_outlook-2017-en.

OECD (2017b), *OECD Science, Technology and Industry Scoreboard 2017: The Digital Transformation*, OECD Publishing, Paris, http://dx.doi.org/10.1787/9789264268821-en.

OECD (2016a), *Getting Skills Right: Sweden*, Getting Skills Right, OECD Publishing, Paris, http://dx.doi.org/10.1787/9789264265479-en.

OECD (2016b), "New forms of work in the digital economy", *OECD Digital Economy Papers*, No. 260, OECD Publishing, Paris, http://dx.doi.org/10.1787/5jlwnklt820x-en.

OECD (2016c), "New markets and new jobs", *OECD Digital Economy Papers*, No. 255, OECD Publishing, Paris, http://dx.doi.org/10.1787/5jlwt496h37l-en.

OECD (2016d), *OECD Reviews of Innovation Policy: Sweden 2016*, OECD Publishing, Paris, http://dx.doi.org/10.1787/9789264250000-en.

OECD (2015), *Back to Work: Sweden: Improving the Re-employment Prospects of Displaced Workers*, Back to Work, OECD Publishing, Paris, http://dx.doi.org/10.1787/9789264246812-en.

OECD (2014), *OECD Employment Outlook 2014*, OECD Publishing, Paris, http://dx.doi.org/10.1787/empl_outlook-2014-en.

Söderqvist, F. (2017), "A Nordic approach to regulating intermediary online labour platforms", *Transfer: European Review of Labour and Research*, Vol. 23/3, pp. 349-352, https://doi.org/10.1177/1024258917711375.

Test Site Sweden (n.d.), "DriveMe", webpage, https://www.testsitesweden.com/en/projects-1/driveme (accessed 21 April 2018).

TUAC (2018), "The Swedish job security councils: A case study on social partners' led transitions", Trade Union Advisory Council to the OECD, Paris.

Vinnova (2018), "Testbeds in Sweden", webpage, https://www.vinnova.se/en/m/testbed-sweden/testbeds-in-sweden (accessed 21 April 2018).

Vinnova (2017), *Annual Report 2017*, Vinnova, https://www.vinnova.se/publikationer/arsredovisning-2017.

Vinnova (2016), *Digitalisering av svensk industry*, Roland Berger AB, https://www.vinnova.se/en/publikationer/digitalisering-av-svensk-industri (accessed 21 April 2108).

Chapter 6.

Policy recommendations

This chapter presents the policy framework being developed by the OECD project Going Digital: Making the Transformation Work for Growth and Well-being, reviews policy recommendations in specific policy areas and addresses the issue of policy coherence in the implementation of the Digital Strategy in Sweden.

This review has examined recent developments in the digital economy in Sweden and has reviewed policy measures to further foster digital transformation. Sweden has been among the best performing economies in the OECD in recent years and is a leading country for the diffusion and use of digital technologies. The information and communications technology (ICT) sector and ICT investments have been the main drivers of labour productivity growth. Through digitalisation, the economy has been able to maintain its international competitiveness in manufacturing while moving up along the value chain towards high value-added services.

As the digital transformation opens up new opportunities and international competition becomes stronger, partially as a result of digitalisation, some changes in policies seem appropriate to maintain Sweden's high performance in the future. Some policy changes are specific to certain areas, as illustrated in the previous chapters of this review. Yet, the most challenging policy issue, for Sweden as for many other countries, is the development of a coherent policy framework for digital transformation, both among ministries and agencies (horizontal co-ordination) as well as across levels of government (vertical co-ordination).

As digitalisation cuts across different policy domains and government levels, further seizing its potential benefits may increasingly depend on Sweden's capability to strengthen a whole-of-government policy approach. This requires overcoming organisational barriers to integration, sharing and horizontal decision making, a greater emphasis on anticipating potential changes and impacts, and greater use of data and digital technologies in policy making.

To address these policy issues, the OECD has launched "Going Digital: Making the Transformation Work for Growth and Well-being". The project aims to help policy makers better understand the digital transformation that is taking place and create a policy environment that enables their economies and societies to prosper in a world that is increasingly digital and data-driven.

This chapter will present the policy framework being developed by the OECD Going Digital project, review the recommendations specific to each policy area, develop recommendations for Sweden's Digital Strategy and finally, address the issue of policy coherence.

Going Digital: An integrated policy approach in the digital age

Digital transformation is challenging almost every aspect of the economy and society, and a wide range of policy areas need to be considered as much as all actors (individuals, firms, governments and other stakeholders) need to be involved in the policy-making process. Individuals must be engaged and firms need to continue to act as a catalyst of transformative change. At the same time, governments need to reach across traditional policy silos and across different levels of government to develop a whole-of-government approach to policy making using the multi-stakeholder model that has underpinned the development of the Internet so well.

One aim of the Going Digital integrated policy framework is to help change the way policy makers think about digital transformation and in doing so change the way policies are developed in the digital age. Rather than considering narrow policy silos, the framework aims to support an integrated approach because policy changes in one domain may have implications in another domain. It is essential to be aware of interconnections and relationships across policy domains and to develop digital policy making with them in mind.

Figure 6.1 shows a preliminary integrated policy framework[1] for making the digital transformation work for growth and well-being (OECD, 2018). This section will briefly discuss its key components and what they mean for policy making.

Figure 6.1. **An integrated policy framework for making the digital transformation work**

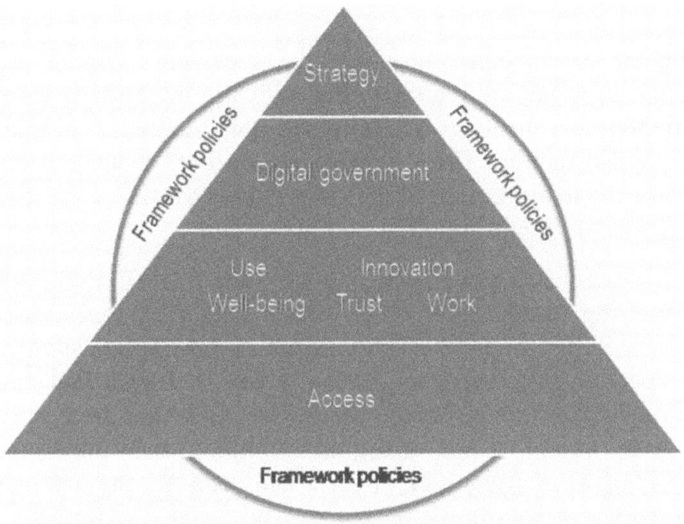

Source: OECD (2018), "Going digital in a multilateral world: An interim report to ministers", www.oecd.org/mcm/documents/C-MIN-2018-6-EN.pdf.

Framework policies

Digital transformation does not occur in isolation; it is shaped by (and helps shape) the broader economy and society as a whole. Framework policies play an important role in ensuring that the right conditions exist for digital transformation to flourish. Open trade and investment regimes can create new avenues for rapidly upgrading technologies and skills, and increasing specialisation. Efficient, open financial markets help to allocate financial resources to firms investing in the digital transformation, while competitive product markets foster consumer welfare, allow new firms to challenge incumbents, efficient firms to grow, and inefficient ones to exit. Well-functioning labour markets can support the inevitable structural change. Sound policies for intellectual property can help foster value creation from digital transformation and support innovation and diffusion. More broadly, sound macroeconomic policies can help reduce uncertainty and create an enabling environment for the digital transformation to thrive. In some cases, framework policies will need to be reviewed to ensure they are suited for the digital age.

Access

Digital infrastructures, including efficient, reliable and widely accessible broadband communication networks and services, data, software, and hardware, are the foundations on which the digital transformation is based. It is essential that governments promote investment in digital infrastructures and competition in the provision of high-speed networks and services, ensuring that key complementary enablers are in place and cover a maximum of territory (e.g. fibre optic backhaul, sufficient spectrum and increasing uptake of IPv6 Internet addresses), and that critical network infrastructures are resilient. Individuals, businesses (including small and medium-sized enterprises [SMEs]) and governments need reliable, affordable, and widespread access to digital technologies and services to benefit from digital opportunities and enable an inclusive digital transformation. Indeed, much of the future growth in demand for devices connected to digital infrastructures is expected to come from the Internet of Things (IoT).

Use

Access to digital technologies provides the technical foundation for the digital transformation of the economy and society, but does not necessarily ensure effective use by itself. Other factors also need to be addressed concomitantly, notably education and skills. Effective use also requires firms to take into account in their decision making and operational processes the management of the risks related to the use of digital technologies, particularly with respect to digital security and privacy.

Moreover, it is crucial that governments enable the diffusion and adoption of digital technologies in fostering complementary investments in data, research and development (R&D), management skills, and other knowledge-based capital such as organisational change. This is especially important for SMEs, many of which lack the know-how but whose participation in the digital transformation is essential in ensuring an inclusive digital transformation. Effective use of digital technologies in an economy can also be affected by a lack of firm dynamics, which can lead to the coexistence of poorly performing firms, with very low levels of ICT use, with star performers.

Innovation

Science and innovation are the source for the digital technologies that are driving the digital transformation, with all of them, and notably the Internet, drawing on a long history of public investment in fundamental research. Continued investment in public and private research and innovation is needed to drive the digital transformation further and develop new technologies and applications. In turn, the adoption and use of digital technologies, including data analytics, are associated with higher innovation performance across the economy.

Technologies, smart applications (including data analytics) and other innovations can also improve services and help address policy challenges in a wide range of areas, including education, finance, health, transportation, energy, agriculture and fisheries, between and within countries. Digital technologies contribute not only to innovation in goods and services, but also to innovation in processes, business models and organisational arrangements, as well as the process of science and innovation itself.

Trust

Trust is fundamental to the digital transformation; without it, individuals, firms and governments won't fully use digital technologies, and an important source of potential growth and social progress will be left unexploited. Countries may benefit from greater cross-border co-operation if they develop comprehensive and coherent national strategies for digital security and privacy to address issues such as the protection of personal data, resilience of essential services (e.g. water, energy, finance, public health and safety), creation of incentives (e.g. cyber insurance, public procurement), support to SMEs, and related skills development, in consultation with all relevant stakeholders. At the same time, it is important to continue promoting effective protection to consumers engaged in e-commerce and other online activities, as this will help the digital economy flourish as well as be inclusive.

Jobs

Digital transformation has already begun to change the nature and structure of organisations and markets, raising important questions about which jobs might disappear and where new ones will come from, what they will they look like and which skills will be required, who might be most affected, and what can be done to foster new job creation. Going forward, low-skilled jobs are likely to be the most at risk of being displaced.

At the same time, technological advances are facilitating the expansion of new forms of work such as "crowd work", "gig work" and other forms of on-demand labour. Digital transformation may increase the already sizeable number of workers (one-third of the OECD labour force) in non-standard forms of employment that are in many cases a poor fit with traditional social protection systems predicated on the archetype of full-time, permanent work for a single employer. As these changes take place, it is important to ensure that effective adjustment mechanisms are in place to help individuals navigate the transition from one job to the next. It is also essential to ensure that complementary policies – in the form of a social safety net, social dialogue between employers and workers, employment regulation and skills policies – are in place to support those people for whom the transition is lengthy, or who are ultimately unable to transition effectively to new skills and jobs.

Well-being

Digital transformation changes how people from different cultures access information and interact with one another and with society more broadly. For example, digital technologies can promote social inclusion by enabling better access to healthcare through online services, as well as new opportunities for skills development by offering access to education, as well as flexible working arrangements for families. They can also help disadvantaged groups connect. On the other hand, the increasing spread and use of some technologies has the potential to reduce face-to-face interactions, thus further isolating some individuals, and in some cases digital services can lead to the creation of like-minded groups that do not interact with others. Security and privacy also become more urgent issues to address as the IoT and intelligent connected objects, such as self-driving cars, become deployed.

Digital government

Digital transformation of governments and public services requires new forms of partnerships and engagement, new skills and accountability models for the public sector. Digital technologies offer opportunities to increase the access to, reach and quality of public services, and to improve policy making itself. In addition, digital technologies and the use of large datasets across the public sector are also raising issues around how to leverage these new digital opportunities to rethink how the public sector functions, including the governance of ICT use in government and the regulatory environment concerning these new (potentially disruptive) areas. This requires overcoming organisational and regulatory barriers to integration, sharing and horizontal decision making, and use of data and digital technologies across the public sector.

Strategy

Digital transformation affects all corners of the economy, society and government activities. As mentioned above, to realise its full benefits, governments need to reach across traditional policy silos and across different levels of government and develop a whole-of-government approach to policy making. This means more co-ordination when taking decisions and implementing policy measures across ministries and levels of government, as well as more active involvement of all key stakeholders, including the business community, trade unions, civil society and the Internet technical community, in the policy-making process as well as in implementation and monitoring. By identifying the inter-dependencies among the policy areas affected by digital transformation, it will be easier to link up the relevant ministries and government bodies that need to be co-ordinated to ensure that policies are mutually reinforcing. At the same time, it is important to assess how the digital transformation is affecting international regulatory co-operation.

National digital strategies (NDS) are a key component of ensuring a whole-of-government approach. Current approaches to governing NDS vary across countries. Information from 35 countries provides an overview of the responsibilities allocated for the development, co-ordination, implementation and monitoring of NDS (Table 6.1). The lead on strategy development is often taken by a ministry or body that is not dedicated to digital affairs, while only a minority of countries so far charge a ministry or body that is dedicated to digital affairs. Almost all countries engage multiple private stakeholders and public bodies to contribute input to developing their NDS.

Table 6.1. **National digital strategy governance**

Number of countries that have allocated respective responsibilities to the bodies and institutions

	Lead the development	Contribute input	Co-ordinate	Implement	Monitor
Government, e.g. prime minister, presidency, etc.	4	0	5	1	6
Digital affairs minister or body	8	1	10	3	8
Minister or body not dedicated to digital affairs	15	2	13	1	11
Several ministries, bodies or institutions	6	14	5	26	7
Multiple public and private stakeholders	1	17	0	3	0

Source: OECD (2017b), *OECD Digital Economy Outlook 2017*, http://dx.doi.org/10.1787/9789264276284-en.

Strikingly, only a few countries (Austria, Luxembourg, Mexico and the Slovak Republic) have a single high-level government official, e.g. in the prime minister's office, presidency or chancellery, or a ministry or body dedicated to digital affairs to co-ordinate their NDS. However, effective co-ordination is essential for developing and implementing a whole-of-government approach with an NDS. The implementation of the NDS is the responsibility of several ministries, bodies or institutions in the majority of countries, and in some, multiple stakeholders are involved in implementing it. Bodies responsible for monitoring the implementation of the NDS tend to be the same as those who lead the development and the co-ordination of the NDS.

Designing better policies for a digital economy and society not only requires better knowledge about the technological changes underway and a holistic strategy, but also further efforts to improve measurement, evidence and analysis. All countries need to work together to fill the data gaps and in doing so enable better benchmarking, evidence building, policy development, and the identification and prioritisation of policy review and action. At the same time, new opportunities are e merging thanks to digital technologies, e.g. through the use of big data analytics and non-official data sources.

Policy recommendations

The previous chapters of this review have analysed recent developments in several policy fields in relation to digitalisation in Sweden. The analysis had led to an assessment of the performances and a set of policy recommendations for each field. These recommendations are discussed below and mapped against the Going Digital integrated policy framework. The components of the framework considered are those requested by Sweden.

Framework policies

The OECD carries out a regular assessment on framework policies in areas that have been identified as priorities to boost incomes in OECD countries. The last assessment for Sweden (OECD, 2017a) recommends reducing housing market distortions and improving the efficiency of the tax structure in order to ease labour mobility and increase productivity.

Strengthening policy labs and regulatory sandboxes

Digitalisation is opening up great opportunities for the economy and society, but seizing these opportunities requires innovative ways to design and implement policies and regulations. Several policy labs have been established in Sweden in recent years, as in a number of many other countries. While these initiatives are interesting and potentially useful, their effects seem limited by a number of factors, including insufficient political commitment in the long run. The government should take a clear stance in favour of policy labs and include them among its policy tools, particularly in relation to digitalisation.

Regulatory sandboxes provide another useful instrument to ensure co-operation between all stakeholders in the development of new regulations better suited to the digital economy. The successful example of the Innovation Centre launched by Finansinspektionen (FI), Sweden's Financial Supervisory Authority, points out the opportunity to broaden the traditional mandate of regulatory agencies (supervision, authorisation and regulations) to include support to innovation.

Through regulatory sandboxes, agencies should engage in a closer dialogue with companies that intend to develop new business models based on innovation. This requires a profound change in the culture and the practice of regulatory agencies, as well as a clearer mandate by the Swedish government, which issues instructions to those agencies.

Access

Expanding connectivity

Connectivity is a building block of the digital economy. In this regard, Sweden exhibits an impressive performance in terms of broadband availability, quality and affordability among OECD countries. Sweden is an historical leader in the OECD in mobile broadband penetration and mobile data usage; it is also one of the most developed countries in terms of next-generation access.

Overall, Sweden is on a solid path to achieve its broadband connectivity targets for 2020. However, some issues still remain. Addressing these issues would further foster the robust deployment of ultra-fast networks in both rural and urban areas. In this way, Sweden would be able to reach its ambitious target of 98% of households and firms with access to 1 gigabit per second broadband connections by 2025.

Enhancing co-ordination among national, regional and local strategies for broadband (fibre) deployment

The broadband market in Sweden is characterised by more than 500 stakeholders and thousands of fibre associations. A plethora of municipal networks exist, using different models in terms of the roles adopted by infrastructure providers, network operations and service providers. The multiplicity of players in the fibre market is a main reason why Sweden has reached the levels of fibre deployment it has today. However, going forward, potential co-ordination issues among different connectivity stakeholders may become a challenge.

The Broadband Forum, which has a steering committee headed by the Ministry of Enterprise and Innovation, has served as an important form of co-operation contributing positively to fibre expansion in Sweden. There is room to enhance the role of this forum in promoting a more co-ordinated approach among several levels of government and the multiplicity of players in the broadband market.

Increasing the robustness of fibre networks

The Swedish National Audit Office (NAO, 2017) pointed out an uneven distribution of "robust" fibre networks due to a diversity of players and municipal networks, also engaging in operating active parts of the network (i.e. bitstream access).

Although there is no harmonised definition or measures of "robust fibre networks", as stated in the ministry's reply to the NAO's report, there seems to be room for improvement. One way to increase the "robustness" of fibre networks is by strengthening the role of the Broadband Forum and the Swedish Post and Telecom Authority (PTS) in this area. The PTS already has taken a number of initiatives in this regard, such as the "Robust Fibre Instructions" and the "PTS Operational Safety Regulations", which are steps in the right direction.

Promoting the deployment of high-speed broadband networks in sparsely populated areas

The Broadband Strategy in Sweden is striving for ubiquitous ultra-fast connectivity. At present, however, access to broadband of at least 100 megabits per second is uneven across the country. In addition, Sweden is facing a technology shift, where the incumbent has announced the replacement of copper networks in rural areas with mobile technologies.

The PTS should remain vigilant as to ensure that all households that will no longer have a digital subscriber line (DSL) connection receive a similar or better technological alternative. This is especially important given the current connectivity targets for 2025 in Sweden.

The government should continue its effort to enhance co-ordination among stakeholders in the administering of the regional funds for rural deployment of broadband (i.e. the European Agricultural Funds for Rural Development and the European Regional Development Fund). The establishment of the Broadband Forum is a move in the right direction. There may also be room for the newly created Digitalisation Council to enhance co-ordination.

Fostering competition in infrastructure provision by private players and municipalities

Low adoption rates of IPv6 in Sweden can be regarded as a symptom of larger issues related to the interoperability of fixed networks stemming from the diversity of municipal network models in place. In addition, incentives to IPv6 adoption may be lower in cases where municipal networks offer bitstream access, i.e. active infrastructure.

Sweden should generalise the model where only passive infrastructure is leased, at least for very small municipal networks. It should also evaluate the incentives that result from the retail and wholesale split of some of the municipal networks providing active infrastructure access as well as those that are vertically integrated providing services to end users.

The PTS, in co-ordination with the Swedish Competition Authority, should assess the geographical definition of broadband markets in order to continue ensuring sufficient competition in infrastructure provision by private players and municipalities.

The Swedish government could also work as an enabler of the IPv6 transition by establishing government promotion programmes to adjust Internet services for which it has responsibility, adapting government purchasing and ensuring multi-stakeholder task forces to foster IPv6 deployment.

Measuring the implications of autonomous vehicles for communication infrastructure

Sweden is a leader in machine-to-machine (M2M) penetration, and is one of the few OECD countries capturing more detailed statistics on M2M, such as revenue and traffic generated by M2M. Many Swedish companies are engaging in the future of the IoT and fifth generation (5G) mobile networks and leading the way forward for the rest of the world. The IoT application that is expected to have the most implications in terms of data traffic, and hence, infrastructure requirements, are autonomous vehicles.

Given its position of leadership in the IoT, Sweden may be the best placed to improve measurement of M2M as to single out the SIM cards related to connected and automated vehicles. This will help policy makers to start measuring an application that may have important implications to communications infrastructure in the near future.

Use

Increase digital inclusion through policies targeted to groups with lower usage levels of digital technologies

Most Swedes are familiar with basic digital tools and, in comparison to other OECD countries, many individuals also engage in more sophisticated online activities. Yet, use of digital technologies is far from being universal. Policies should foster usage among individuals with a lower education and low income and promote the uptake of online activities in remote areas.

An important condition for higher sophistication in online activities is a simple and secure digital identity (e-ID). Government should work to improve interoperability between different e-IDs. It should also ensure that newcomers in Sweden have access to a trustworthy and secure e-ID.

Promote the diffusion of advanced digital technologies in firms, in particular among small and medium-sized enterprises

Swedish firms are ahead of many other countries in the use of basic digital technologies and more advanced digital tools. Yet, there is room to improve the use of digital tools in firm operations, in particular supply chain and customer relationship management. The "digital lift" programme implemented by Sweden's Agency for Economic and Regional Growth could be re-enforced with a focus on digital business processes.

Swedish firms also seem to be late in the adoption of big data analytics and data-driven innovation (DDI). Sweden should develop a strategic approach and effective actions to increase the use of big data analytics in Swedish firms, in particular in SMEs. It should also improve conditions to attract foreign talent, e.g. through centres of excellence and by building on existing efforts to integrate newcomers.

Upgrading skills for the digital transformation

Several reforms of the education system have been carried out over the past decade to address Sweden's declining school performance, including reforms aimed at improving digital skills. Reform efforts should be continued to improve school performance in mathematics and science and to support effective use of digital tools in schools. The focus of the reforms should be on information-processing skills, in particular writing, numeracy and ICT skills, to enable more sophisticated digital activities in life and at work.

It is important to ensure that vocational, high school, college and university educations provide sufficient training in advanced digital skills and are co-ordinated with industry, for example, by building on the "knowledge lift" programme. Policy efforts to develop lifelong learning should be continued, including through support to municipal learning centres. Incentives for firms, particularly SMEs, to invest in training their employees should be strengthened.

The evidence of a shortage of ICT specialists in Sweden calls for decisive action at several levels: foster more interest in science-related careers, in particular in ICTs, mathematics and technology-related teaching; increase the number of training places with a digital focus or component at universities and polytechnic schools as well as in adult education; strengthen incentives for firms, particularly SMEs, to provide ICT specialist training to their employees; increase the responsiveness of higher education institutions to the evolving skills needs of industry.

Current policies do not address the demand for complementary skills to thrive in a digital economy, e.g. problem solving, self-direction, interaction, co-operation, management and leadership skills. Education reforms should include such skills more firmly in curricula and syllabuses.

Policy actions are needed to reduce the gender gap in digital skills, for example among ICT specialists, but also in relation to numeracy and generic ICT skills.

Innovation

Set clearer priorities for digital innovation

Sweden is an international hub of scientific excellence and technological leadership. A large number of initiatives, publicly funded and in co-operation with business, exist to foster research in ICT technologies and promote the adoption and development of advanced digital tools for businesses.

While this high dynamism combined with a bottom-up approach are very valuable for research and innovation, it would be useful for the government, through its innovation and research agencies, to provide stronger guidance about innovation priorities in the field of digitalisation.

The establishment of the Innovation Council and the innovation partnership programmes are a useful step towards setting strategic priorities, streamlining activities and fostering synergies of innovation programmes. There is, however, room for further improvement in this direction.

Scale up the size of programmes for digital innovation

Public funds to research activities related to digitalisation seem to be scattered among a plethora of programmes. Reaching a critical mass is particularly important for innovations related to digitalisation, as challenges and solutions are common to many sectors and industries. Also, digital solutions often require large investments and it is less costly to develop common test environments that can be shared for different technologies.

Too many projects may result in too little funding for at least some of the projects. As available resources are limited, it is critical to focus on areas with high importance to Sweden and where Swedish firms can gain or sustain a leading position.

Improve the assessment of innovation policies

The Research and Innovation Bill 2017 points to the need for a closer and more systematic evaluation of the variety of projects and initiatives supported by Swedish innovation policies. Indeed, evaluation studies of the effects of innovation policies provide a mixed picture of their results, with self-assessment based studies resulting in a positive evaluation more often than quantitative studies.

While assessing innovation policies is a complex task, it is essential that the large number of programmes active in Sweden are systematically analysed, as they may not only be ineffective, but may also lead to undesired outcomes, e.g. rent-seeking, distortion of competition, excessive administrative costs, etc.

Trust

Sweden should promote a clear vision of digital security risk management

The general digital security risk management approach in Sweden focuses on systems and networks rather than economic and social activities. Despite its early awareness of digital security, Sweden has been slow to recognise digital security as a strategic policy issue. In this regard, the adoption of the first National Cybersecurity Strategy and the inclusion of digital security in the 2017 Digital Strategy mark a turning point.

To become a world leader in harnessing the opportunities of the digital transformation, Sweden needs to devise and promote a clear vision of digital security risk management as an economic and social responsibility for public and private organisations' leaders and decision makers. They should approach digital security risk management as an essential tool to increase the likelihood of success, make informed economic and social choices, prioritise actions, and distinguish among alternative courses of action.

Policy leadership on the economic aspects of digital security requires stronger ministerial co-ordination

There is lack of clear policy leadership with respect to the economic aspects of digital security in Sweden. This probably explains why strategic policy documents do not yet reflect a vision in this area and why other economically oriented digital security policy initiatives seem uncoordinated (e.g. research and innovation) or limited (e.g. towards SMEs or in relation to education).

Currently, digital security is primarily about crisis management preparedness, an area led by the Ministry of Justice (MoJ). The MoJ also co-ordinates digital security policy making more broadly. Constitutionally, however, the MoJ has a duty to address digital security in areas falling under the mandate of other ministries, such as economic prosperity. Stronger ministerial co-ordination on the economic aspects of digital security is essential to promote a clear vision and strong policy leadership.

The Digitalisation Council could become a hub for co-operation on digital security

The policy leadership on digital security for prosperity should be clear. As all facets are interrelated, it is important that the vision is developed jointly by all ministries and agencies with a mandate and expertise on digital security. Strong co-operation between ministries and agencies with mutually reinforcing and complementary mandates is essential to foster a holistic approach to digital security policy.

The Digitalisation Council might be a useful platform to foster such co-operation, bringing together the stakeholders involved in digital security to promote a common vision and more co-ordinated agenda.

Sweden should develop adequate mechanisms for policy co-ordination around digital security

There is no one-size-fits-all model to digital security governance. Governance arrangements vary and reflect cultures and styles of government. Governments have taken different approaches to establish a policy co-ordination mechanism. Over time, there has been a trend towards bringing together scattered operational bodies and resources to achieve critical mass and generate synergies, and to foster public-private partnerships with businesses across all sectors for information sharing and better situational awareness. Sweden could build on the experience of other OECD countries to develop better co-ordination mechanisms.

Jobs

Strengthening labour market institutions

Effective labour market policies and institutions are essential to accompany workers during the digital transformation. The Swedish model, based on the strong dialogue between the social partners and the active role of job security councils (JSCs), seems well-equipped to facilitate a smooth transition for workers affected by this transformation. However, there is room to improve the coverage and the quality of the JSCs' and the Public Employment Services' (PES) services.

Social partners may want to:

- extend the provision of JSCs' services to all displaced workers, including blue-collar, youth and other vulnerable groups
- promote successful job-transition services, e.g. the Early Risk Service offered by the TRR, among all the JSCs
- improve co-ordination between the JSCs and the PES at an early stage of the dismissal procedure, in co-ordination with the government.

In an increasingly integrated global economy, digital technologies are enabling firms to segment work in new ways and to increase the use of temporary labour. Platform-based workers are likely to face some of the same problems as those in non-standard work, such as temporary, part-time or short-term jobs, i.e. lower wages, greater job insecurity and fewer work-related benefits. In Sweden, employment protection legislation (EPL) is well developed but the gap in EPL between permanent and temporary workers is among the highest in the OECD.

To meet these challenges, governments and social partners should improve their ability to detect emerging labour market trends and explore ways of developing existing labour market programmes and safety nets, in which eligibility is tied to standard employment models, so as to ensure inclusive growth and job quality in the new work organisation enabled by the digital economy:

- Social partners may want to take initiatives to promote the establishment of a negotiation council where job platforms and trade unions may negotiate collective agreements fit to the new forms of work enabled by digitalisation.

The government may want promote a regulatory sandbox on the labour market, based on the model of the Innovation Centre established by the FI. To this purpose, the Ministry of Labour may consider issuing instructions for the National Mediation Office (Medlingsinstitutet) to map innovations in the labour markets and review issues that platforms and trade unions may have in relation to the agency's core activities.

Digital government

Enhance digital government

Sweden's policy to improve digital government and manage the digital transformation of the public sector is bearing fruit. However, progress is not equally distributed. Policies should enhance digital public services in remote areas, in particular by strengthening capacity at the local level. Efforts should be focused on making online interactions with the public sector more user-friendly, by building on existing initiatives under Digital First and implementing the "once only" principle. It is crucial to agree on common standards across level of government and agencies and to increase interoperability between different systems, in particular for essential services such as healthcare.

While policies are strongly committed to opening up public sector information and open government data to citizens, as confirmed by several new initiatives in the 2018 budget, Sweden seems to lagging behind many OECD countries. Policies to promote access to public sector information and open government data should focus on increasing the interoperability of data resources; improving the use of data within the public sector; and enhancing the integration of data from regions and municipalities, including through capacity building at the local level.

Strategy

In June 2017, the Swedish government launched its Digital Strategy (Government Offices of Sweden, 2017a). The strategy's overall goal is for Sweden to be the best in the world in the use of digitalisation opportunities. In order to achieve this overall goal, the strategy sets five targets: digital literacy, digital security, digital innovation, digital leadership and digital infrastructure (Table 6.2). A few key policy areas are identified under each target.

The Digital Strategy provides an ambitious goal for the Swedish economy and society. Its approach is very close to the rationale underlying the OECD Going Digital policy framework while its targets focus on the policy areas that are crucial for the potential benefits from digitalisation to unfold. The strategy, however, needs to be made more operational by linking its targets to concrete policy instruments, assigning institutional responsibilities for them, providing for an appropriate budget appropriation and, most crucially, setting up stronger co-ordination mechanisms.

Table 6.2. **For a Sustainable Digital Sweden: Five targets**

Targets	Description
Digital competence	**In Sweden, everyone will be able to develop and use their digital skills.**
	The ability and opportunity to contribute and participate in the digital society
	Modernisation of the education system
	Matching skills
	Digital literacy in the public sector and state-owned companies
Digital security	**Sweden will provide the best conditions for everyone to safely participate, take responsibility and have confidence in the digital society.**
	A digital identity
	Strict security requirements
	Privacy in the digital society
	Democracy is preserved in digital environments
	A safe and mobile labour
	Well-functioning digital markets and confident consumers
Digital innovation	**In Sweden, the best conditions exist for digitally driven innovations to be developed, disseminated and used.**
	An increased focus on data-driven and digitally driven innovation and research
	A stronger innovation environment for data-driven and digitally driven innovation
	Effective intellectual property
	Strengthening national and international competitiveness through digitalisation
	A modern social structure
Digital leadership	**In Sweden, improvements in efficiency and quality through digitalisation should be relevant, purposeful and lawful.**
	A clearer state leadership for change
	Simplification by digitalisation
	A continuous analysis of digital maturity and need for action
	Leading towards a resource-efficient society through digitalisation
	Strengthening local and regional engagement
Digital infrastructure	**The whole of Sweden should have access to infrastructure allowing for fast broadband, stable mobile services and supporting digitalisation.**
	Improved access to hard infrastructure
	Development of soft infrastructure

Source: Government Offices of Sweden (2017a), "For a sustainable digital transformation in Sweden: A digital strategy", www.government.se/49c292/contentassets/117aec2b9bf44d758564506c2d99e825/2017_digitaliseringsstrategin_faktablad_eng_webb-2.pdf.

Link the Digital Strategy targets to concrete policy instruments

All five targets and most policy areas in the Digital Strategy are defined at a fairly high level. In fact, the targets propose a vision For a Sustainable Digital Sweden rather than a set of policy objectives. For instance, the target "digital skills" is "In Sweden, everyone will be able to develop and use his/her digital skills".

The key areas under each target highlight specific features of the target but provide little guidance on the policies that will be implemented to achieve it. For instance, the key areas identified under the target "digital skills" (ability and possibility of contributing to and participating in the digital society; modernisation of the education system; skills matching; and digital skills in the public sector and state-owned companies) help to characterise the target but leave open the issue of what policies should be pursued in these areas.

By its very nature, a strategy is not an action plan with quantified objectives and budget appropriations. However, both its political strength as a societal vision and its effectiveness as a policy agenda would be strengthened by a clearer identification of its high-level targets and of the policy instruments to achieve them. These targets are already identified in areas where the Digital Strategy refers to policies currently in place, such as the Smart Industry (Government Offices of Sweden, 2016) for the target "digital innovation" or the Agenda 2030 for the target "digital infrastructure".

It seems urgent that the Digital Strategy be translated into an action plan, with well-defined and quantifiable objectives under each of the strategy's targets. The action plan should also establish monitoring mechanisms to assess progress towards the objectives and trigger policy responses when appropriate.

Assign institutional responsibilities for the Digital Strategy's targets

As any other policy in Sweden, digital policies are a shared responsibility of the Government Offices, which forms a single, integrated public authority comprising the prime minister's office, the government ministries and the Office for Administrative Affairs. Within this "collective government decision making", three ministers have the main responsibility for digital policies: the Minister for Housing and Digital Development, the Minister for Enterprise and Innovation, and the Minister for Public Administration. The first two ministers sit in the Ministry of Enterprise and Innovation while the third is in the Ministry of Finance.

The Minister for Enterprise and Innovation leads policies to promote the uptake of digital technologies by businesses and to foster innovation in the digital field. The Minister for Public Administration leads policies to enhance digital government as well as to promote innovation, collaboration and the uptake of digital technologies by the public administration. He/she is also responsible for general governance of the public sector (public administration policy), public procurement (strategy for public procurement), municipalities (Law of Municipalities) and human resources (skills and competencies). Finally, the Minister for Housing and Digital Development leads policies to enhance access to, and the quality and use of broadband and telecommunications infrastructures. He/she also has the overall responsibility for digital policies that are not explicitly addressed by other ministers.

The current allocation of responsibilities for digital policies within the Government Offices seems to map fairly well into some of the Digital Strategy's targets, notably innovation, infrastructure and leadership. However, the responsibilities for the other two targets – competence and security – are less clearly defined.

The definition of the Digital Strategy's targets in more operational terms should be accompanied by the identification of the institutions – ministries, agencies and levels of government – responsible for the implementation of the strategy in relation to each target. The assignment of institutional responsibilities within the Digital Strategy does not require the definition of a specific set of actions to be undertaken by each institution. It simply needs to indicate which institutions bear a shared responsibility in relation to each target.

A clearer assignment of institutional responsibilities would have three main benefits. First, the process would help to identify areas where the implementation of the Digital Strategy requires co-ordination among ministries and agencies and between the central and local governments. This would set the basis for improved co-ordination in the actual implementation of these policies.

Second, the assignment of institutional responsibilities requires consultation with and the agreement of all institutional stakeholders. This process, therefore, would strengthen their political commitment to the Digital Strategy.

Finally, clear responsibilities in the implementation of the Digital Strategy would also increase the political accountability of each institutional stakeholder and increase their incentives to play their role according to the strategy.

Provide for clear budgetary appropriations for the Digital Strategy

Allocating a budgetary appropriation to each target goes beyond the scope of the Digital Strategy. However, not providing an adequate level of resources would weaken its political credibility in the short run and delay its implementation in the long run.

The Digital Strategy should indicate an overall budgetary appropriation, with a breakdown for the five targets. Central government expenditure in Sweden is divided into 27 areas known as expenditure areas. Each area shows the amount of resources allocated to state-controlled activities. The Digital Strategy's budget, therefore, should be linked to the relevant expenditure areas of the state budget.

At present, it is difficult to identify the resources devoted to policies contributing to the achievement of the Digital Strategy's targets. These targets do not appear among the policy reforms of the 2018 Budget Bill (Table 6.3). Similarly, the press release and the statement accompanying the 2018 Budget Bill 2018 do not make an explicit reference to digitalisation (Government Offices of Sweden, 2017f).

Table 6.3. **Reforms and financing in the Budget Bill 2018**

SEK million

	2018	2019	2020
More people in work	7.3	10.1	11.4
Sweden will have equitable knowledge-based education	2.4	4.6	7.0
Sweden will be a fossil-free welfare nation	5.0	7.9	10.0
The welfare system must be strengthened	7.8	13.6	18.9
Sweden's economic strength to benefit everyone	11.9	18.5	22.9
Sweden must be secure	6.7	8.3	9.7
Other reforms	2.7	1.9	2.0
Total reforms	**43.8**	**64.8**	**81.7**
Total financing	**3.4**	**4.9**	**8.8**

Source: Government Offices of Sweden (2017e), "Budget Bill for 2018: Building our society – investing for the future", www.government.se/press-releases/2017/09/budget-bill-for-2018-building-our-society--investing-for-the-future.

The Budget Bill 2018 itself (Government Offices of Sweden, 2017b) provides more details on the policies related to the Digital Strategy's targets. However, the resources allocated these policies are singled out only in a few areas, particularly those where a minister has clear responsibility for digitalisation: the Minister for Housing and Digital Development, the Minister for Enterprise and Innovation, and the Minister for Public Administration (Box 6.1).

Digital skills have a prominent place in the budget area "Education and university research", although the allocation of resources for these policies is not detailed in the budget. Despite the attention devoted to these issues in the Digital Strategy, the budget area "Labour market and working life" does not make any mention of digitalisation and does not provide any explicit allocation for policies in this field.

The strategy's overall goal is for Sweden to be the best in the world in the use of digitalisation opportunities. The ambition of this goal is such that it may justify considering the creation of a new expenditure area "Digitalisation". This would imply that some of the resources allocated to the existing 27 expenditure areas should be transferred to the newly created one. Such a transfer would increase transparency about the targets of the Digital Strategy, signal the government's commitment to it and strengthen the political credibility of the strategy. More transparency would also help with implementing the strategy.

Box 6.1. Selected budget expenditures for the Digital Strategy

The Budget Bill establishes a budget for the "information society policies" (Budget area 22.4), as shown in Table 6.4. These cover general issues of digitalisation and use of information technology; electronic communication, mail and basic payment services. It also includes the PTS, which is the regulatory authority in the field of electronic communications and postal services; the Broadband Forum; and the Digitalisation Council.

The appropriation for information society policy, net of the resources reallocated to the "Agency for Digital Government" (see below in this chapter) is expected to increase significantly, from SEK 351 million (EUR 34 million) in 2017 to SEK 437 million (EUR 43 million) in 2018 and 2019. The increase is mainly due to higher expenditure for "data and communications", which will increase from SEK 19 million to SEK 73 million (EUR 1.85 million to EUR 7.10 million). This budget line, which may be used for the implementation of digitalisation policies as well as for analysis and policy evaluations, is expected to finance the activities of the Broadband Forum and the Digitalisation Council.

The resources of the PTS have also considerably increased, from SEK 29 million to SEK 4 million (EUR 2.8 million to EUR 4.1 million) to enhance digital security in communication infrastructure.

Table 6.4. **Budget expenditures for information society policy, 2016-20**

SEK million

		Outcome 2016	Budget 2017	Forecast 2017	Budget 2018	Forecast 2019	Forecast 2020
2:1	Swedish Post and Telecom Authority	28	29	29	42	43	43
2:2	Special services for people with disabilities	133	140	139	140	140	140
2:3	Basic payment services	20	34	33	36	36	36
2:4	Data and telecommunication	11	23	19	73	73	73
2:5	Reliable and available communications	115	126	131	146	146	140
2:6	Common e-government project[1]	54	75	65	x	x	x
Total	Information society policy	361	427	416	437	437	432

1. Allocation transferred to the "Agency for Digital Government" from 2018 onwards.

Note: x = not applicable.

Source: Government Offices of Sweden (2017b), *Budgetpropositionen för 2018*, www.regeringen.se/rattsdokument/proposition/2017/09/prop.-2017181.

The Budget Bill 2018 also sets up a budget for the digitalisation of the public administration (Budget area 2.6), in line with the targets of the Digital Strategy. The appropriation for this area includes the transfer of resources allocated to "information society policy" until 2017 and additional allocations for national digital infrastructures, open data and the "Agency for Digital Government" to be established in September 2018.

The total budget for the digitalisation of the public administration is forecast to increase from SEK 75 million (EUR 7.3 million) in 2017 to SEK 177 million (EUR 17 million) in 2018.

Setting up stronger co-ordination mechanisms within government

Fostering digitalisation requires a coherent policy framework both among ministries and agencies (horizontal co-ordination) as well as across levels of government (vertical co-ordination). Developing a whole-of-the government policy approach to digitalisation is a challenge for all countries and the appropriate mechanisms to ensure co-ordination depend on the institutional settings specific to each of them.

As discussed in Chapter 1, the Swedish government system is characterised by two features. The first is administrative dualism: a clear division of roles between ministries in charge of strategic policy development and oversight, on the one hand, and autonomous agencies tasked with policy implementation, on the other. The second feature means a high degree of decentralisation for largely autonomous county councils and municipals governments, which are responsible for key components of the Swedish welfare system.

Sweden's political and societal culture towards co-operation is crucial to ensure a smooth policy-making process in such an institutional setting. Yet, the speed and the scope of the economic and societal transformations driven by digitalisation seem to be challenging the responsiveness of this institutional setting. Changes triggered by digitalisation are rapid and pervasive while policy co-ordination in a largely decentralised decision-making system takes time. The gap between the speed of the digital transformation and the pace of the policy response calls for more formal co-ordination mechanisms.

The implementation of the Digital Strategy

In recent years, three of the Swedish government's policy initiatives have tried to set up more formal co-ordination mechanisms. The first initiative is the creation of a Digitalisation Council in the first half of 2017 (www.digitaliseringsradet.se/en).

The council consists of ten people under the leadership of the Minister for Housing and Digital Development. Its undertaking is to promote the implementation of the government's digitalisation policy while enhancing co-ordination between different governmental and public organisations and subject areas, as well as between public and private actors.

Several governmental councils and fora related to digitalisation already exist in Sweden, in areas such as e-health, digital government, broadband, smart grids, digital security and innovation. In order to avoid duplications, the Digitalisation Council must consult with these councils and fora.

The Digitalisation Council is mandated to support the government in the implementation of its Digital Strategy. This involves setting the basis for the Digital Strategy, identifying key initiatives for the five strategic targets, and monitoring and analysing the implementation. In particular, the council will:

- evaluate the effects of the government's initiatives
- monitor and analyse digitalisation in Sweden
- compare Sweden's performance in the area of digitalisation
- produce data to support the implementation of the government's initiatives
- propose new initiatives as required
- consult with other councils and similar bodies set up by the government in order to promote, implement or develop digitalisation in other areas.

A group of secretaries of state in the Cabinet Office will contribute to the horizontal organisation necessary for the implementation of a policy when several policy areas are concerned. The Secretary of State Group is responsible for co-ordinating the work of the digitalisation policy.

The mandate of the Digitalisation Council is clearly meant to improve the evidence base for policies and to increase exchanges among different institutions with a mandate related to digitalisation. This is a useful step to increase the effectiveness of digitalisation policies by sharing good practices and reducing duplications. However, the council comes short of addressing the issue of co-ordination. Lack of co-ordination is not only due to limited information about the measures taken by other institutions and their outcomes, it is mainly the result of two other features.

The first is a different appreciation of the opportunities created by digitalisation and the appropriate policies to seize them. The appreciation is largely dependent on the specific position of each agency and each local government. As digitalisation is not a purpose in itself for these institutions but a means to achieve economic and societal objectives, agencies and local governments may take different approaches to digitalisation policies to the extent their position and their objectives are different.

The second feature that may hamper co-ordination is the opportunity cost of policies related to digitalisation. As the opportunity cost of a given measure tends to vary among policy fields and across levels of government, the scope for co-ordinated policies will be narrowed.

Both of the above features – different policy objectives and different opportunity costs – provide the main rationale for the autonomy of agencies and local governments. Therefore, in order to be effective, co-ordination mechanisms should be designed as to address these two issues.

The second initiative taken by the Swedish government to increase co-ordination is the establishment of an "Agency for Digital Government" on 1 September 2018. This initiative follows the report of an independent investigation released in March 2017 (Government Offices of Sweden, 2017c). The report notes that Sweden is lagging behind comparable countries in terms of digitisation of the public sector and ascribes this outcome to two circumstances. The first is the government's choice to delegate responsibility for the digitalisation of public administration to several agencies. The second is the lack of clear instructions from the government to the agencies with regard to digitalisation. As a result, the report argues, agencies have approached digitalisation mainly as a tool to improve their internal efficiency rather than as an opportunity to provide new and better services to final users. Based on this assessment, the government has decided to establish an agency with the overall responsibility for the digitalisation of the public sector.

The agency will consist of 50-70 staff and will receive directives from the Ministry of Finance. It shall be responsible for supporting the government in developing, co-ordinating and promoting the digitalisation of the government agencies, municipalities and county councils, with the exception of the defence authorities.

In particular, the agency will assist the government to promote greater digitalisation of the public sector, including through the analysis and monitoring of developments in this field. It will also co-ordinate, develop, manage and provide a national digital infrastructure for the public sector, as well as promote its use; for example, by increasing the standardisation of public sector information exchanges and developing simple and secure e-credentials.

The agency will promote open government that supports innovation and participation by, for instance, promoting the availability of open data and DDI in the public sector. It will also co-ordinate and support public sector work with user-driven business developments, including support to digital investments.

The agency is also taking full responsibility for the e-Identification Board, as well as for certain tasks and assignments that have been carried out by the Swedish Tax Agency, the Swedish Financial Supervisory Authority, the Expert Group on Digital Investments, the National Archives of Sweden, the Swedish Agency for Growth, and the National Post and Telecom Agency.

The establishment of an agency is a positive step towards better co-ordination of digitalisation policies within the public sector. In particular, gathering in one institution tasks previously scattered among several agencies and bodies is welcome. Also, the positive reactions by the Swedish Association of Local Authorities and Regions (SKL in Swedish) to the creation of the agency and the SKL's close involvement in the preparatory work are essential to its success.

By putting forward a more compelling vision and a stronger political commitment, the agency is likely to help improve co-ordination. However, according to the current proposal, it has the power to "issue regulations on the national digital infrastructure, such as the use of standards, formats and specifications for information, information technology systems and basic data, *insofar as this does not infringe on other agencies' regulatory powers*" (Government Offices of Sweden, 2017d). The agency, therefore, will enhance coherence in the design of digitalisation policies for the public sector but its capability to implement such policies will depend on the willingness and the capability of all other institutions to adopt them. There may even be the risk that the creation of yet another agency may result in an additional silo. As will be discussed in the next section, a more direct approach, possibly based on incentives for all public sector institutions to adhere to the regulations issued by the agency, may prove more effective.

Finally, at the beginning of 2018 the Swedish government appointed a Chief Digital Officer (CDO) responsible for promoting the implementation of its digital strategy and strengthen its overall ability to lead the digitalisation process. The CDO's main task is to co-ordinate and communicate the government's work on digitalisation; create synergies between different initiatives and areas; identify the need for further initiatives; and be a catalyst for action.

While both the Digitalisation Council and the Agency for Digital Government are positive initiatives to increase policy co-ordination in the field of digitalisation, further steps appear necessary to build a whole-of-government approach. The agency's mandate is limited to the public sector and this is entirely coherent to it receiving directives from the Minister of Public Administration, within the Ministry of Finance. No other institution in the Swedish policy-making machinery has a mandate to enhance co-ordination among agencies and across levels of government in relation to digitalisation policies. Complementarities and trade-offs between labour and taxation, employment and education, innovation and technological diffusion, competition and jobs should be addressed in a more co-ordinated manner. This may be the natural role of a multi-stakeholder body like the Digitalisation Council. However, as discussed above, the Digitalisation Council has the mandate to consult stakeholders, advise the government and propose policies, but it does not have the power or the resources to design and implement them. The same limitations are likely to apply to the newly appointed CDO, although this position was created too recently to allow any assessment.

Political leverage vs. incentives: A typology of co-operation arrangements

In general, there are two, non-exclusive mechanisms for policy co-ordination. The first is based on "political leverage": the implementation of co-ordination is devoted to an institution with *de facto* sufficient political power to command other institutions to co-ordinate their actions towards a well-defined outcome. In a presidential regime, for instance, the president is typically empowered with such a degree of power: he/she can command several ministers to take a certain course of action, even if each minister has discretion about the definition of policies in his/her own area. In a parliamentary regime, this level of policy leverage may pertain to the prime minister alone and/or to some council composed of a small number of ministers.

The second co-ordination mechanism is based on "incentives": the implementation of co-ordination is devoted to an institution that can set incentives for other institutions to co-ordinate their actions towards a well-defined outcome. Often incentives take the form of budgetary allocations. For instance, the central government may set a matching grant, i.e. a grant for a specific use conditional upon additional resources by the recipient, as an incentive for subnational governments to implement certain policies. Similarly, the president or the prime minister may allocate an additional budget, i.e. a kind of co-ordination premium, for policies that are implemented through co-ordination between several ministries.

These two mechanisms – political leverage and incentives – can be used as a grid to analyse co-ordination arrangements, as shown in Table 6.5.

Table 6.5. **A typology of co-ordination arrangements**

		Budget	
		High	Low
Political leverage	High	Plenipotentiary Digitalisation Minister	President/prime minister-led council
	Low	Digitalisation Co-ordinator	Digitalisation Advisory Group

Source: OECD (2018), "Going digital in a multilateral world: An interim report to ministers", www.oecd.org/mcm/documents/C-MIN-2018-6-EN.pdf.

In the bottom-right quadrant (low budget/low political leverage), the "Digitalisation Advisory Group" has the mandate to promote greater co-ordination between different governmental and public organisations and subject areas, as well as between public and private actors. While it may be led by a minister, it does not have sufficient policy leverage to affect the policies implemented by the central government, independent agencies and the local governments. It cannot set incentives, in particular budgetary incentives, to affect policies carried out by other institutions. It can be regarded as the weakest co-ordination arrangement.

In the top-left quadrant (high budget/high political leverage), the plenipotentiary Digitalisation Minister appears as the strongest form of co-ordination. The minister concentrates the policy authority and the budget to implement all policy measures related to digitalisation, across the policy fields of all other ministers, agencies and local governments. This arrangement should be considered as a purely theoretical case as it seems unlikely that any political system may be willing to concentrate so much power over such a large range of policy domains to a single institution or person.

The other two co-ordination arrangements provide intermediate cases. Low budgetary discretion but strong policy leverage is typical of a council led by the president or the prime minister (top-right quadrant). The council does not have a dedicated budget to implement a coherent set of digitalisation policies across different policy areas but has sufficient policy leverage to command ministers, agencies and local governments to implement certain policies. This co-ordination arrangement is suited for policy regimes where the president or prime minister has strong political authority but it is less appropriate for political regimes with stronger local governments.

The final arrangement is the one exemplified by a "Digitalisation Co-ordinator" (bottom-left quadrant). Unlike a minister, the co-ordinator does not have the political authority to implement any policy. However, she/he has a discretionary budget that can be used to co-finance policies, according to the targets set by the government, implemented in co-ordination among two or more institutions: ministries, agencies or local governments. Budgetary allocation by the co-ordinator would typically take the form of a matching grant, i.e. a grant that has to be used for a specific purpose and is conditional to additional resources by the receiving institution. This arrangement seems best suited for political systems where power is diluted among a variety of institutions and across levels of government.

A "Digitalisation Co-ordinator" appears to be a promising mechanism in an institutional setting like Sweden's, characterised by administrative dualism and a high degree of decentralisation. A "Digitalisation Co-ordinator" would guarantee the autonomy of agencies and local governments, while, at the same time, provide monetary incentives to co-operate. The co-ordinator may be a single person, with a small office, or a small agency, receiving instructions and appropriations by the government or the prime minister but autonomous from them in the implementation of these instructions. The co-ordinator's budget would not require additional resources, but a reallocation of the appropriations currently allocated to digitalisation policies under different lines of the state budget. A clearer budgetary allocation, as discussed above, is therefore a prerequisite for the establishment of this co-ordination arrangement.

Note

1. While still work in progress, this framework is based on input from the 14 core OECD committees involved in the Going Digital project and a group of leading experts (Steering Group).

References

Government Offices of Sweden (2017a), "For a sustainable digital transformation in Sweden: A Digital Strategy", Factsheet, N2017/03643/D, Ministry of Innovation and Enterprise, June, www.government.se/49c292/contentassets/117aec2b9bf44d758564506c2d99e825/2017_digitaliseringsstrategin_faktablad_eng_webb-2.pdf (accessed 22 April 2018).

Government Offices of Sweden (2017b), *Budgetpropositionen för 2018* (in Swedish), Prop. 2017/18:1, Government Offices of Sweden, Stockholm, www.regeringen.se/rattsdokument/proposition/2017/09/prop.-201718l (accessed 22 April 2018).

Government Offices of Sweden (2017c), *Digitalforvaltning.nu* (in Swedish), SOU 2017:23, Government Offices of Sweden, Stockholm, www.regeringen.se/4948a6/contentassets/b1285825f50548eb83e23667b5130bc2/digitalforvaltning.nu-sou-201723 (accessed 22 April 2018).

Government Offices of Sweden (2017d), "Inrättande av en myndighet för digitalisering av den offentliga sektorn" (in Swedish), Dir. 2017:117, Government Offices of Sweden, Stockholm, www.regeringen.se/4ae5ed/contentassets/ca8f6b4f3d5d4e09a518430b7e988ae8/inrattande-av-en-myndighet-for-digitalisering-av-den-offentliga-sektorn-dir.-2017117-.pdf (accessed 22 April 2018).

Government Offices of Sweden (2017e), "Budget Bill for 2018: Building our society – investing for the future", Government Offices of Sweden, www.government.se/press-releases/2017/09/budget-bill-for-2018-building-our-society--investing-for-the-future (accessed 23 March 2018).

Government Offices of Sweden (2017f), "From the Budget Bill for 2018: Budget statement", Government Offices of Sweden, https://www.government.se/information-material/2017/09/from-the-budget-bill-for-2018-budget-statement.

Government Offices of Sweden (2016), "Smart industry: A strategy for new industrialisation for Sweden", N2016.06, Ministry of Enterprise and Innovation, www.government.se/498615/contentassets/3be3b6421c034b038dae4a7ad75f2f54/nist_statsformat_160420_eng_webb.pdf (accessed 22 April 2018).

NAO (2017), "World class broadband? The government's measures to achieve the broadband policy objective", Swedish National Audit Office, Stockholm, https://www.riksrevisionen.se/en/Start/publications/Reports/EFF/2017/World-class-broadband---The-Governments-measures-to-achieve-the-broadband-policy-objective-/ (accessed 20 November 2017).

OECD (2018), "Going digital in a multilateral world: An interim report to ministers", OECD, Paris, www.oecd.org/mcm/documents/C-MIN-2018-6-EN.pdf.

OECD (2017a), *Economic Policy Reforms 2017: Going for Growth*, OECD Publishing, Paris, http://dx.doi.org/10.1787/growth-2017-en.

OECD (2017b), *OECD Digital Economy Outlook 2017*, OECD Publishing, Paris, http://dx.doi.org/10.1787/9789264276284-en.

ORGANISATION FOR ECONOMIC CO-OPERATION AND DEVELOPMENT

The OECD is a unique forum where governments work together to address the economic, social and environmental challenges of globalisation. The OECD is also at the forefront of efforts to understand and to help governments respond to new developments and concerns, such as corporate governance, the information economy and the challenges of an ageing population. The Organisation provides a setting where governments can compare policy experiences, seek answers to common problems, identify good practice and work to co-ordinate domestic and international policies.

The OECD member countries are: Australia, Austria, Belgium, Canada, Chile, Colombia, the Czech Republic, Denmark, Estonia, Finland, France, Germany, Greece, Hungary, Iceland, Ireland, Israel, Italy, Japan, Korea, Latvia, Lithuania, Luxembourg, Mexico, the Netherlands, New Zealand, Norway, Poland, Portugal, the Slovak Republic, Slovenia, Spain, Sweden, Switzerland, Turkey, the United Kingdom and the United States. The European Union takes part in the work of the OECD.

OECD Publishing disseminates widely the results of the Organisation's statistics gathering and research on economic, social and environmental issues, as well as the conventions, guidelines and standards agreed by its members.

OECD PUBLISHING, 2, rue André-Pascal, 75775 PARIS CEDEX 16
(92 2018 02 1 P) ISBN 978-92-64-30224-2 – 2018

www.ingramcontent.com/pod-product-compliance
Ingram Content Group UK Ltd.
Pitfield, Milton Keynes, MK11 3LW, UK
UKHW051501290926
15471UKWH00008B/1347

9 789264 302242